SUNLIGHT AND SHADOW

CULTURAL STUDIES

A series of books edited by Samir Dayal

Crisis of the European Subject
Julia Kristeva

*Three Mothers, Three Daughters:
Palestinian Women's Stories*
Michael Gorkin and Rafiqa Othman

*Sunlight and Shadow:
The Jewish Experience of Islam*
Lucien Gubbay

SUNLIGHT AND SHADOW

The Jewish experience of Islam

LUCIEN GUBBAY

Other Press
New York

First softcover printing 2000

Copyright © 1999 Lucien Gubbay

10 9 8 7 6 5 4 3 2

All rights reserved, including the right to reproduce this book, or parts thereof, in any form, without written permission from Other Press, LLC, except in the case of brief quotations in reviews for inclusion in a magazine, newspaper, or broadcast. Printed in the United States of America on acid-free paper. For information write to Other Press, LLC, 377 W. 11th Street, New York, NY 10014. Or visit our website: www.otherpress.com.

Library of Congress Cataloging-in-Publication Data

Gubbay, Lucien.
    Sunlight and shadow : the Jewish experience of Islam / Lucien Gubbay.
      p. cm.—(Cultural studies)
    Originally published: London : Sephardi Centre, 1999.
    Includes index.
    ISBN 1-892746-69-7
      1. Jews–Islamic countries–History. 2. Islamic countries–Ethnic relations.
3. Judaism–Relations–Islam. 4. Islam–Relations–Judaism. I. Title. II. Cultural studies (New York, N.Y.)

DS135.L4 G83 2000
909'.04924—dc21

00–055777

CONTENTS

SERIES EDITOR'S INTRODUCTION BY SAMIR DAYAL   VI
ACKNOWLEDGEMENTS   X
FOREWORD BY DR ZAKI BADAWI   XI
INTRODUCTION   1

Part 1   The coming of Islam

1 THE PRE-ISLAMIC WORLD   7
2 MUḤAMMAD, MESSENGER OF GOD   14
3 CONQUESTS OF THE ARABS   20
4 ISLAM, JUDAISM AND THE JEWS   26
5 THE DHIMMA   31

Part 2   Jews in the World of Islam – The first 500 years

6 SOURCES   39
7 HISTORICAL BACKGROUND   43
8 JEWS IN THE EARLY CENTURIES   47
9 JEWISH INSTITUTIONS AND OFFICIALS IN ABBĀSID BAGHDAD   51
10 JEWISH-ARAB SYMBIOSIS   65
11 AL-ANDALUS   73
12 MASSACRES AND FORCED CONVERSIONS   83

Part 3   Jews in the World of Islam – The later period

13 TURKISH AND MONGOL INVASIONS   88
14 THE OTTOMAN TURKS AND THE JEWS   96
15 THE JEWS IN OTTOMAN SOCIETY   105
16 OTTOMAN AND JEWISH DECLINE   112
17 REDEMPTION   120
18 PROVINCIAL LIFE IN 18TH CENTURY ALEPPO   129
19 WESTERNISATION   143

Part 4   Dissolution

20 COLONIAL PERIOD AND INDEPENDENCE   149
21 ISLAMIC FUNDAMENTALISM   154

Sources and further reading   160
List of quotations   161
Significant Dates   164
Index   170

SERIES EDITOR'S INTRODUCTION

A curious division is opening in commentary about the contemporary international cultural landscape. On the one hand there is the much-vaunted globalization of culture, the increasing permeability of national borders, and the deflation of any purist notion of "race." On the other hand, conflicts around the world suggest that tensions between and among groups, especially tensions generated by burgeoning ethnonational ideologies, continue to grow in some quarters, as in the Balkans, in Rwanda, in South Africa, in Asia, and in the Middle East and Near East. Nowhere does the social and cultural gulf yawn more alarmingly than between societies aligned with Islam and societies adhering to Christianity, or between Muslims and Jews. It is on this latter conflict between Muslims and Jews that Lucien Gubbay sheds light.

The perspective that Gubbay provides is at once refreshing and historicizing. It is a perspective obviously grounded in his wide reading of the historical records and expert commentary. His chief burden is to remind or inform his readers that while today Islam and Judaism seem mortal enemies in Palestine and Israel, for instance, Muslims and Jews have had an extraordinarily long history of living more or less in mutual tolerance. This was true, historically speaking, even when Jews were afforded only enclavic space within a majoritarian Muslim society. The book suggests that there is historical precedent that Jews, Muslims, and others *can* live together, something that many contemporary cultural studies theorists have been arguing.

There was often respect between the two groups; and during the High Middle Ages of Islam (950 – 1250), Jews were treated with great liberality by Islam, and given broad rights to travel and conduct business. People, books, and ideas circulated freely as a result, and Gubbay sees the richness of this social interchange as a possible model for multicultural life. He observes that there were periods in which Muslims regarded Jews as far more agreeable than Christians, both in a political sense and in a very visceral sense. Jews rarely lost their rights under Islam. They were treated well in times of Islamic prosperity and very badly in times of adversity. While Jews fared badly under the repressive regimes of Turkish mercenary soldiers, they flourished under the Ottoman Turks in the sixteenth century (p. 98). For centuries, over 90 per cent of the world's Jews lived under Islamic political power, at a time when there were few Jewish communities under Christian rule (p. 6).

There is much indirect, but little direct, evidence that Jews and Muslims lived harmoniously despite, or perhaps because of, cultural *difference*. Gubbay notes that Jews tended not to preserve extensive records of their cultural life, contrasted with their Christian contemporaries or even contrasted with the Muslim communities among whom they lived, on more or less friendly terms. There are tantalizing glimpses of direct evidence of everyday Jewish life afforded by the discovery of the magnificent Fustat (Old Cairo) *geniza* or storehouse (pp. 41–42). Islamic records suggest, as do some Christian sources, that despite the undeniable differences in religious ideology, Jews were often more helpful to Muslim rulers than were Christians (p. 29). And of course this means also that sometimes when Jews too strongly asserted their cultural difference, there was (in 1066 for instance) a Muslim backlash—beginning as it often does from within the masses, Gubbay notes. He is realistic, and proposes no quick fixes for the difficult problem of anti-Semitism or ethnonationalism, but contents himself with suggesting that understanding the historical pattern in these violent upsurges of ethnic hatred may yet have value.

But the lesson to be derived here is not merely that Jews and other minorities must always be self-effacing and "mind their fences," metaphorically speaking. There may be better ways of being good neighbors. Tracing the vibrant commercial and intellectual life of Jews under Islam, Gubbay shows that in many cases the ethnically separate communities were *interested* in each other, willing to learn from each other, not just to do business with each other. In the tenth century, the Jewish mercantile power in Baghdad and Cairo, as in Spain, was clearly a force recognized by political leaders. But as in more recent times, the Jews' reputation for financial prowess was always matched by a reputation for intellectual activity. Gubbay points to the shifting centers of Jewish learning—from ninth century Baghdad to Cairo to Cordoba to Istanbul being tied to Muslim wellbeing and occasionally even to some financial patronage. The respect accorded to the Geonim, the Jewish heads of academies in Babylon, was echoed by the high regard for Jewish culture and learning in evidence during the extraordinary, if brief, golden age of Spanish Islam under Abd al-Rahman III (929–961) and his successor Hakam II (961–976). In Ottoman Istanbul, leading Jewish physicians and some of the great Jewish international traders were often able to gain a sultan's confidence and then act as his valued personal advisors; in later times, Jewish women (*kiras*) became purveyors to the imperial harem and in that capacity were also able to exert indirect influence on the sultans. The Ottoman rulers behaved with exemplary leniency even toward the Messianic and apostate Jewish leader, Shabbetai Zvi, who had sought to displace the sultan from his throne. After Shabbetai had converted to Islam on pain of death, his apocalypse-hungry Jewish followers, who had seen a messiah in Shabbetai, were not persecuted. Gubbay comments that had "a similar event occurred within the boundaries of Christian Europe, the outcome would have been very different and the end result too terrible to contemplate" (p. 125). Readers will find this corrective view of Islam to be a welcome tonic against the overwhelmingly Christian and Eurocentric perspective of the contemporary West.

But perhaps what is most exceptional about the coexistence of Jews and Muslims in the same spaces and places is how unexceptional that coexistence seems to have been for them, and the degree to which each found the other unexceptionable. Is it possible for the contemporary world to learn this version of "tolerance" where as a result of massive migration and demographic shifts so many groups live together in close physical proximity but not necessarily in real sympathy with and openness to one another's worldviews?

This is not to forget that there was never a question of equality of power, this particular political equality being a modern and Western idea. There was for instance the *Dhimma*, a treaty of surrender formalizing the relationship and the power differentials between Islamic conquerors and their vanquished, first established in 638 when Jerusalem's Christian patriarch turned over the keys to the city to Kalif Umar I in surrender, offering a very specific set of terms. The *Dhimma* was subsequently incorporated as an eternal principle for the treatment of all subjects under Islam. Those monotheists who submitted to the rule of Islam, but chose to follow their own religion rather than convert to Islam, nevertheless had to follow a strict code of deference to Muslims in all outward matters. There were times, too, when Jews were considered inimical to Islam. During the Prophet's period in Medina, Jews were seen as enemies of the message that Muhammad was bringing to the Arabs, and it was he who commanded Muslims to face not Jerusalem (as in the past) but Mecca when they prayed (p. 17). Gubbay points out further that "the Qur'ān and the Hadīth are far more hostile to Jews than to Christians" (p. 28). So the history of toleration of Jews under Islam has not been an uninterrupted terrain of blissful symbiosis; but it is remarkable that this long and deep history of coexistence has so infrequently been written about. Gubbay's book is an attempt to fill in these historical and cultural lacunae.

Yet Gubbay's interest is not only antiquarian. He touches upon the varied fortunes in more recent times of Jews in Aleppo and Calcutta, two cities where a substantial Jewish community has grown, complete with synagogues and cemeteries. He traces the increasing Westernization of the Jews in the Near East, British India, and Egypt, and describes the diasporization of Jews resulting from the "rising tide of Arab and Islamic nationalism" (p. 148) as well as from the contemporary conflicts in Jerusalem, Gaza, and the West Bank. Gubbay discusses the recent rise of fundamentalism as the "present malaise in the Islamic world"; he is aware of the geopolitical asymmetries when he writes that there is an understandable desire of a minority to return to a "mythical golden age when confronted with the huge problem of corruption in their own society with its immense disparity between rich and poor." While he is cautious about marking a precise turning point in the shifting cultural hegemony from East to West, he is not partisan when he writes that the Christian West has, since the mid-seventeenth century at the latest, dominated the world and that Islamic fundamentalists cannot live in denial of the (to them potentially unsettling) democratic vistas of a Jeffersonian model, the sexual revolution inaugurated by Freud, or the scientific-paradigm shift instituted by Einstein (pp. 158–159).

Gubbay is under no romantic illusions about the prospects of a return to a harmonious relationship between Muslims and Jews, and is careful not to present their coexistence as a utopian idyll. Besides, he goes so far as to say that "what might have been a tolerably fair attitude to Jews in the tenth century is monstrously inappropriate [today] and best forgotten" (p. 159). Gubbay's book adds much, in short, to a contemporary cultural studies perspective, because its framing concerns include a desire to understand the prospects for a multicultural or multiethnic community, an openness to the politics of recognition, and an engagement with the ethics of the self's openness to the "other."

SAMIR DAYAL

ACKNOWLEDGEMENTS

Based on a course of non-specialist lectures given in the Sephardi Centre (London) for students new to the subject, this book follows closely in the tracks established by the acknowledged experts in the field. I am deeply indebted to the published works of many distinguished scholars ranging from Bernard Lewis, Salo Baron, S D Goitein and Philip Hitti to S Fawzi, Walter Fischel, Ronald Nettler, Stanford Shaw, Gershon Scholem, Norman Stillman, Aron Rodrigue, Yosef Yerushalmi and others too numerous to mention here. I am glad to have been given the opportunity of using the results of their research and re-stating some of their ideas and conclusions, even if in simplified form. Principal sources are listed and explained in the bibliography, in the hope that readers will be attracted to the original books.

I am obliged to Naim Dangoor for bringing John Evelyn's pamphlet to my notice: also to Professor Bernard Lewis for drawing my attention to the most recent scholarly work on the subject. Sheikh Dr Zaki Badawi is warmly thanked for kindly reading the draft and thus enabling me to correct some misunderstandings.

I am grateful to Abraham Levy for persuading me to undertake the original course of lectures, to the Directors of the Sephardi Centre for commisioning the book and to Cesare Sacerdoti in particular for his valued encouragement and advice at all stages.

SPELLING OF ARABIC AND HEBREW WORDS

Compromises have been adopted in the rendering into English of Arabic and Hebrew words, most of which have been spelt in the manner roughly approximating to their correct pronunciation. Some few of the words most commonly mispronounced have been specially marked in the text – but this has been done sparingly so as to guide but not burden the general reader.

Thus ḥ represents the guttural, such as in Muḥammad; and the top bar indicates a stressed syllable, such as in Abbāsid.

DATES

Dates are quoted in Jewish style. Thus BCE corresponds to BC and CE to AD.

FOREWORD

It is refreshing to read an account of the relationship between Muslims and Jews over the centuries that is without the cant or rancour which one often finds when the topic is discussed. Lucien Gubbay writes clearly and fairly on the close and continuing relationship between Jews and Muslims – ties which are historical, cultural and psychological.

Close ties are not always happy and Gubbay does not evade the issues of contention that exist between Jews and Muslims. Hatred and distrust rumble like desert thunder between them. Moral criticism in such cases is not enough, however edifying: we must understand the reasons for the rise of fundamentalism in both religious traditions

Gubbay has highlighted the profoundly humanising principle held dear by Jews and Muslims which is to respect God's creation and to treat all other people – no matter what their belief or faith – as individuals deserving respect as human beings created by the God we all worship.

Gubbay has written a valuable and thought-provoking summary of the enriching and problematic relationship – the Sunlight and Shadow – between Muslims and Jews.

DR ZAKI BADAWI
Principal of the Muslim College, London
10th May 1999

INTRODUCTION

Active hostility between the religious communities of Muslims and Jews recently rose to a peak not experienced before in history. But now at last, people of goodwill on both sides are looking anew at those they once saw as implacable foes; and for the first time in many years, despite the many ups and downs of Middle Eastern politics, there is again some talk of living together in peace.

"Sunlight and Shadow" traces the condition of Jews living under the rule of Islam, through good times and bad times, from the age of Muḥammad to the present struggles between Arabs and Israelis. It was written in the hope that the lessons of the past may lead to better understanding now and in the future.

Muslims and Jews have lived together and reacted to each other for the past fourteen hundred years; but few Jews today have much idea of how their brethren fared under Muslim rule.

A balanced view is that, in return for accepting a subordinate position in society, Jews were granted security for their lives and property, freedom of worship and a large measure of self-government. Though now little remembered, they experienced golden ages in Baghdad, Egypt and the Ottoman Empire, as well as in Spain – to name just the highlights. They participated in the flowering of the brilliant international civilisation made possible by the almost world-wide conquests of the Arabs, and bound together by Islam and the Arabic language. In its turn, early Judaism was enabled to develop and then to crystallise into very much the religion we know today.

That relatively optimistic assessment of Muslim-Jewish relations is often challenged by those who tend to view the Jewish condition in absolute terms and out of context; but interestingly enough, it has only recently been confirmed by the happy memories of many middle-class Jews forced to flee their homes in the Middle East in the decades following the establishment of the modern State of Israel. On the other hand, those who came from less Westernised backgrounds speak of the ground rules of Jewish inferiority being simply accepted as part of life, with each side knowing precisely how far to go in the game: no Jew, for example, would ever have thought of protesting if pushed aside to allow a Muslim to step in front.

Of course there were major disasters, riots, persecutions and massacres, especially on the fringes of the Muslim world; but those were violent times in which every section of society was subjected to very similar tribulations and when the poor of all nations suffered continuing hardship. No doubt Jews, being utterly defenceless, were especially vulnerable to the savagery of enraged mobs – but wherever possible they were protected by Islamic law or by the pragmatism of Muslim rulers. It is all too easy to compile lists of fearful massacres, forced conversions and gross humiliations from over fourteen hundred years of living together with Muslims; but far harder to uncover the other side of the picture. Jews, never at all interested in recording the history of their own times, barely mentioned the many centuries of peaceful coexistence; and it is only the occasional horrors that successfully penetrated the veil of time to enter into their collective memory.

On the whole, the Jews of Islam fared well when times were good and relatively badly in periods of hardship and decline. Though second-class subjects of the countries in which they lived, they hardly ever lost their rights. Unlike the Jews of Christendom, they suffered few economic restrictions, were not expelled arbitrarily from their countries of residence and only rarely were they forced to abandon their religion. On the whole, their disabilities and even their humiliations must have seemed a relatively small price to pay for their freedom to live full Jewish lives within their own communities; and there can be little doubt that until the nineteenth century their lot was a far happier one than that of most of their brethren under Christian rule.

The wider world, within which the complex web of Muslim-Jewish relationships developed, has changed in several fundamental ways during the past few centuries. "Whoever claims that all people are equal must be hopelessly mad" – so wrote a cultivated eighteenth-century inhabitant of Aleppo in his journal. Aleppo in Syria, though by then in decline from its former position as one of the leading cities of the Middle East, was still a centre of learning and culture in an old, old Islamic world as yet untouched by the spirit of modern Europe. Those of us living in the West have become accustomed to a world dominated by English speakers, a world whose centre of power has shifted from Europe to North America, a world in which human expectation was so nobly summarised in the words of the American Declaration of Independence: "We hold these truths to be self-evident, that all men are created equal..." But it was not always so! In none of the great civilisations of the past, whether of Mesopotamia, Egypt, Greece or Rome, was there any notion of the fundamental equality of human beings. On the contrary, inequality was part of the natural order, woven into the very fabric of society – with the rulers and the ruled, the superior castes and the inferior castes, the women and the slaves.

The civilisation of Islam was no exception; and it is unfair to judge past times only in terms of the ideal standards of today, still not always achieved. When the Arab empire was first established in the seventh century, it would have been inconceivable for the Jews – a distinct people living in lands conquered by Islamic warriors – to have been assigned an equal status to that of the triumphant Muslims. What is remarkable though, and in striking contrast to Christendom, is that they were granted well-defined rights, guaranteed by law.

Six hundred years is a comparatively short time span in history; and the world was a very different place six hundred years ago. Then, the heartland of Islamic civilisation comprised North Africa, the Middle East and Central Asia. To the south lay India, soon to be conquered for Islam by a descendant of Genghis Khan; and to the east lay the ancient empire of China. Travel within that vast area was mostly by land; and the old caravan routes were still the principal channels though which flowed much of the trade, the people, the ideas and the culture. Western Europe, just starting on its struggle for ascendancy, was on the very edge of the known world; and the continents of America and Australia had yet to be discovered and exploited.

Christopher Columbus's crossing of the Atlantic to find America and Vasco da Gama's rounding of the Cape of Good Hope to reach India were the first signs of the rapid technological advance of the previously backward countries of Western Europe. The supremacy of the land-bound realm of Islam was doomed just as soon as the fragile sailing ships of Western Europe – eventually to be replaced by more formidable steam ships – encircled and outflanked it. There can be no doubt that it was by means of its vastly superior technology that Europe first seized world markets for itself and then went on to dominate the globe.

As an example of the changing balance of power, it is amusing to recall that as late as 1793 the Emperor of China reacted with incredulity to a proposal from King George III of England to establish diplomatic relations with him on an equal footing. To him, Western Europe was still a barbarian land, beyond the pale of civilised life; and he regarded the King's letter as a gross impertinence. Of course we can now smile at the Emperor's attitude, for we know that it was not so many years later that tiny, faraway England was able to impose its will on mighty China in the Opium Wars.

The Muslim world reacted to the reversal of roles between West and East with a crisis of confidence so deep-seated that it continues to this day as the driving force behind Islamic fundamentalism. Islam turned in on itself, becoming more intolerant in the process; and the position of its Jews deteriorated.

The Jews' own perception of themselves has also changed radically over the years and it may now be in the process of changing yet again. For example, until comparatively recently it was by no means unusual for a French Jew to consider himself a Frenchman in every respect – no different from all other Frenchmen except in his profession of the Jewish religion. Such an idea would never even have occurred to the Jews of Islam. They were part of a separate nation and, what is more, a nation in exile. They constantly longed for a Redeemer to lead them back to their own land and were not backward in flocking to the banners of many would-be messiahs who promised much but in the end accomplished nothing. Their nationality as Jews was fully recognised by the Muslim rulers, who encouraged them to live as self-governing entities within the larger Islamic states.

Before the immigration into Israel of large numbers of Jews from the Middle East and North Africa, a common view was that the bulk of the Jewish people originated in the heaving semi-destitute masses of Eastern Europe: Sephardim were rare creatures, exotic but scarcely relevant. But only six hundred years ago the majority of the Jewish people, as well as much of its religious, secular and intellectual leadership, came from the Babylonian/Sephardi tradition – and not from that of the Ashkenazim of Christian Europe.

Babylon, home to the first great community of Jewish exiles, became the acknowledged centre of Jewish life after Roman oppression had rendered life intolerable in the Holy Land. It was in the Babylonian academies that the Talmud was composed; and that compendium of knowledge, law, religious practice and morality has remained a foundation of Judaism ever since. With the coming of the Arabs in the seventh century, Baghdad became the hub of a Muslim empire stretching from Spain to India. Its Jews, comprising by far the larger part of the Jewish nation, looked to Baghdad for its religious development, for the confirmation in office of high officials and for the settlement of difficult litigation. Following in the steps of the sages of the Talmudic era, the Geonim of Baghdad continued to uphold the unchallenged primacy of Babylonian Jewry, which lasted for close on seven hundred years before their mantle of leadership shifted to new centres of achievement in

The Babylonian/Sephardi and the Ashkenazi traditions

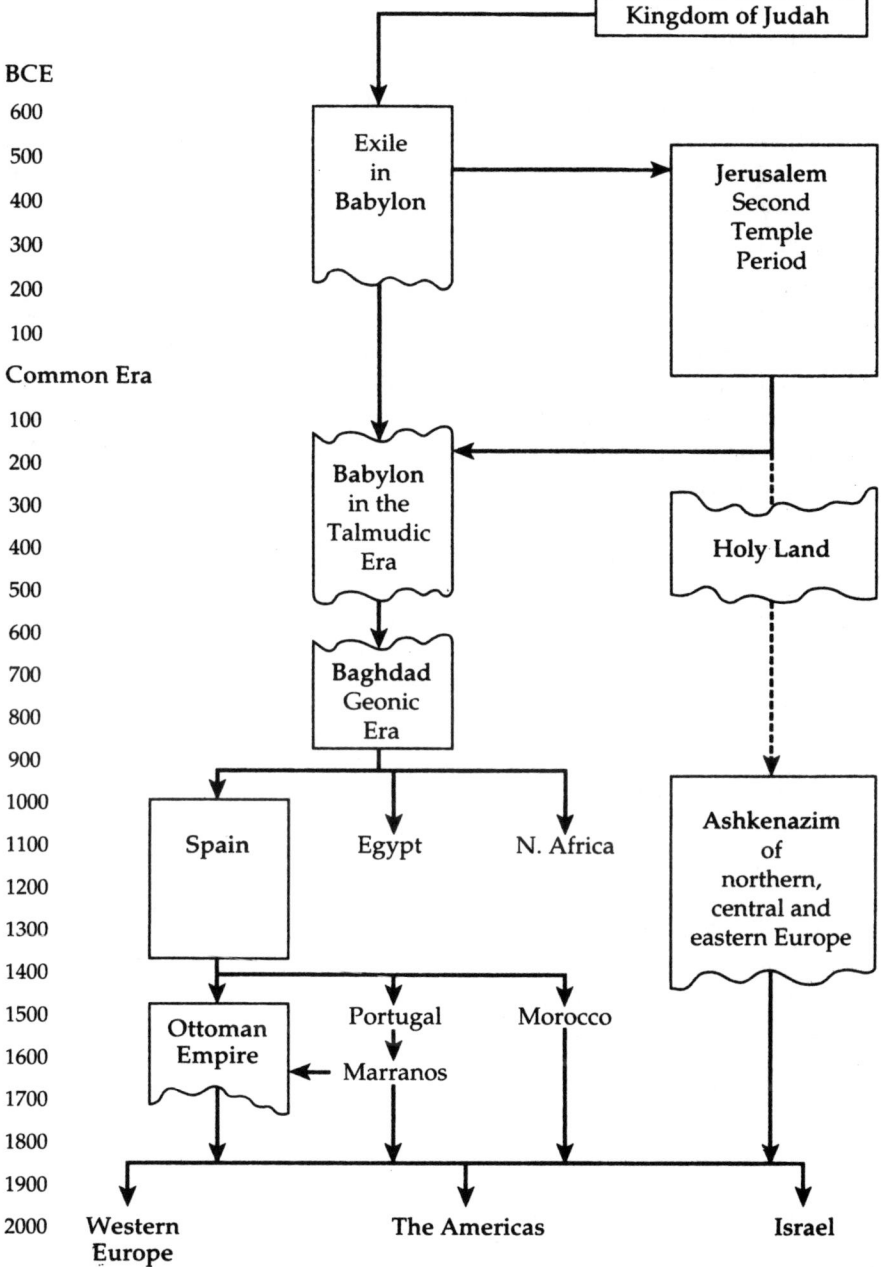

Muslim North Africa, Spain and Egypt – and then eventually to Christian Spain, Germany and France.

For many hundreds of years, over ninety per cent of the Jewish people lived under the sway of Islam at a time when the Jewish communities of Christian Europe were relatively insignificant. The growth of the Ashkenazi tradition – that of the Jews of Christian Europe – started in the eleventh century; but even in the sixteenth century there were still over twice the number of Jews in the Ottoman Empire than in the territory of Poland, Lithuania and the Ukraine to which most Ashkenazim had by then fled. Eventually the expulsion from Spain, the decline of the Ottoman Empire and a Jewish population explosion in Eastern Europe altered that balance dramatically: and later, in a contrary direction, so did the tragedy of the Holocaust. But as already observed, six hundred years is not too long a period in history for us to be able to disregard what occurred before; and the nuances of the relationship between Muslims and Jews can only be understood in the context of the complete picture.

Part 1

The coming of Islam

CHAPTER 1

BEFORE ISLAM

The world was ready for change in the seventh century as conflict everywhere undermined the old-established patterns of society.

Civilised urban life, with its luxurious centrally-heated villas, Roman roads and aqueducts, was already a distant memory in Western Europe; and it would be hundreds of years before the crude barbarian tribes, who had finally overrun the western half of the Roman Empire in 476, became capable of producing the first glimmering of medieval civilisation.

The surviving eastern half of the Roman Empire, ruled from the splendid city of Constantinople, still controlled a broad swathe of territory in the Balkans, North Africa and the Middle East. But the Christian Byzantine emperors, obsessed by the finer points of religious belief, had alienated large sections of their own population by relentless persecution of those they considered heretics. In consequence many Christians whose beliefs varied from those of the Orthodox Church lived in constant fear, while others fled to the Persian Empire for refuge.

The Persian Empire also seethed with discontent as civil wars, popular disturbances and bouts of state-inspired religious fanaticism alternately flared and subsided, leaving behind a residue of disillusion and despair.

To make matters worse, the Persian and Roman empires had been locked together for centuries in a state of perpetual hostility, interrupted only by short periods of peace. In the latest full-scale war, which had lasted for twenty-six long years, the Byzantines had first been brought to their knees by an unprecedented advance of the triumphant Persian army, before it was the turn of the Persians to suffer a similar fate. As a result, both empires were utterly exhausted and impoverished.

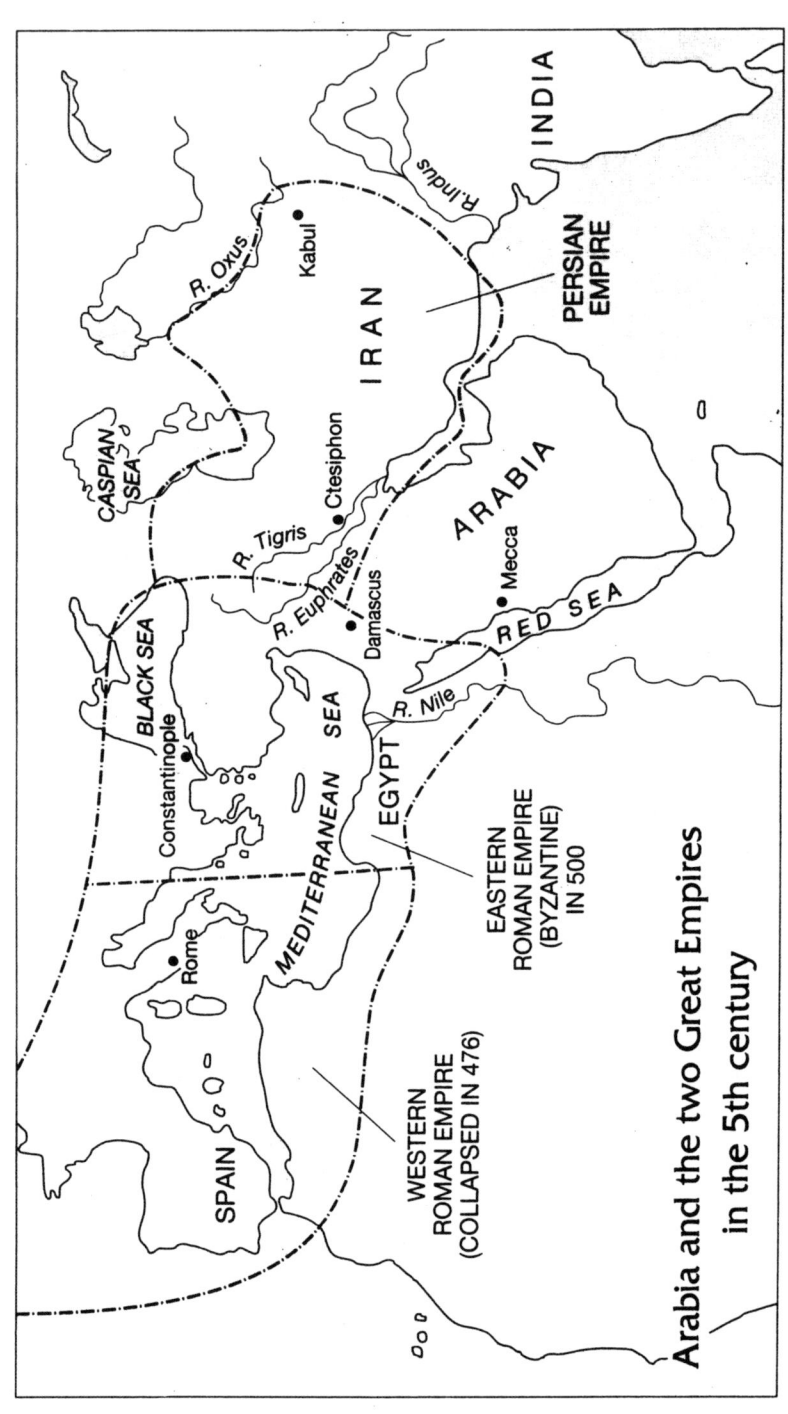

The Jews of the world were physically divided by the struggle between the great empires. Life for those in the Christian West was fast being made intolerable by increasing persecution. Byzantine Jews had interpreted the seemingly irresistible advance of the Persian army as a sign of the approaching Messiah. They had actively helped the Persians in their war against the Christians, especially in their conquest of Jerusalem in 614 after which the city was temporarily handed over to Jewish rule. The Byzantines exacted their revenge when they recaptured Jerusalem in 629. With some justification, Jews came to be regarded as disloyal and pro-Persian. They were ordered to convert to Christianity throughout the Empire; and even the king of the Franks was persuaded to issue a similar decree.

The barbarian tribes of Western Europe were also turning against the Jews with increasing ferocity as they moved from the Arian to the Orthodox form of Christianity. A horrible climax was reached in Spain in 613 when its Visigothic king gave his Jewish subjects the stark choice of baptism or exile.

Conditions were generally far better for Jews in the Persian Empire which had a long history of toleration; but now for the first time, its Jews too were experiencing sharp reversals of fortune. The forty years between 445 and 485 were the worst; and the first Babylonian Jewish martyrs appeared as observance of the Sabbath was banned, synagogues closed and Jewish children snatched from their parents by Magian priests. Another period of repression followed the revolt of the Exilarch Mar Zutra and his setting up of a short-lived independent Jewish kingdom. But soon after that, the situation had so changed that we read of a Persian general asking his Byzantine foe for a temporary truce in the war to enable his own Jewish soldiers to celebrate Passover.

ARABIA, CRADLE OF ISLAM

The vast and mostly arid peninsula of Arabia, as big as Spain, France, Germany and Italy combined, continued in its old role as a buffer between the Roman and the Persian empires.

Fertile oases with plantations of date palms and small areas of cultivation punctuated the bleak plains of central and northern Arabia in which nomadic Bedouin tribes eked out a frugal existence. The only extensive stretches of irrigated land lay in the deep south, where the kingdom of Ḥimyar (Yemen) was successor to a series of ancient civilisations which had lived off trade and agriculture. Ḥimyar however had been plunged into anarchy and ruin by invasions, first from Christian Ethiopia (as proxy for the Byzantines) and then from Persia.

Though Arabia was in itself too poor to justify the effort of conquest, both sides eyed it warily for it lay astride an important trade route to the East. Strange as it may seem today, the import of silk from China, of spices from India and South-east Asia (both for preservation and to mask the taste of badly preserved food), of incense (for use in pagan temples and Christian churches) and slaves, was of vital importance to the West and figured large in imperial policy. The merchants of Mecca controlled much of the transit trade between east and west. They bought goods off the ships at Aden and then transported them along caravan routes for sale in Egypt, Syria and Persia. The proceeds were used to buy manufactured goods, which were then brought back to Mecca and sold at the trade fairs which accompanied the annual pilgrimage to the Ka'aba (the haj).

The shrine of the Ka'aba in Mecca housed a black stone sacred to all Arabs: this was most probably a meteorite that had once fallen flaming from the skies. The rudimentary and barely developed pagan worship of the Arabs was centred on the god Hubal and the three hundred and sixty idols which surrounded the Ka'aba, to which the Bedouins flocked in annual pilgrimage. The haj, later to be taken over by the Muslims together with the Ka'aba itself, was a period of truce from tribal warfare, during which pilgrims could travel freely for the purposes of prayer and trade.

Al-Llah, the High God of the Arabs, was also associated with the Ka'aba; and it has been suggested that Arabs may have regarded him as the same God as that of the Jews and Christians – for with no written scriptures of their own and no belief in an after-life, some of them had developed a grudging admiration for those more developed religions. This feeling manifested itself in signs of spiritual discontent and in the rejection of idol worship by a small number of seekers after the one God who practised an ascetic religion of their own. There were also converts to both Judaism and Christianity in the settled populations of the desert oases and in the deep south.

The Jews of Arabia, few in number, are scarcely mentioned in Jewish sources. They dominated several of the main oases; and there was a tiny community with its own cemetery in Mecca. The Jews spoke Arabic, were organised into clans and tribes just like the Arabs, and had assimilated the values and customs of desert society. For example, they

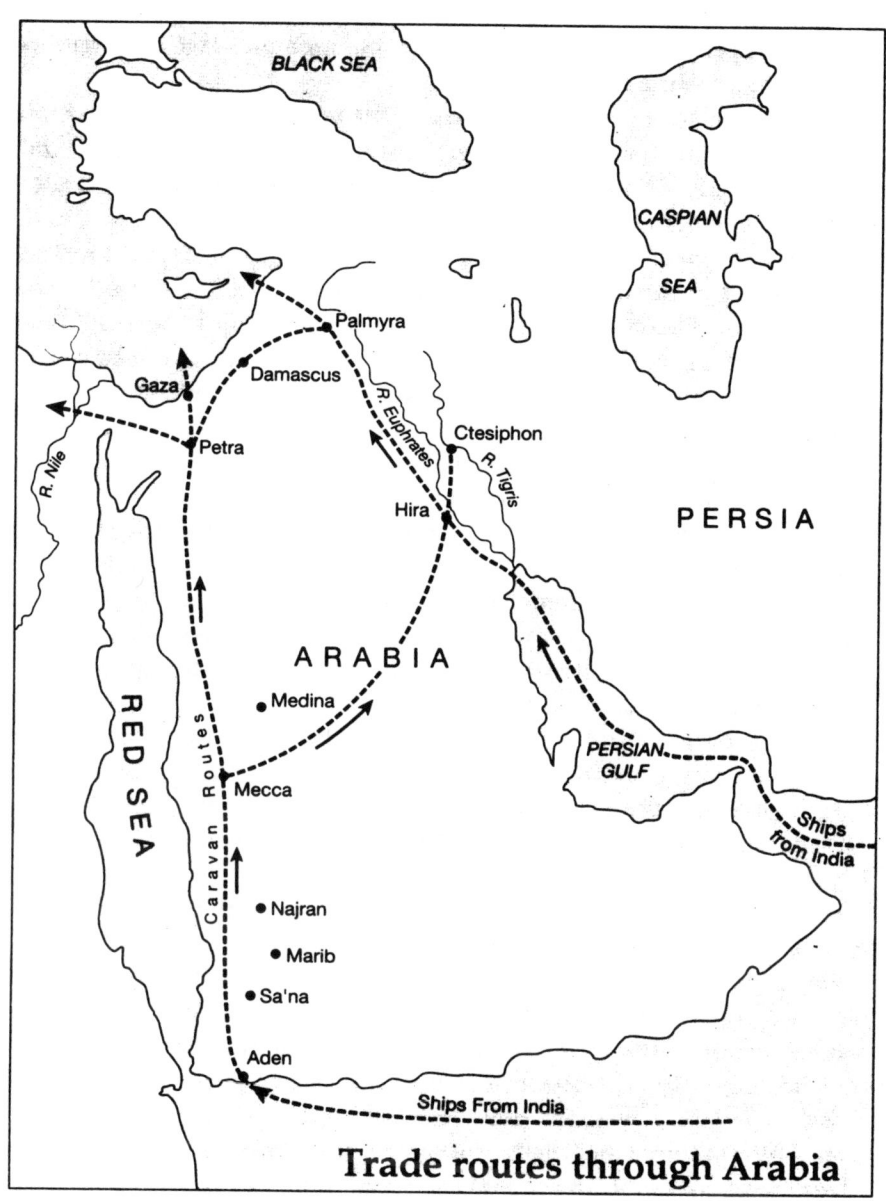

freely competed in the great poetry competitions which were so prominent a feature of Bedouin life.

There is some controversy concerning the origin of the Jews of Arabia who, apart from their religion, were so similar in culture to their Arab neighbours. The most likely explanation is that they were descended from refugees from persecution in the Holy Land and Babylonia, augmented by local converts. The Jews were engaged in agriculture, not in trade; and ancient Arabic writings credit them with the introduction into Arabia of the date palm and the honeybee as well as the techniques of advanced irrigation. Some Jews appear to have been educated; and the Qur'ān mentions learned Jews who taught the Torah. It was their ability to read that made bible stories, midrashim (rabbinic legends) and belief in the coming of the Messiah familiar to the pagan Arabs; and those were the seeds from which Islam grew.

There is firm evidence of a Jewish presence in the southern kingdom of Ḥimyar as well as in many of the desert oases. The burial place established at Beth Shearim (near Haifa in Israel) in about the year 200 had a chamber reserved for Jews from Ḥimyar; and they are mentioned with much irritation in letters from Christian visitors to the kingdom in the third and fourth centuries.

Arab legend ascribes the conversion to Judaism of the king and people of Ḥimyar to two Jewish rabbis from the oasis of Medina who cured the king of a terrible illness on an expedition to the north of Arabia. The king was so impressed by the rabbis that he and his generals converted to Judaism on the spot. He then took the rabbis back with him to Ḥimyar where they also converted part of the population – presumably members of the court and leading families.

We know that a Jewish king of Ḥimyar executed some Byzantine traders passing through his country in the year 516, allegedly in retaliation for ill-treatment of Jews in the Byzantine Empire; and also that he seized on the murder of two Jews in neighbouring Najrān to massacre its Christian inhabitants in an attempt to re-assert his authority over that rebel territory. The Byzantine emperor retaliated to avenge the Christians and, more important, to protect his vital trade route to the East. He conquered the pro-Persian Jewish colony on the island of Tirān at the mouth of the Red Sea and urged Christian Ethiopia to invade Ḥimyar. Ḥimyar fell to the Ethiopians in the year 525, when its Jewish king was reported to have "finally spurred his horse and plunged into the waters of the sea, never to be seen again".

It was not until 574 that a Jewish prince travelled to Persia and appealed to its king to rescue his country from the Ethiopians. According to legend, instead of promising help, the king sent him away with a gift of 10,000 silver dirhams. The Jew was recalled to court in haste after the king learned that he had distributed the entire sum in tips to the servants. " Of what use is this to me" the prince explained, "We have an inexhaustible supply of gold and silver in my country". Persia consequently sent an expedition to expel the Ethiopians and take control for itself; and that was followed by a period of internal strife, which was ended only by the coming of Islam.

CHAPTER 2

MUHAMMAD, MESSENGER OF GOD

All we know about the life of Muhammad and the early years of Islam comes from Muslim sources. First and foremost is the Qur'ān, comprising verses claimed to have been revealed by God to Muhammad. These were dictated by him to his disciples, who wrote them down on palm leaves, stones and whatever else was to hand, and collected together into a single volume twenty years or so after the Prophet's death in 632. The final version of the Qur'ān was fixed from seven different readings in the year 933.

The other main sources, based on material repeated by word of mouth for many years before finally being committed to writing, are the Histories and the Books of Traditions (Hadīths). The principal Histories were produced one hundred and twenty years after Muhammad's death; and the six standard Books of Traditions over a hundred years later. Of course they suffer from contradictions caused by lapses of memory and the differing viewpoints of their writers; but taken as a whole, they present a coherent and convincing account of those early years.

Muhammad was born in Mecca in the year 570, at a time when guardianship of the Ka'aba and successful international trade had greatly enriched its ruling clans. We are told that the Meccans were swollen with pride and their society was an unhappy one, differing from that of other Arabs because of its rivalries, greed, and great disparity between rich and poor.

Muhammad came from one of the poorer and less influential of the ruling families of Mecca. Orphaned at an early age, he had a reputation for honesty and reliability. Muhammad had already accompanied his uncle on trading missions to Syria, where he had come into contact with Christian monks and with Jews, when he was asked to lead a similar expedition himself on behalf of the wealthy widow Khadījah. This was successful; and he accepted Khadījah's proposal of marriage on his return to Mecca. The marriage was a happy one. Khadījah bore him six children; and Muhammad took no other wife or concubine until after her death.

Thus freed from financial anxiety for the first time, Muhammad was able to devote himself increasingly to spiritual concerns. He distributed much of his money to the poor, making his own family live frugally, and was conspicuously kind to slaves. He used to retire alone to an isolated mountain cave for days at a time in order to meditate and pray.

Muslims proudly claim that Muḥammad was unable to read or write, which enhances the miraculous nature of God's revelations to him. The Prophet's inability to read was not that unusual for a successful merchant of that time, or even of today, in some parts of the Middle East. But as one of mankind's most outstanding and charismatic religious leaders, Muḥammad was very, very far removed from the "ignorant camel driver" or the "dangerous madman" portrayed in some Christian and Jewish writings.

Muḥammad received his first revelation in the year 610, when he was forty years old. An angel appeared to him in his cave and commanded "Iqra" – recite! When Muḥammad demurred, the angel "overwhelmed me in his embrace until I reached the limits of my endurance". Then the angel proclaimed:

Recite in the name of your Lord, the Creator,
who created man from clots of blood.
Recite: your Lord is the most bountiful one,
who by the pen has taught mankind things they
did not know.

At first Muḥammad recoiled in horror from the memory of what had happened and doubted his own sanity. It was only three years later, when other revelations began to follow in quick succession, that he recovered his self-confidence and commenced his mission to the Arabs as the "Messenger of God".

The revelations, transmitted by the angel Gabriel to Muḥammad when in a state of trance, were taken down in writing by his followers as he repeated them later. They were collected together after the Messenger's death to form the sūras (verses) of the Qur'an.

The message of the Qur'ān is similar in essence to much Jewish and Christian teaching – there is no god but Allah, the all-powerful Creator, and Muḥammad is his Messenger: there will be a Day of Judgement: there is an afterlife in which the good will be rewarded and the wicked will burn in hell: life is to be lived according to divine law, with prayer and fasting, the giving of alms and the supporting of widows and orphans. When he secretly persuaded a number of pilgrims from Medina to accept his authority, Muḥammad's terms simply required them to accept the one God and to refrain from stealing, from fornicating, from burying alive newly born female babies and from slandering their neighbours. In addition they had to promise total obedience to the Messenger of God in "what is right".

Though Muḥammad had some success with the young and the poor, he was ridiculed by the leaders of Meccan society. The fact that he could not work miracles was held against him. The required total allegiance to the new community of Islam cut right across traditional tribal loyalties; and Muḥammad's teaching that their idol-worshipping ancestors were in gross error outraged the Arabs, who venerated their forefathers. Above all, the concept of only one God, and the resulting rejection of idols, seemed almost to have been designed to ruin the basis of Meccan prosperity: it would, quite simply, have been bad for business.

Some converts to Islam had been made amongst pilgrims who visited Mecca on the haj. A group from Medina, a desert oasis some two hundred and fifty miles away, secretly invited Muḥammad and his followers to join them there as their judge. So, in the year 622, Muḥammad and seventy of his followers fled from Mecca to Medina.

Medina was occupied by three Jewish tribes and two pagan tribes who had once forced their way into the oasis: each tribe lived in its own fortified village. Muḥammad was soon accepted as leader by the pagans and reached a modus vivendi with the Jews.

Unlike the Meccans, the pagans of Medina – who had long lived alongside Jews – were not shocked by the rejection of their gods under the new order. It did not affect their livelihood; and they were thrilled by the presence in their midst of the Prophet for the Arabs, with his revelations in their own tongue. There was a rapid tide of conversions to Islam.

It is clear that Muḥammad knew the Torah only from hearsay and cannot have read it for himself. The Jews of Medina probably assumed that the newly arisen Prophet was much confused by his imperfect knowledge of scripture and rabbinic legend – while to the Muslims, the Messenger's knowledge derived from divine revelation and it was the Jews who had confused and distorted their own version of the divine message.

As a fellow monotheist, Muḥammad looked to the Jews as his natural allies; and he no doubt hoped they would come to accept him as their long-awaited Messiah. He promptly adopted the Aramaic name "Medinta" used by the Jews ("al-Madinat" in Arabic) in place of Yathrib, the old name of the oasis. His followers were directed to face towards

Jerusalem in prayer and to recite three daily prayer services and special Friday evening prayers as did the Jews. Ablutions and forms of worship followed the Jewish pattern. It seems that the Muslims may have misunderstood the solemn Jewish fast of Kippur to be a celebration of victory over Pharaoh, for they too adopted the same day to celebrate their own successes. Above all, the Qur'ān itself is full of elements that had previously appeared in Jewish sources.

Though respecting Christians and accepting Jesus as a major prophet, Muḥammad vehemently rejected the notion that Jesus was the Son of God as well as all idea of a Trinity. In fact he compared himself to Moses many times and clearly regarded himself as his successor. According to the Qur'ān:

Before this book there was Moses's book ... and this book confirms it in the Arabic language.

And again, in response to taunts arising from the Jewish origin of one of his wives, Muḥammad proudly declared:

Aaron was my father and Moses my uncle.

Sadly for them and for future generations of their people, the Jews of Medina not only refused to accept Muḥammad but also subjected him to increasing criticism and mockery. Realising how little he knew about events described in their own Bible, they lost no opportunity of exposing what they took to be his ignorance. In repeated attempts to make him look ridiculous, they harassed him with trick questions such as "Name the nine plagues of Egypt". The Jews were also accused of conspiring with Muḥammad's enemies among the pagan Arabs, and among those who had recently converted to Islam, in order to undermine the new faith.

The Messenger was a proud man who could not tolerate public ridicule; and so, only eighteen months after his arrival in Medina, his attitude changed radically. Arab poets who had satirised him were assassinated together with certain Jews who had opposed him in one way or another.

Muḥammad demonstrated his displeasure with the Jews as a whole, and his growing self-confidence and independence of them, by adopting measures designed to steer his followers firmly against Jewish practices. Muslims were ordered to turn towards Mecca in prayer and no longer towards Jerusalem – now with five daily prayer services instead of the Jewish three. All traces of the Sabbath were eliminated when Friday was declared a day of public prayer on which work was allowed. Ramadan was instituted in place of Kippur. In a complete change of emphasis, Muḥammad began to lay far greater stress on Abraham, whom he claimed as the first Muslim, than on Moses. He also took over Christian arguments against Jewish interpretations of scripture and repeated the Christian calumny that the Jews had killed their prophets.

Non-Muslim scholars disagree as to whether Muḥammad was influenced more by Jewish or by Christian ideas. Although Moses is mentioned over one hundred times and Jesus only twice in the Meccan period of the Qur'ân, Muḥammad's often repeated dread of the Day of Judgement and hellfire is certainly more akin to Christian monasticism than to rabbinic Judaism. A suggestion has been made that he may have been swayed by the doctrines of a deviant Jewish sect – there were many around at the time – which might explain the sharp hostility to him displayed by the Jews of Medina. To Muslim scholars, it is of course inconceivable that the Prophet was influenced by any source other than the divine: his revelations came from God alone.

The three Jewish tribes of Medina, by then considered a threat to the Muslim community in its struggle against its enemies in Mecca, were accused of treachery. Curiously enough, the Jewish tribes made no attempt to defend one another against the common foe when pretexts were found to attack and besiege each of their villages in turn. They were eliminated one by one.

The first tribe was expelled from the oasis in 624, leaving much of its property behind to be shared out amongst the Muslims. The following year saw the expulsion of the second tribe which, being originally in a less vulnerable position, marched out of Medina with their heads held high and carrying their possessions with them. The remaining tribe did not fare so well. In a rare bout of savagery after their surrender, they were offered the choice of Islam or the sword. Even some Arabs admired their courage as the seven hundred men who had refused to convert were lined up alongside a trench and beheaded: their women and children were enslaved.

Muḥammad's actions were prompted by the politics of the situation and not by hatred of Jews as such. Individual Jews, not perceived as a threat to Islam, continued to live freely in both Medina and Mecca.

The Muslims spent the years between 623 and the Messenger's death in 632 in a series of raids and minor wars, first against the Mecca and the

Jewish tribes, and then against other tribes and oases.

Muḥammad did not always have to fight to get his way, for news of his great achievement in forcing the submission of Mecca soon became known throughout Arabia. In 631 he declared war against all idol-worshippers; and his reputation was by then sufficient for that declaration to be taken seriously. A stream of deputations flocked to Medina from all over the peninsula, there to be both awed and charmed by the charismatic new leader. Without exception they bowed to his authority and returned home bearing gifts and the faith of Islam. It is claimed that the leader of the Jewish tribes of Afghanistan, who proudly claimed and still claim descent from King Saul, visited the Prophet at this time and accepted Islam for himself and his people.

The Messenger offered generous terms to Jews and Christians to persuade them to submit quietly to the new order. Typical, and forming a precedent for the later conquests of Islam, were those contained in his long letter to the Christians of Najrān and the Jewish princes of Ḥimyar:

If a Jew or Christian becomes a Muslim he is a believer with the same rights and obligations as other Muslims. Those however who hold fast to their own religion, whether Jews or Christians, will not be obliged to change it. They must pay the poll tax, one dinar for every adult ... He who pays this tax to God and his Apostle has his security guaranteed ... but he who withholds the tax is an enemy ...

Muḥammad died of natural causes in the year 632, leaving Arabia united under Islam.

CHAPTER 3

THE CONQUESTS OF THE ARABS

By definition, Muḥammad – as Messenger of God and the last of the Prophets – was irreplaceable: yet a new leader had to be found at once if his achievements were not to be squandered. The Arabs found it very difficult to elect a successor and bitter struggles between rival clans resulted in the violent death in office of three out of the first four khalīfs. Those early controversies persisted; and it was the refusal of some to accept the legitimacy of any but a descendant of the murdered Khalīf 'Alī (cousin and son-in-law of the Prophet) that created the Shi'a movement, which permanently split Islam.

Welded together by Islam, their poverty and their greed, the half-starved Bedouin nomads erupted from Arabia with extraordinary vigour. The Byzantine Empire was humbled and the Persian Empire totally destroyed during their first twenty years of warfare.

By 732, one hundred years after the death of Muḥammad, the Arab Empire stretched from the Atlantic in the west to modern Pakistan in the east. At one stage, the vanguard reached a point in France only two hundred and fifty miles from Dover before falling back into Spain. Progress was slower after that, with Sardinia, Sicily and parts of Southern Italy gradually added to the Islamic world.

In retrospect, it is not too difficult to find convincing reasons for the astonishing success of the comparatively small body of Bedouin tribesmen in defeating the armies of two mighty empires and then going on to conquer much of the civilised world. There can be no doubt that Muḥammad had the rare ability to inspire unlimited devotion in most of those who met him in Arabia. Also the essential simplicity and egalitarianism of Islam suited the mentality of the Arabs, already discontented with their primitive form of paganism and aspiring to a nobler expression of their religious yearnings. The new creed of Islam, combined with the old fighting traditions of the Bedouin tribes, provided the Arabs with the self-confidence they needed to challenge the rest of the world.

Once the invasions started, belief in the one God who had chosen the Arabs and rewarded them with success after success became inspirational. Fighting, Arab-style, seemed to be the way of God as the Bedouin warriors used the deserts like seas – appearing suddenly from nowhere and, whenever necessary, retreating back where none could follow.

Looked at in another way, the Arab conquest was a classic invasion of the world's settled lands by semi-starved nomads, seeking bread and booty – but this time, spurred on by the powerful missionary zeal of Islam.

It should not be forgotten that the Arabs exploded into a world exhausted by twenty-six years of constant warfare, a world whose inhabitants longed for peace and stability and had come to believe that great changes were inevitable. Christian heretics and Jews in the Byzantine Empire, to whom almost any change must have seemed for the better, welcomed the Arabs with open arms. The Christians and Jews of the Persian Empire too, weary of civil and religious strife, also willingly accepted the prospect of change.

Another important factor in the overwhelming success of the Arabs was the generosity of their surrender terms. For most pagans, the choice of Islam or the sword was not onerous: they too could join the ranks of the conquerors by simply declaring: "There is no God but Allah, and Muḥammad is his Messenger". Also it soon became widely known that Jews, Christians and Zoroastrians would not be harmed by the triumphant Muslims so long as they submitted to the new order by paying the poll tax, which often amounted to no more than the tax demanded by the former regimes.

The result was that, in time, almost all the defeated nations aspired to the name "Arab". Though strict social barriers between Arabian and non-Arabian Muslims were erected in the first century following the conquest, those dissolved and merit alone became the key to advancement for Muslims in the expanding empire.

The Arabs themselves remained nomads or travelling merchants at heart and very few of them settled down in the conquered territories to cultivate the land. Some remained in the new garrison towns, at first well-insulated from the local populations: others continued to lead the wave of conquest onward, as the original Arab armies were replaced by native troops recruited from the defeated nations; and the remainder simply returned home with their loot.

According to surviving records, Jews helped the Arabs in many places. From Syria to Spain, they opened city gates to the besieging armies; and in Spain, they often garrisoned the captured cities to enable the Muslims to sweep on to further conquests.

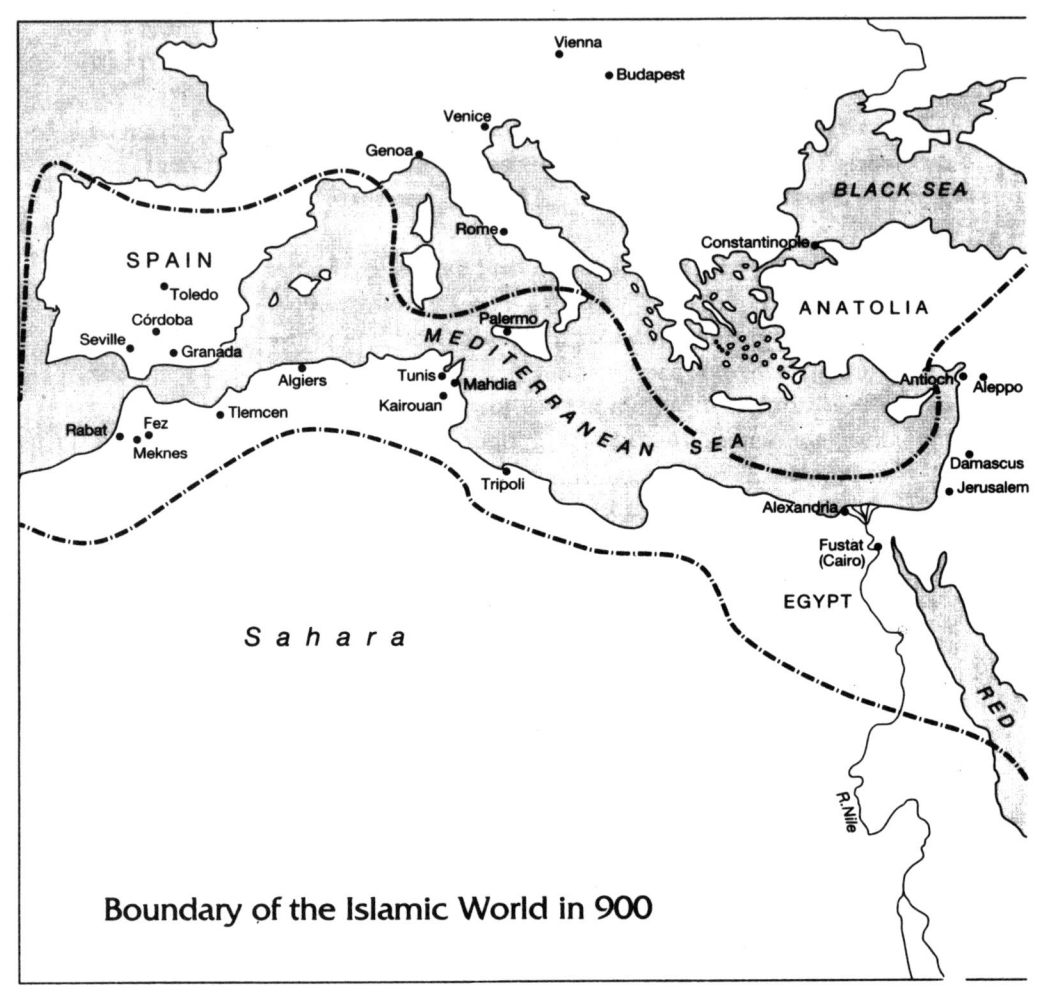

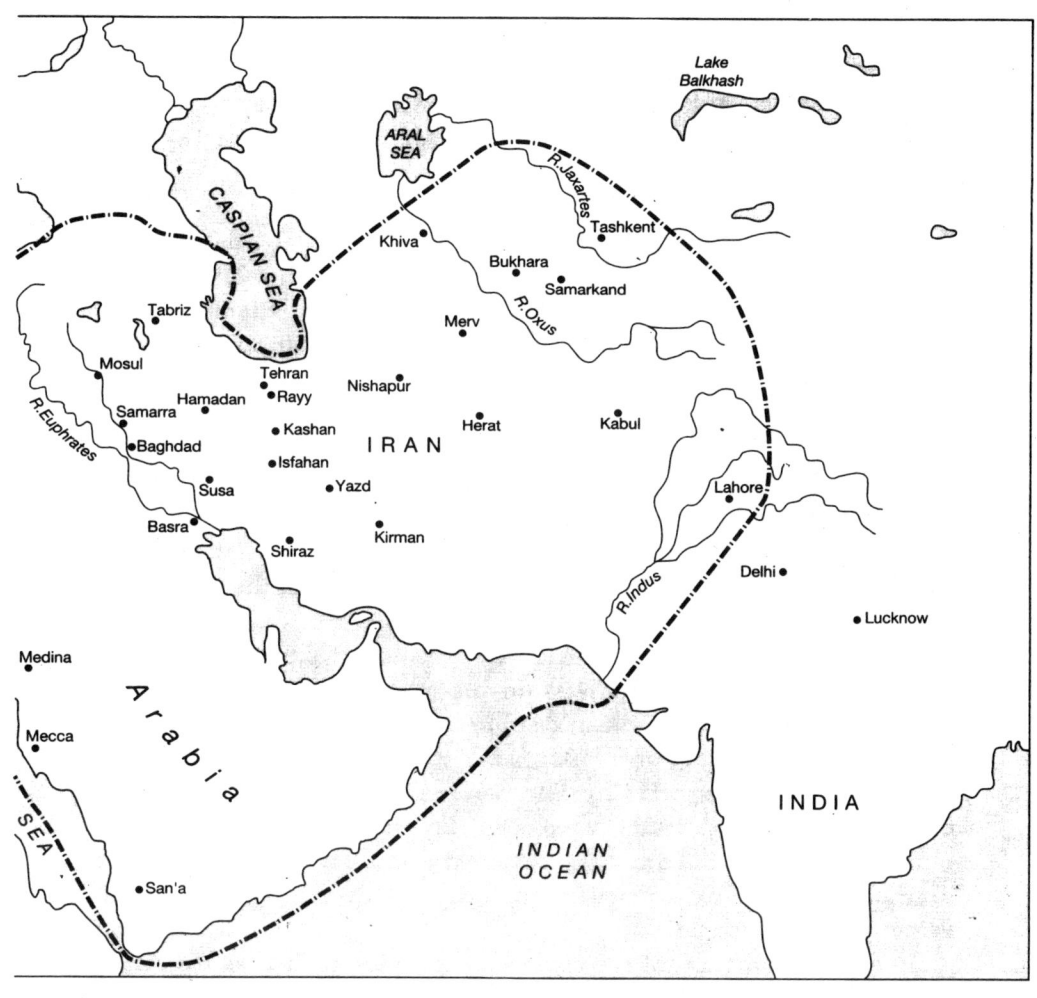

It had become their custom to gather the Jews in each town and set them as a garrison over the municipality ... while most of the men would march on ... They did this in Granada and Elvira, but not in Granada or Reijo because they could not find any Jews in them. (3.1)

In 658, Gaon Yizhak of Pumbedītha, at the head of 90,000 Jews, was reported to have welcomed Khalīf 'Alī into Firuz-Shapūr. The Exilarch Bustānay was even awarded one of the Persian King's daughters by the grateful Arabs – and as another daughter was given to Husain, grandson of the Prophet, that was no mean gift.

The conquests of Islam united both halves of the Jewish people under a single political and cultural system. Arabic became the universal language, replacing the Aramaic, Persian, Greek and Latin they had previously spoken. Jews, accustomed to adversity, found their change of masters an improvement. They survived the hardship brought about by the conquest and were eventually able to participate in the creation of the new Arabic civilisation that followed.

The Zoroastrian religion, previously an integral part of the power structure of the Persian state, was unable to survive its utter defeat by the Arabs. Though the Persian people later re-asserted its genius in Islamic guise, the religion of Zoroaster dwindled rapidly and never recovered. The persecuted Christian heretics of Syria and Iraq survived the conquest, though much weakened. Some Christians (Copts) also remained in Egypt; but the shock of defeat was too much to bear for the dominant Orthodox Christian majority of North Africa, which eventually disappeared.

Times were hard for all the conquered peoples at first, as the Arabs reaped the spoils of victory. The conquest, after all, had been at least partly for gain; and the empire was maintained primarily as a source of wealth for the Bedouin troops and their descendants. Conditions did not improve until the new masters learned that, to quote an old Arabic proverb, "One cannot slaughter a cow and milk it at the same time".

The Arabs, being predominantly warriors and merchants, despised agriculture and took no interest in the land. The very heavy burden of taxation they imposed on the countryside caused large numbers of poverty-stricken peasants to flee to the towns despite strenuous efforts to prevent them. The very mechanics of the conquest encouraged commerce, industry and bureaucracy, as did the Arab mercantile leadership that replaced the former imperial aristocracies. The many new garrison towns built by the Arabs, such as Kufa, Basra, Qomm,

Fustāt (Old Cairo) and Kairouān stimulated consumer demand. The provisioning of large-scale military expeditions, the building of the necessary roads and the development of sea transport brought a great expansion of trade in their wake, as did the gradually increasing purchasing power of the Christian West.

The result of all this was a large increase in activities connected with trade and industry at the expense of agriculture. At a time when Europe was in the grip of the feudal system, with its lords and serfs, the Islamic world was fast becoming an urban, bourgeois society.

The effect of these changes on the Jews was startling. They had been an agricultural people since time immemorial, both in the Holy Land and in exile. But in the centuries following the conquest, they were transformed into a nation primarily engaged in commerce and manufacture.

CHAPTER 4

ISLAM, JUDAISM AND THE JEWS

Islam, claiming to be God's last and perfect revelation to mankind, extended limited toleration to members of the older monotheistic faiths on condition they submitted humbly to its rule. In contrast, the only choice open to polytheists was Islam or the sword – though the less wasteful alternative of slavery was often substituted for the sword.

The Qur'ān frequently refers to Jews and Christians, who had received earlier revelations from God but had then distorted and corrupted them. Though some of its suras (verses) mention Jews and Christians in friendly terms and are quoted in support of Islam's tolerant attitude to fellow monotheists, others display very different sentiments. The Qur'ān, it must be remembered, came to Muḥammad in stages throughout the many years of his ministry – from the time he was a persecuted outcast to that of his final role as the undisputed master of all Arabia.

Zoroastrians, mentioned once only in the Qur'ān, were included with the monotheists for practical reasons. Later, again because of political imperatives, other peoples that would be far harder to describe as monotheists – such as Hindus – were also granted toleration on the same terms.

Non-believers, though protected by Islam, were generally despised because of their wilful persistence in refusing to accept the words of God recorded in the Qur'ān. However, unlike Jews in Christian Europe, they were neither hated nor demonised.

Mainstream (Sunni) Islam and Judaism have more in common with each other than with Christianity. First and foremost, they both share the basic concept of the absolute unity of God. Though Muslims accept Jesus as a major prophet, they strenuously deny that he was the Son of God. In the words of the Qur'ān:

... Allah is one, Allah the eternal. He begets not and is not begotten. Nor is there anyone like him.

Abraham is accepted as the first man to have received God's revelations; and most other Jewish patriarchs and prophets are also revered by Islam.

Both religions are based on divinely given books. The Qur'ān, like the

Torah, is the unchanging word of God; and every letter of its text is holy. Sunni Muslims go even further and believe that the Qur'ân is eternal and uncreated – as is the view of the Torah held by some Jewish mystics.

Muslim forms of worship are closer to those of the Synagogue than the Church. Neither Islam nor Judaism employs priests with supernatural powers to serve at symbolic altars of sacrifice. Indeed, Jewish rabbis and Sunni alim receive similar training and perform much the same function. Other concepts such as the sanctity of Jerusalem, forbidden and permitted foods, and many others, appear to have come directly from Judaism.

The equivalent position of law in Islam and Judaism may not be a coincidence, for Islamic law first developed in Iraq, home to the great academies of Jewish learning. In both faiths, holy law governs every aspect of human activity and its very study is an act of worship. Both distinguish between "written" and "oral" law in much the same way; and in the development of "oral" law, the mufti's fatwa serves the same purpose as the rabbi's teshuvah (an authoritative statement of the law on an obscure or disputed point). Another common feature of the two systems is that neither was imposed by the state or by a central ecclesiastical authority – as was the canon law of the Church – but was developed by the deliberations of independent scholars.

Muslims deny that Islam owes anything to Judaism – for as a faith coming directly from God, any outside influence is inconceivable. Similarities are attributed to the common origin of the two religions in divine revelation, and differences to corruption in Jewish texts and interpretations.

Jews were much influenced by Muslim methods when they set about the formidable task of codifying Talmudic law, which had never been attempted before the Arab conquest. The Talmud contains accounts of the discussions of groups of sages who finally reached consensus on different issues in Jewish law. The idea of extracting the individual laws from those accounts, summarising them and then setting them out in ordered sequence, was entirely new. The logical thought processes of the Greek philosophers, alien to Jews of the Talmudic era, were absorbed from the Arabs after the conquest. Jewish poetry, literature, philosophy, science and theology were also revived and quickened as the result of the same influence.

It was contact with the Arabs – obsessed with their own language and with the text of the Qur'ân – that stimulated similar fascination amongst Jews. They turned to the Hebrew language and studied it systematically for the first time in their already long history. Hebrew grammar, lexicology and philology were then created in direct imitation of the work being done with Arabic. Sacred Hebrew texts were subjected to intensive scrutiny in order to eliminate errors and establish definitive versions; and the science of pschat, that of determining the literal meaning of the Hebrew text, owed its initial impetus to Arab influence. Pschat later spread to the Ashkenazim, of whom Rashi was the outstanding master.

Islam's attitude to the Jews was, and still is, governed by a contradictory two-pronged approach. On the one hand, Muslims shared the old pre-Islamic Arab feelings of friendship for their Jewish neighbours, who were praised in early Arabic literature for their loyalty, hospitality, generosity and usefulness. Even in modern times, Muslims unhesitatingly formed business partnerships with Jews and lived with them on terms of mutual respect and trust. Jews and Christians are both Peoples of the Book. They worship the same God as do Muslims; and their prophets, from Abraham and Moses to Jesus, are the same prophets. Providing they submitted to the rule of Islam, Jews and Christians were guaranteed freedom of worship and the protection of the Muslim community.

The other parallel approach uses the same facts but interprets them in a negative way. Though worshipping the same God, Jews and Christians refused to accept the authenticity of his revelation to Muḥammad. Instead, they perversely falsified their sacred books and distorted God's message. Jews in particular are to be distrusted because the Jewish tribes of Medina, by rejecting the Prophet and refusing to support him in his war against Mecca, became his enemy. There is no doubt that the Qur'ān and the Hadīth are far more hostile to Jews than to Christians. To quote the Qur'ān:

... the most hostile to believers are Jews and idolaters ... the greatest affection (for believers comes) from those who say: we are Christians.

Present-day fundamentalist thinking goes much further in its portrayal of the Jews as eternal enemies of Islam, forever plotting its destruction.

Christian belief in the Trinity was highly offensive to the Muslim concept of the unity of God. It may seem strange therefore that Islam preferred Christians to Jews; but the fact that the Christians of Arabia had little contact with Muḥammad and never came into conflict with him, was decisive. To be fair, it would have been easy for the Muslims to have carried their dislike into action, when they took over the reins of government after the conquest, by simply confirming the old Byzantine anti-Jewish laws; but in fact Islamic law makes no distinction between Jews and Christians.

There is a great deal of evidence to suggest that, despite the negative religious attitude, Jews were often treated with less suspicion than Christians. In practice, Jews were often extremely useful to the Muslim rulers and were therefore exempted from some of the burdensome regulations heaped on non-believers.

Christians, because of their contacts and sympathies with the Byzantine Empire, and later with Christian Europe, always presented a potential threat to the Muslim state, while Jews did not. It was not unusual therefore, in the early years of the conquest, for the Arabs to deport entire populations of doubtfully loyal Christians from sensitive locations and replace them with more reliable Jews. The Ottoman Turks repeated the same policy many centuries later during the expansion of their own empire.

After all, Jews had demonstrated their friendship during the conquest by helping the Arabs against the Christians almost everywhere. Islamic law developed in Iraq, the ancient centre of Jewish scholarship, where mutual influences between the two faiths were strong. Iraq was also the seat of the Exilarch, leader of all Jews, who as a descendant of King David – a revered Muslim prophet – occupied an honoured position at the Khalīf's court. Despite religious reservations, practical ties between followers of the two faiths often remained strong.

Muslim hostility to Jews was not based on theology. Though part of the birth pangs of Islam, it was not a vital part as it was in Christianity. Jews were always a small minority in the Muslim world: they presented no threat and could largely be ignored. Though often despised as unbelievers, and envied when they became too successful, there was seldom much reason to hate them.

THE SHI'A BRANCH OF ISLAM

The Shi'a movement started after the murder of 'Alī, the fourth khalīf and first cousin and son-in-law of the Prophet. Its followers, comprising about 15% of all Muslims, insist that succession to the leadership of Islam belongs only to the descendants of 'Alī. Denying the legitimacy of others who occupied that position, they split Islam – and that split continues to this day.

The doctrines of this important minority differ from those of mainstream Sunni Muslims in one very important respect. Shi'ites, though themselves divided into different sects, all believe that divine revelation did not cease with the death of Muḥammad – the last of the prophets – but that it has continued in human form ever since.

The first leaders after Muḥammad – called the Imāms – were recognised as manifestations of the primordial light that sustains the universe. As such, they were free from sin and their interpretations of the true hidden meaning of the Qur'ān were infallible. The last Imām – and the Shi'a sects differ as to how many there were before him – did not die but disappeared or went into hiding. It is this hidden Imām who guides succeeding Shi'a divines in their interpretations of the Qur'ān; and it is he who will re-appear in the world at the end of time as a kind of messiah.

For Shi'ites therefore, it is the continuing and divinely inspired interpretation of the Qur'ān – and not the consensus of independent scholars – that defines their belief and practice. The Sharī'a (holy law of Islam) is not necessarily binding on Shi'ites in all its aspects, as some may be modified by an infallible ruling from the hidden Imām through his proxy.

This doctrine of infallibility can work in opposite directions in so far as the treatment of minorities is concerned. The Fātimids of Egypt, for example, were one of the most tolerant Muslim dynasties ever towards the Jews; and many generations of their khalīfs contributed funds towards the upkeep of the Jewish academy of Jerusalem. On the other hand, the Shi'ites of Iran developed a theory of impurity in which Jews were considered ritually unclean. Their very touch was polluting; and at one time Jews were even required to remain indoors when it rained, lest Muslims be contaminated by water that had come into contact with them.

CHAPTER 5

THE DHIMMA

According to tradition, when the Christian Patriarch of Jerusalem surrendered his city to Khalīf 'Umar 1 in 638, he offered detailed terms of submission which were accepted by the Arabs with only minor additions.

... to Allah's servant 'Umar, Commander of the Faithful ... When you advanced against us, we asked you for a guarantee of protection for our persons, our offspring, our property and the people of our sect, and we have taken upon ourselves the following obligations ... (5.1)

This treaty of surrender, called the Dhimma, was incorporated in the holy law of Islam and became the basis for the treatment of all monotheists forced by conquest to submit to the rule of Islam. Historians, pointing to the many inconsistencies in the traditional account, consider it far more likely that the Dhimma was a later summary of the security precautions adopted by the Arabs warriors during the first century of Islam. However the idea of the Dhimma as a treaty between conquerors and conquered persisted for many years until it was replaced by the harsher concept of a one-sided concession to non-believers by the victorious Arabs as an act of clemency following conquest.

For Muslims, the purpose of the Dhimma was to guarantee the superior status of Islam for all time. During the first centuries after the conquest, when Muslims were still a minority, it was also used to preserve the well-being of the non-Muslim subject peoples, depended on to provide the revenue required to sustain the new ruling class and swell the coffers of the state. This policy was clearly set out in a letter from Khalīf 'Umar 1 to one of his governors:

The Muslims of our day will eat from the work of these people as long as they shall live. And when they die, our sons shall eat from their sons for ever ... Therefore ... do not let the Muslims oppress them or harm them or consume their property except as permitted, but faithfully observe the conditions you have accorded them ... (5.2)

In return, the dhimmīs (protected people) were guaranteed their lives, property and religious freedom. They were free from economic restriction and could follow any occupation. Except in the Hejaz, they could live wherever they chose; and only rarely were they forced into ghettos. The rights of dhimmīs were protected by Islamic law and Muslims were forbidden to disregard its provisions. Thus the 11th century Khalīf al-Zahir:

... be assured that they (dhimmīs) will enjoy protection and care and retain their position as protected communities ... and it is the duty of all members of the Muslim community to protect him (the dhimmī) ... (5.3)

Dhimmīs lived within their own communities, which enjoyed almost full autonomy in internal affairs. Each small community of Jews was ruled in accordance with Jewish law, administered by its own elected rabbis, judges and officials. Providing they paid their taxes and kept the peace, the ordinary people were left undisturbed and only their leaders had much contact with the Islamic state.

Though the internal affairs of the dhimmīs were regulated by their own courts, disputes with Muslims usually came before Muslim courts. There, some schools of Islamic law allowed dhimmīs almost full equality in civil and criminal proceedings; but other schools would not accept the evidence of a dhimmī against that of a Muslim and put a lower value on a dhimmī than on a Muslim when assessing compensation for death or injury.

Submission to the rule of Islam was demonstrated by the paying of the jizya (poll tax). The jizya, demanded on the authority of the Qur'ān, was imposed everywhere without exception until European notions of equality began to prevail in the latter part of the nineteenth century. According to the Qur'ān:

Fight against those ... who do not practice the true religion, among those who have been given the Book, until they pay the jizya from their hand, they being humbled.

Ancient regulations specified that the act of paying the poll tax shall involve the public humiliation of each and every dhimmī:

... the dhimmī shall appear (in person) with bent back and bowed head. The tax collector must treat him with disdain, even with violence, seizing his beard, slapping his cheeks and the like ... (5.4)

In practice however, most Muslim rulers were concerned more with the efficiency of their tax-collecting system than with imposing petty humiliation on the tax payers; and so the extreme demands of Islamic theology were disregarded more often than not. Indeed, it made sense to keep dhimmīs sweet when the success of the economy depended so much on their efforts; and two early authorities directed that:

... they should be treated with leniency ...
and

... they must not be burdened beyond capacity ... nor must they be caused to suffer ... (5.5)

Here we come across the typical Muslim contradiction in their attitude to minorities. The harsh rulings of the religious authorities, when applied rigorously, resulted in the humiliation of those affected; but when tempered by the goodwill or the pragmatism of Muslim rulers, they were transformed into relatively minor disabilities. It depended very much on the prosperity and self-confidence of the particular Islamic society as to which view prevailed at any one time or place.

Though the jizya was applied in different ways throughout the empire, two distinct traditions emerged. The first was a uniform tax of one gold dinar for all adults – men and women, free or enslaved. The second was a graded tax comprising one dinar for the poor, two dinars for the middle class and four dinars for the wealthy. In the latter system only one in four of the Jewish population paid the jizya, as women, children, cripples and slaves were exempt.

The jizya, by itself, could not satisfy the ever-growing cash demands of the state and so a land tax, the kharāj, was also imposed – first on dhimmīs alone and then eventually on Muslims too. As the kharāj often amounted to as much as one-fifth of the total crop, it became an almost intolerable burden on the already impoverished peasants and was responsible for a mass flight from the countryside to the towns.

With the growth of trade, customs dues became an increasingly important source of revenue. In theory, dhimmīs were obliged to pay at twice the rate as Muslims – 5% on a minimum value of 20 dinars, as against 2.5% on a minimum value of 40 dinars. But here again, the differential rate was not always imposed. For example, it was not collected in Fātimid Egypt; and when Saladin tried to re-introduce the tax, the protests of foreign merchants soon forced him to change his mind.

According to law, those were the only special taxes paid by dhimmīs. But that did not prevent greedy officials, far from central authority, from enriching themselves by imposing special levies on defenceless dhimmī communities.

The visible display of respect for Islam and for Muslims was fundamental to the Dhimma. Lack of respect for Islam or its Prophet was a serious crime, punishable by flogging in some Islamic schools of law and by death in others. Though prosecutions were not common, the threat of denunciation was real enough and at times contributed to a climate of fear. Nevertheless Maimonides, in the 12th century, felt secure enough to describe Muḥammad in the most unflattering terms in his famous letter (written in Hebrew characters) to the Jews of the Yemen.

An incident with far-reaching consequences for Tunisia occurred 1857 when a Jew, Batto Sfez, was accused of insulting Islam by a Muslim with whom he had quarrelled. The Bey insisted on his being brought to trial in the most rigorous of the four Islamic courts, where his evidence could not be accepted against that of a Muslim and the death sentence was mandatory. The Bey's refusal of a reprieve, despite pressure by the French consul and the promise of heavy bribes, resulted in the arrival of a French naval squadron at La Goulette and the subsequent proclamation of a European-type constitution.

Deference to Muslims was incorporated in numerous sets of regulations. One of the most recent and shocking, issued in Hamadan in 1892, declares that a Jew must never overtake a Muslim in the street or talk loudly to him. He must claim his debts from Muslims in a quavering voice; and must hang his head and remain silent if insulted. He must never defend himself against Muslims, not even against unruly children.

The Dhimma existed to preserve the primacy of Islam and the superiority of Muslims in the world. In the egalitarian world of Islam, there was no bar to any Muslim rising to the highest rank, other than his ability or luck. A dhimmī, in contrast, lived outside society: though his basic rights were guaranteed, he could never become a full member of society by achieving the status of a Muslim.

The ability to bear arms was a crucial demonstration of that difference. A dhimmi, certainly not a warrior (or "gentleman"), was absolutely forbidden to bear arms in any circumstances – that being the exclusive privilege of Muslims. The dhimmi was also required to ride on an ass and not on a horse, side-saddle and not astride, to emphasise his inferior status. A direct consequence of the situation in which dhimmīs were forbidden to bear arms and compelled always to rely on the Muslim state for protection is that they were exempt from military service – a very considerable relief and at least part-compensation for the disability.

Dress too became important. Each nation, including that of the Arabs, maintained its own distinctive manner of dress with some pride; and at first, when the Arabs were a tiny minority living in their own garrison towns, there was little danger of any blurring of identity. However, Islamic law anticipated future laxity by strictly forbidding non-believers from imitating Arab dress, manners and customs. Arabs too were urged to differentiate themselves in all ways possible from dhimmīs.

This suited the Jews very well for they preferred to remain a nation apart, awaiting redemption. To this day observant Jews may be seen on the streets of New York, London and Jerusalem, clad in the fashions of the Polish nobility of hundreds of years ago. The mode of dress adopted is incidental: what is important is that they dress in a distinctive manner, different from other people on the street. The wearing of a kippah (skullcap) outdoors is a lesser symbol of that same difference.

As times changed and the Arab mode of dress became fashionable and spread throughout the Muslim empire, further regulations became necessary to prevent dhimmīs from resembling Muslims in appearance and forgetting their inferior status. Jews and Christians were ordered to wear distinctively coloured outer garments, or special turbans, belts or badges, to distinguish them from Muslims. They were also forbidden to wear costly fabrics and jewellery in public. When imposed by rulers with particular reasons to punish dhimmīs, such regulations multiplied to a ridiculous extent. The "mad" Khalīf al-Hākim, for example, once forced all Christians to wear a cross two feet long and one finger wide on their clothes, while Jews had to hang a wooden ball weighing at least five pounds around their necks: as may be imagined, the enforcement of such rules soon lapsed.

Dress regulations were more often disregarded than strictly enforced where Jews were concerned, especially during the early self-confident years of Arab rule and again during the heyday of the Ottoman Empire. Whatever Islamic jurists may have decreed, most Muslim rulers were not interested in humiliating their subjects, except sometimes to swell their coffers by making rich dhimmīs pay for exemptions. The records reveal stark contrasts. We read of richly dressed Jews, wearing the distinctive clothing of the Islamic nobility, proudly riding their horses through the streets in some places – while in other places and at other times, particularly on the fringes of the Muslim world, Jews were made to dress and bear themselves as outcasts from society.

Though Khalīf 'Umar 1 had urged:

Do not appoint Christians or Jews to public office ... (5.6)

and Islamic lawyers all supported that view, the prohibition was widely ignored by Muslim rulers. Many dhimmīs were appointed to high office in some Muslim states; and once, very exceptionally, a Jew even attained the top position as Vizier to the Muslim King of Granada.

Dhimmīs could not build new places of worship but were allowed to repair existing ones. It is clear from the number of synagogues and churches in the Muslim world that this rule must sometimes have been ignored. Its existence, however, resulted in permanent feelings of insecurity; and during periods when extreme views prevailed, offending churches and synagogues were actually destroyed. Worship had always to be quiet to avoid offending Muslims – no bells, clappers or other noisy devices, and no processions or display of crosses in the streets.

Graves had to be level with the ground so as to be lower than Muslim graves; and that is probably the origin of the flat memorial stones still used in the Sephardi tradition. Cemeteries themselves were not usually attacked during riots, when trouble was focused on the actual burial processions through the streets.

There was also a general rule that the dwellings and the houses of worship of dhimmīs must be lower in height than those of neighbouring Muslim buildings. Historians have concluded that these regulations affected Christians more than Jews, for though surviving Jewish documents are full of complaints about iniquitous taxes, there is little mention of these particular matters.

A dhimmī was protected for so long as he remained in the faith to which he was born; but he was forbidden to convert to any faith other than Islam – the argument being that he was blameless at birth, having no choice other than to follow in the religion of his parents.

A dhimmī must not attempt to convert a Muslim, on pain of death. Apostasy from Islam was punishable by death and the confiscation of all wealth; but here again, the recommended policy was one of leniency. The apostate should be invited to return to Islam and goes free if he accepts. If not, he is made to lie on a plank and goes through the same process. If he still persists in his refusal, he is tied to the plank and a spear put to his heart. Only then does a refusal result in instant death.

It was a capital offence for a dhimmī man to marry a Muslim woman; but a Muslim man could marry a dhimmī woman.

In theory, people could only inherit within their own religious community. Thus, a dhimmī could not inherit from a Muslim; and a convert to Islam could not inherit from an unconverted dhimmī kinsman or leave money to a dhimmī on his death. However, as may be imagined, the rule that a Muslim cannot inherit from a dhimmī was sometimes circumvented. Intolerant Shi'ites caused great hardship during periods of forced conversion by insisting that a Muslim heir always took precedence over a dhimmī heir.

The rule on slaves, often disregarded, is that a dhimmī cannot own Muslim slaves. Muslims could of course own dhimmī slaves.

Dhimmīs remained the majority of the population during the first few hundred years of Islam. Their number was steadily eroded as more and more of the subject peoples embraced Islam until, by the middle of the 10th century, they had become a minority – but a minority that still contributed substantially to the economy, the government and the culture of the Muslim world.

From the 11th century onwards, the time of the Crusades, pressure from the outside world began to grow; and by the 13th century, much of the empire had fallen into the hands of Turkish dynasties descended from mercenary soldiers formerly employed by Arab masters. These alien rulers oppressed their local Muslim populations with remarkable lack of sensitivity and caused widespread economic decline. Jealousy and resentment of dhimmīs by the Muslim masses grew as their own conditions worsened – and the governments responded by treating dhimmīs harshly. Their position deteriorated and remained low until the rise of the Ottoman Turks in the 15th century.

The expansion of the Ottoman Empire brought much relief to the Jews for very similar reasons to those that prevailed during the Arab conquest. Jews then enjoyed nearly two centuries of well-being under the Ottoman Turks at a time when their brethren in western and central Europe were experiencing the deepest misery: they fared badly however during the long decline of the Ottoman empire, losing their privileges and gradually descending into obscurity and poverty. In the later years of the 19th century, roles were reversed for the first time in history as emancipated Jews of Christian Europe began coming to the aid of their oppressed Sephardi brethren.

The progressive breakdown of traditional Muslim attitudes in the face of egalitarian European influences led to the formal abolition of the Dhimma by the Ottoman Sultan in 1856, when all his subjects were declared equal under the law.

The fall of the Ottoman Empire after the First World War of 1914-1918 ushered in the colonial period, after which the different countries of the old Islamic empires gained their independence. Though the concept of the Dhimma remains deeply engrained in Muslim thought and attitudes, it now hardly exists in practice except possibly in Iran.

Part 2

Jews in the world of Islam
The first 500 years

CHAPTER 6

SOURCES

The great problem confronting anyone attempting to picture the Jewish condition in the centuries before the coming of Islam and in its early years is the almost complete lack of Jewish records, other than religious writings that ignored contemporary events. What little we do know has been gleaned from fragmentary mentions in mainly unfriendly sources such as Christian decrees against the Jews. Sad though it may be to accept, the barest outline of the Jewish story can only be pieced together with the help of the spiteful comments of sworn enemies.

For example, we know of the part played by the Jews of Arabia in the drama accompanying the rise of Islam and its Prophet only from later and distinctly hostile Arab accounts. Even earlier, our knowledge of the continued existence of the great Babylonian Jewish community after the return to Zion of some of its members in the 5th century BCE comes only from occasional references in Palestinian writings and from the much later Roman-Jewish historian Josephus (1st century CE).

History, as we now understand the term, was considered a sheer waste of time by the rabbis; and it is clear that the Jews of the period displayed no interest at all in recording and preserving accounts of the times through which they were living. Historical writing, so brilliant in the Biblical era, ceased altogether with Josephus in the 1st century CE; and even his works were promptly forgotten by Jews. Attention to history only resumed, and falteringly at that, in the 16th century after the expulsion of the Jews from Spain.

According to the historian Yosef Yerushalmi, this striking indifference to history was due to the Jewish view of the Bible solely as a record of the nation's encounters with God – God's challenges and its responses. For Jews, eagerly awaiting the end of the historical process by redemption at the hands of the Messiah, the Bible with its prophesies was the divinely revealed pattern of what had been and what was still to come: nothing else mattered. The rise and fall of mighty empires, as well as daily events of lesser consequence, could all be clearly understood in the light of the prophesies, and then related directly to the underlying pulse of history described in the Bible. Their actual details must have seemed so unimportant as not even to be worth noting.

The first 200 years after the Arab conquest, from about 650 to 850, are the most obscure in the whole of Jewish history. The Arabs were far too busy to interest themselves in a small and non-threatening minority: the Persian empire had disappeared: the Christian Byzantines recorded no more than some anti-Jewish legislation and a few unflattering stories; and the Jews themselves wrote nothing. As a result we have few clues concerning the everyday lives of the Jews of the early Islamic empire and what little we do know can be interpreted in more than one way.

Later, the picture clears. In the year 751 a paper mill was built in Samarkand by a group of Chinese craftsmen captured by the Arabs. That was a pivotal event in the development of Islamic culture; for by the end of the same century a paper mill had been established in Baghdad and that was followed by the opening of others in Egypt, Morocco and Spain. Paper did not come into common use in Europe until the 15th century and until then books were rare and costly luxury items in the West: some of the older manuscript bibles preserved in museums must have each required the skins of a large flock of sheep to provide the parchment on which they were written. The information explosion in the Muslim world following the availability of paper and cheap books can justly be compared to those that resulted from the much later inventions of printing and of the computer. Though no doubt an exaggeration, an Arab historian claimed that there were many hundreds of bookshops in 9th century Baghdad – and all this at a time when no European king could read or write.

By the 9th century, Arab historians were busily at work; and as their wide-ranging interests encompassed the affairs of the Christian and Jewish minorities, a steady trickle of valuable information about the Jews of the empire began to emerge from Arab sources.

There were also some chinks in the heavy curtain of Jewish indifference to the recording of history. According to tradition, the

Written Law (the Five Books of Moses) and the Oral Law (the detailed body of later legislation) were both handed to Moses on Sinai. The Rabbis saw no contradiction between the theory of a divine source and the fact that the Oral Law had been developed (interpreted, they would say) throughout the ages. To defend the Oral Law against Jews such as Karaites who rejected the very concept, it was vital for the Rabbis to be able to validate the chain of authority that underpinned it – all the way back to Moses. Lists of names of the sages of the Talmudic era, and then of those of the later Exilarchs and Geonim were therefore prepared. The most valuable lists were contained in two 10th century letters, one from Nathan ha-Babli and the other from Gaon Sherīra of Pumbedītha in Baghdad in response to an inquiry from the Jews of Kairouān in North Africa: though now known to contain errors, those documents were of crucial importance to later historians.

Ancient legends, whether based on fact or otherwise, were also useful in trying to build up the picture of an age. For example, it matters little whether or not Sultan Mehmet, conqueror of Constantinople, actually wrote his famous letter inviting Jews to settle in the ruined city, possess it and live off the fat of the land. What is important is the state of mind at the time, which allowed belief in such a letter to impress itself so deeply on Jewish memory.

It was however the discovery of the Cairo Geniza at the end of the 19th century that did most to give us a clear picture of Jewish life in the Middle Ages. It also shed much needed light on the Geonic period as well as on history of the Jews of Palestine and Egypt in the centuries following the conquest

Such is the veneration accorded by Jews to the Almighty that papers, letters, manuscripts or printed books in which the name of God appears are not destroyed after use like other waste paper, but are either buried reverently in a cemetery or else deposited in a store called a geniza (usually attached to a synagogue) for future burial. This practice continues to the present day.

The geniza of the Palestinian synagogue of Fustāt (Old Cairo), undisturbed for very many hundreds of years, contained pages and fragments of documents dating from the 8th to the 15th centuries, with the bulk of its material deriving from the 11th century onwards. There are over 140,000 such pages and fragments in Cambridge alone, with many others scattered in learned institutions throughout the world. This random deposit of papers ranges in content from ancient manuscripts and autograph letters of famous rabbis to records of business transactions and ordinary family gossip.

In the Middle Ages it would have been hard to write any kind of letter, even on a matter of business, without mentioning God at least once – either in thanks for favours received or in invoking a blessing on the person addressed. Cairo, being the pivot of communications between the eastern and western wings of the Islamic world, thus generated a great deal of commercial and other correspondence, which ended up in the Geniza. This was invaluable to scholars attempting to reconstruct a realistic model of the everyday life of Jews of the period.

It is difficult to exaggerate the importance of the Geniza in our understanding of the condition of the Jews of the Mediterranean basin in the Middle Ages. Indeed, the absence of similar sources of information prior to the 8th century is far more keenly felt because of the Geniza's revelations.

CHAPTER 7

HISTORICAL BACKGROUND

The first 500 years of Islam was a time of conquest, consolidation and solid achievement. It saw the flowering of an advanced international civilisation united by the rule of Islam and the use of the Arabic language – one that built on those of Persia, India, ancient Greece and Rome, to create a peak of human endeavour. Though the civilisation proudly bore the name "Arab", the role of the conquerors themselves was limited to providing the conditions in which it could develop and thrive. Few of its administrators and historians, mathematicians and scientists, poets and artists, were descended from Arab warriors: most came from the ranks of the conquered peoples who had rushed to participate in the new Islamic world order.

In time Jews too, by no means excluded from society as were their brothers in the Christian West, were able to contribute to the wider Arabic culture they shared with their neighbours. They also made great strides in developing a pattern of Jewish religious life that has largely endured to the present day.

Following the death of Muḥammad in 632 the first Khalīfs (Commanders of the Faithful) ruled from Medina and led the Arab armies in their destruction of the Persian Empire and their serious defeat of the Byzantines. This was a period of internal strife between the Bedouin tribes and no fewer than three out of the first four of the Prophet's successors were killed in office.

THE UMMAYAD DYNASTY

In 661 the leadership of Islam passed to the Ummayad dynasty, originally from the south of Arabia. They ruled from Damascus for the next ninety years, during which time the Arab empire expanded to almost its greatest extent – from Western Europe all the way across North Africa, the Middle East and Central Asia into India – and after which the pace of conquest slowed considerably.

It was very much an Arab empire, with the Bedouin troops and their descendants enjoying the fruits of conquest. Non-Arab converts to Islam from amongst the conquered peoples were largely excluded from power and its benefits, which caused increasing resentment.

The Arabs themselves were split into many competing factions, with inter-tribal rivalry – particularly between clans from the north and the south of Arabia – resulting in a seemingly endless series of uprisings. Religious differences also became endemic, in turn leading to ever more bitter struggles for power between mainstream Sunni Muslims and dissident Shi'ites.

In time, the luxury of the Umayyad court in Damascus – with its limitless wine, slaves and women – aroused the hostility of the more austere Arab tribesmen as well as that of members of the former Persian aristocracy excluded from the favoured élite. The last of the Ummayad khalīfs spent more time on the affairs of the harem, on music and poetry, than on government. Luxurious living arising from excessive wealth sapped their vitality and made them no match for the powerful combination of opponents that gradually built up against them. This coalition of tribes from the north of Arabia was led by descendants of the Prophet's uncle Abbas and was supported by bitterly discontented Shi'ites as well as by many Persian converts to Islam.

The Abbāsids rose in revolt, conquering Damascus and killing the reigning khalīf in the year 750. This was followed by the slaughter of eighty members of the former ruling clan, murdered during the course of a banquet to which they had been invited by the victorious Abbāsid general. Particularly horrifying is the account of the general and his officers finishing their meal to the accompaniment of the groans of the dying – not removed from the room but simply covered over with leather blankets. Surviving members of the family were pursued and killed wherever they could be found in a determined effort to extirpate all traces of the dynasty; and the hatred was so intense that even the corpses of its khalīfs were exhumed, scourged and then burnt to ashes.

THE ABBĀSID DYNASTY

The removal of the Khalifate from Damascus to the newly built city of Baghdad in Iraq marked the beginning of the end of the exclusive rule of the Arabs over Islam. People from the conquered nations, particularly the Persians, increasingly came to share in the power structure of what, though still described as "Arab", was soon to become a truly international Islamic empire.

By the year 820 more authority was concentrated in the hands of the

Abbásid Khalíf of Baghdad than in those of any other person; and Baghdad itself had become the most civilised and luxurious city in the world. Drawing heavily on the cultures of the conquered peoples, as well borrowing from China, India, ancient Greece and Rome, the Muslims built up an advanced urban civilisation.

The introduction from India of so-called Arabic numerals, including the zero and the numbers 10, 100, 1000, etc., revolutionised mathematics and enabled the Arabs to make great advances in geometry and trigonometry and to invent algebra. Again, starting from an imported Indian treatise, Muslim astronomers measured the circumference of the earth a full 800 years before Europe first accepted that it was not flat.

Significant advances were also made in philosophy, medicine and ophthalmology; and the House of Wisdom in Baghdad was the centre of a systematic programme of translating the scientific work of the ancient Greeks into Arabic – and thus preserving them for posterity.

Literacy, encouraged by the need to study the Qur'án and facilitated by cheap books made possible by the introduction of paper-making from China, was commonplace in the cities; and just as in pre-Islamic Arabia, poetry was Queen of the Arts.

At a time when Europe had declined into the barbarism of the Dark Ages with no industry to speak of, Muslims were producing textiles, weapons and pottery on a large scale. Muslim skills in geography and map-making were put to good use by merchants, whose commercial vessels plied the world for trade; and who even had their own special reservation in Canton. When Europe's illiterate kings could do no better than hoard their wealth in sacks of coins, the Islamic world was benefiting from a well-developed banking system in which a merchant could, for example, write a bill in Canton or Spain with full confidence that it would be encashed in Baghdad.

FRAGMENTATION

Seeds of decay were present in the very act of conquest. The Arabs were far too few in number and too divided amongst themselves to be able to impose more than superficial central control over their vast empire; and a type of government that existed only to enrich a small élite at the expense of the masses could not last.

The failure of the Arabs and their Muslim successors to move on from the policy of exploitation adopted in the first flush of conquest to a more measured approach that took account of the welfare of the people and encouraged farming and industry, proved fatal in the long term. The high Islamic culture in which the rulers took such pride was confined to the cities, while the countryside on which the economy depended was allowed to decline even further into ignorance, poverty and obscurity.

Another important cause of decay was the inability of the ruling class to maintain its traditional Muslim lifestyle when confronted with the great wealth that poured into its coffers. Lack of self-discipline, eroded by the luxurious trappings of the court with its many young girl and boy slaves, its concubines and eunuchs – doctored outside the borders of Islam and then imported – led to the physical and moral degeneration of the élite and the subsequent neglect of firm government. Gradual fragmentation of the empire resulted directly from these failures.

'Abd al Raḥmān, who had survived the massacre of the Ummayads, arrived in Spain in 756. There he founded a brilliant dynasty of his own, independent of Baghdad. At the peak of its power in 929, the rival Khalifate of Córdoba was established, eclipsing that of Baghdad in its learning and culture.

Religious differences also contributed to the break up of the empire. In 785 Idrīs ibn Abdullāh, a great great grandson of 'Alī, revolted and fled to Fez where he threw off the yoke of the Abbāsid Khalīf and established the first Shi'ite dynasty in history. The Idrīside kingdom lasted for about 200 years; and it was succeeded by several shorter-lived Sunni dynasties, which conquered Sardinia, Malta and Sicily, and shared some of their revenues with the Abbāsid Khalīf in Baghdad.

The Fatimids – another Shi'ite dynasty – started from Tunisia in 909, conquered Egypt sixty years later and then proceeded to extend their rule over the rest of North Africa, Palestine, Syria and Arabia. Under al-Aziz (975-996) their newly built city of Cairo overtook Baghdad as the most powerful and prosperous city of the Muslim world; and its Fatimid Khalīf then commanded the obedience of many Muslims formerly subject to his rival in Baghdad.

In the eastern wing of the empire a succession of Persian and Turkish officers also humiliated the Khalīf in Baghdad by establishing their own virtually independent states within his empire. And so by the 10th century, the Abbāsid Khalīf held but a shadow of his former power and his empire had been largely dismembered. By 1258 Baghdad itself lay in ruins and the authentic Khalifate was no more. With its fall, the Arabs too finally disappeared from their by then nominal position at the head of Islam.

CHAPTER 8

JEWS IN THE EARLY CENTURIES OF ISLAM

The scarcity of direct information on Jews who lived during the first two centuries of Islam was discussed in an earlier chapter of this book. What little we do know has been gleaned from outside sources.

The Talmud occasionally mentions of movement of scholars between the major Jewish centres of East and West; but this appears to have ceased after the year 500 when something like an iron curtain seems to have descended between the two mutually hostile empires of Persia and Byzantium. Spontaneous movement between major centres of Jewish population became very difficult in the years following the Arab conquest, for the Arabs did their best to discourage mobility in order to stem the flight from the countryside caused by poverty and heavy taxation. A tax receipt was the necessary passport to travel anywhere; and in Iraq such certificates were sometimes branded on the necks of the unfortunate would-be travellers.

There is some mention of the mass transfer of Jewish populations in the first century of Islam when Jews, considered more reliable than Christians, were moved into areas thought vulnerable to Christian attack. Jews, for example, were moved to the coastline of Palestine and Syria to help defend the region from the incursions of the Byzantines; and seventy Jewish families were moved from Tiberias to Jerusalem following its conquest by the Arabs. In later times the Ottoman Sultans resorted to a similar policy, sometimes compelling Jews to move to recently conquered areas and on other occasions offering them all kinds of inducements to do so voluntarily.

Jewish and Christian populations were also forcibly moved to newly built garrison towns in order to provide the conquerors with the necessary framework of administration and support services: one instance of this is Kairouan in North Africa, to which the governor of Egypt was ordered to send a thousand Jewish and Coptic Christian families.

The Jews were still predominantly an agricultural people at the time of the conquest, as they had been in the Land of Israel and in the Babylonian Exile. The Talmud provides the clearest evidence of this in its detailed legislation concerning all the kinds of transactions involved in the buying and selling of land, crops and animals, as well as in the regulation of working conditions. Indeed the Babylonian custom of Yarhei Kallah – when many thousands of Jews gathered twice a year to study Torah at the great academies of learning – occurred after the harvests when work in the fields came to a virtual standstill.

The Arab conquerors were only interested in the land as a source of wealth to be tapped for their own immediate benefit. They themselves despised agricultural pursuits and lacked the sense to realise that the well being of the countryside was essential for long-term stability and prosperity. The upheaval of the conquest and the subsequent heavy taxation caused great hardship on the land and resulted in mass poverty. The Jews, engaged mostly in farming, must have fared particularly badly and become one of the most wretched sections of the population.

The Jewish condition also seems to have been low in the towns. The early 9th century historian al-Jahiz – himself of negro extraction – commenting on reasons for the menial occupations of the Jews, wrote that they were even uglier than Christians and quite incapable of abstract thought because of their inbreeding. From other sources we learn that the Babylonian Jews of the period worked only in such lowly occupations as tanners, barbers, butchers and executioners, while Christians occupied the higher positions of physicians, bankers and administrators. Scanty though the information is, the general conclusions reached by modern historians seem reasonably convincing.

Jews interpreted the conquest of Persia and the humbling of the Byzantine Emperors by the Arabs as necessary events preceding the coming of the Messiah; and this prompted a fresh outburst of messianic hope and activity. The disappointment experienced when nothing happened was so acute that it caused great despair, leading in some cases to apostasy and conversion to Islam.

An entire literature devoted to messianic prophecies came into being at about that time. In one late 8th century book the sage Simon bar Yohai is pictured as questioning God in despair:

Have we not suffered enough through the dominion of wicked Edom (Rome) that the dominion of Ishmael (Arabs) should now rise over us?

only to be answered by the angel Metatron:

Fear not, son of man, God sets up Ishmael (Arabs) only to free you from wicked Edom (Rome)... and there will be great hatred between them and the sons of Esau (the Christians). (8.1)

All accounts agreed that Arab rule would falter eventually, to be succeeded by a cruel Byzantine emperor. Then, after a period of messianic warfare, the New Jerusalem would descend from heaven to house all Israel in peace and righteousness for two thousand years until the Day of Judgement dawns to herald the end of time.

Messianic activity was not restricted to the fevered fantasies of religious writers, for in the 8th century several groups of enthusiasts actually took up arms in the belief that the Messiah had arrived, or at least was on his way.

In the year 720, a Syrian Jew called Serene announced that he was the Messiah and promised to restore the Kingdom of God by liberating Jerusalem from the Arabs. His military venture failed ignominiously and after searching cross-examination the Khalīf, with fine show of contempt, handed him over to the Jews for punishment. The Syrian Jews, uncertain of how to proceed, appealed to Babylon for a ruling. In the end Serene and his followers were thoroughly flogged and made to declare their repentance in public.

Abu Isa, an illiterate tailor from Isfahan in Persia, was a far more serious contender for the messianic crown, though he claimed to be only the forerunner of the Messiah. With a reported 100,000 followers he raised the standard of revolt and managed to hold the Muslim armies at bay for several years before meeting his inevitable end in 775.

Yudghan from Hamadan, also in Persia, was hailed by his followers as Messiah and then went so far as to abolish the laws of Judaism. Members of his sect, attempting to impose their views by force, bravely marched out of Hamadan to inaugurate the new age; but as the heavenly hosts did not intervene on their behalf, the expedition ended like all the others in defeat and death.

The historian S.D. Goitein used the words "bourgeois revolution" to describe the great change that overtook the Jews and other peoples of the Middle East during the hidden centuries following the Arab conquest. By the start of the 10th century, the Jews were already emerging from obscurity – but no longer as an agricultural people, for in the interval they had somehow been transformed into a nation of merchants, craftsmen and artisans. Not only had they been changed by being freed from dependence on the lowly occupation of farming, but they also appear to have increased in numbers and influence throughout the Islamic world, with Jewish communities flourishing everywhere – even in North Africa where the Christian presence had by then all but disappeared.

One sign of Jews beginning to mount the social ladder comes from a late 9th century Arab geographer who reported that in Egypt and Syria:

Most bankers, dyers, money-changers and tanners here are Jews. Most medical men are Christians. (8.2)

And, as study of surviving records confirms, there were still very few Jewish doctors and certainly no leading ones.

The Jews, curiously strengthened by their centuries of adversity and obscurity, were at last ready to take part in the still developing Arab civilisation; and, with the doors of the Muslim world wide open to them, they took full advantage of that opportunity.

CHAPTER 9

JEWISH INSTITUTIONS AND OFFICIALS IN ABBĀSID BAGHDAD

THE EXILARCH

King Jehoiachin of Judah, a direct descendent of King David, was deported to Babylon with most of his people by Nebuchadnezzar in the 6th century BCE. At first he was held under a mild form of imprisonment or house-arrest: archaeologists have found the clay tablets on which the food requisitions for the captive king and his household are inscribed. He was later released and elevated to a position of some dignity at the Babylonian court. Communal leaders, known as Elders of the Exile, maintained traditional authority and preserved the former clan structure of the Jews.

The bulk of the Jews in Babylon did not join in the later return to Zion sponsored by Cyrus the Great. Advised by the prophet Jeremiah to settle down and work for the welfare of the country, they struck deep roots and performed useful service throughout what had by then become the Persian Empire. There is for example a surviving letter from the Persian military governor of Egypt, written in the name of King Darius II in the year 419 BCE, instructing the Jewish garrison of Elephantine (modern Aswan in Upper Egypt) how to observe the festival of Passover.

The Resh Galuta – head of the Exile, or Exilarch – was always chosen from descendants of the House of David, thus maintaining royal legitimacy. There is no surviving written mention of an Exilarch before the 2nd century CE; but rabbinic tradition claims that the office of Exilarch had been continuous since the time of King Jehoiachin, some seven hundred years before.

By the time Exilarchs first appeared in written history, the Jewish community of the Persian Empire had achieved a large measure of self-government in internal affairs, with its own separate legal system and administration. The Exilarch governed the Jewish people of the empire: he represented their interests at court and in turn passed on and enforced government regulations, especially in the field of taxation. The existence of this Jewish prince was thus highly convenient, both for the Persians and for the Jews.

The Arabs confirmed the authority of Exilarch Bustānay when they conquered Iraq; and they allowed the Jewish community to continue to govern itself under his direction. As a direct descendent of King David – revered as a prophet in Islam – the Exilarch was always respected by the Arabs. The Khalīf specially honoured Bustānay, presumably for services rendered during the conquest, by giving him one of the former Shah's captive daughters for a wife: another daughter was awarded to no less a person than Ḥusayn, grandson of the Prophet.

The office of Exilarch took on increased significance after the Abbāsids seized power in 750 and built Baghdad as their capital. Established at the centre of the Islamic world, there was no Jewish leader anywhere to compare to the Exilarch, who then ruled at least nominally over more than ninety percent of the Jewish nation.

The authority of the Exilarch over Jews outside Iraq and Iran declined as Abbāsid grip on power slackened and their empire began to fragment. However the existence of a Jewish prince, to whom Muslims showed respect, continued to grip the imagination of Jews everywhere and remained a constant source of pride.

There was a long and painful struggle for leadership within the Jewish community between the Exilarchs, supported by the traditional aristocracy, and the Geonim who headed the two great academies of learning. As part of the bourgeois revolution described earlier, the rising families of prosperous merchants and bankers, themselves often former students of the academies, in the end compelled the Exilarchs to relinquish most of their power to the Geonim; and the close alliance between learning and commerce long continued as a feature of Jewish life. Even in decline, the office of Exilarch remained surrounded by an aura of reverence, as confirmed by the 12th century traveller Benjamin of Tudela:

Horsemen, Jewish and non-Jewish escort him every Thursday when he goes to visit the great Khalīf. Heralds go before him proclaiming "Make way for our lord the son of David, as is his due". He is mounted on a horse and dressed in robes of embroidered silk ... the Khalīf rises and places him on a throne ... and all the Muslim princes rise up before him. (9.1)

And in Baghdad itself the Exilarch was so respected that, when called to the reading of the Torah in synagogue, the Torah was brought to him at his seat rather than the other way round. This is confirmed by the following account by Nathan ha-Babli of the installation of Exilarchs in 10th century Baghdad.

Nathan first explained that a new Exilarch was chosen in the house of the most prominent merchant of Baghdad, at a meeting attended by the Geonim (heads of the two academies), other distinguished scholars and the leaders and Elders of the community. The successful candidate was installed in the main synagogue on a Thursday morning by the laying on of hands and the sounding of the shofar (trumpet of ram's horn). The wealthier leaders then sent him presents of fine clothes, jewellery and gold and silver vessels; and the Exilarch prepared a great feast in their honour.

On the following Saturday morning the Exilarch went in procession to the synagogue where a raised dias – covered in blue, purple and crimson silk – had been prepared for him: a choir chosen from the sons of the leading families stood beneath the platform. The Sabbath morning service then proceeded almost exactly as in a Sephardi synagogue today. Only after the Amidah prayer did the Exilarch take his place on the dais, with the Gaon of Sūra on his right and the Gaon of Pumbedītha on his left, each bowing to the others as he entered; and a splendid canopy was stretched over the Exilarch's head. At this point the cantor leaned his head under the canopy and blessed the Exilarch quietly, the choir responding "amen" and the congregation remaining silent. Then the Exilarch either gave an address himself, expounding on the Biblical portion for that Sabbath, or more probably gave the Sūra Gaon permission to preach. The Sūra Gaon would politely defer to the Pumbedītha Gaon, who in turn would defer back to the Sūra Gaon. Finally, with closed eyes and prayer shawl wrapped about his head, the Sūra Gaon delivered the address in an awe-inspiring manner with the congregation maintaining an unbroken silence: an interpreter standing beside him translated his words to the Congregation. (The word "translated" here is not fully understood; it means either literal translation from Aramaic into Arabic or, and more likely, repetition in a loud voice – acting as a kind of human loudspeaker in the vast synagogue). After the recital of Kaddish, the Exilarch was blessed again, this time together with the Geonim; and a list of the cities and villages that contributed to the upkeep of the academies was read out and each was blessed. When it was the Exilarch's turn to be called to the reading of the Torah, the Cantor brought the scroll down from the pulpit over to him: everyone stood while the Exilarch read from the scroll in his hands, the Geonim beside him and the Sūra Gaon translating from the Hebrew. The service continued with more blessings, the scrolls were returned to the Ark and the Musaph prayer was recited – as is still done today.

Crowds of people singing praises accompanied the Exilarch back to his house. The heads of the academies did not return with him, for no scholars were permitted to leave the house until after the conclusion of celebrations, which lasted for seven days. If the Exilarch had to go out for one reason or another, he rode in a litter similar to that used by the Khalīf. He was accompanied by an escort of fifteen men; and in the streets was greeted by the touching of hands by as many as a hundred or more people on each journey.

The Exilarchate, though by then stripped of nearly all its authority, lingered on after the destruction of Baghdad and the abolition of the Abbasid Khalifate by the Mongols in 1258. The institution was finally brought to an end by Tamberlane who again sacked Baghdad in 1401. It was never revived; and from that time on Jews were no longer governed by their own prince from the royal House of David.

ACADEMIES AND GEONIM

The Jewish academy of Pumbedītha in Babylon, which succeeded a previous one in Nehardea, was already centuries old at the time of the Arab conquest: so too was the later academy at Sūra, founded by Abba Arikha in 219 CE

The return of Abba Arikha (known to Jews simply as "Rav") to Babylon from a period of study in the Holy Land was the turning point of the process in which Babylon replaced the Land of Israel as the focus of Jewish religious life. Within a few years there were said to have been 1200 regular scholars at Sūra alone; and thousands of Jews also flocked to study Torah in the academies during the two periods of the year when work in the countryside came to a standstill after the harvests. Membership of the academies and methods of study were organised on formal lines, which became models for the Muslim madrasa.

The contents of the Babylonian Talmud resulted from discussion between the leading sages of the time. Their work was summarised and edited at Sūra during the long presidency of Rav Ashi (371- 427), and finally completed, also at Sūra, in the year 499. The Talmud ranks second only to the Bible as the authoritative statement of Jewish law, wisdom,

The Sway of the Geonim in the World of Islam (mid 8th Century C.E.)

practice and belief.

Rabbi Yizḥak of Pumbedītha, at the head of 90,000 Jews, was reported to have welcomed the arrival of Khalīf 'Alī in 658. But it was the establishment of Baghdad as the political and economic hub of the vast Islamic empire about a century later that placed the Babylonian academies at the physical centre of Jewish life. Both academies transferred to Baghdad itself at the beginning of the 10th century.

The academies of Sūra and Pumbedītha, maintained by subscriptions from Jewish communities all over the world – including a few from Christian Europe – were the highest religious, legal and intellectual centres of Judaism. They functioned as legislative bodies and high courts of judicature as well as colleges of religious learning; and in their heyday they jealously guarded their claim to supremacy against those of the Palestinian academy and outside scholars such as Maimonides in Egypt.

The Palestinian rabbis did not give up the struggle when so many of their best scholars moved to Babylon. They persevered despite the extreme hardship of Roman occupation and Christian persecution to produce a Talmud of their own which is highly valued despite lacking the supreme authority of its Babylonian counterpart. From the Holy Land too came a steady stream of midrashim (narrative literature) of the highest quality, other fundamental scholarship and the superb liturgical poetry which forms the basis of Ashkenazi religious services today.

The head of each of the two Babylonian academies was called Gaon (Excellency): the Gaon of Sūra occupied the senior position, sitting on the right hand side of the Exilarch at formal ceremonies while the Gaon of Pumbedītha sat on his left. The Geonim, claiming to be the latest links in an unbroken chain of tradition stretching back to Moses, literally reigned over Jewry – for they and they alone interpreted divine law from which there is no appeal. Thus their rulings often ended with the phrase:

This is the halacha (religious law) and there is no moving from it.

Even the moderate Sherīra Gaon of Pumbedītha (d. 942) proclaimed:

He who opposes anything the Geonim say is like one who opposes God and his Torah. (9.2)

The Geonim succeeded in persuading all Jews who acknowledged the legitimacy of the Oral Law – and only the Karaites denied it – to accept the authority of the Babylonian Talmud; and it is said that the Amoraim (sages of the Talmudic era) created a Talmud but that it was the Geonim who made it into *the* Talmud. The Geonim transmitted their rulings and interpretations by means of a two-way correspondence – called responsa – with rabbis throughout the Jewish dispersion. They interpreted law, dictated practice, settled difficult litigation, prepared and distributed standard forms of prayer and took the first steps to codify the law. Students from far and near travelled to Baghdad to study under them.

As well as personal rivalry between the Geonim, there were sometimes differences of interpretation and practice between their two colleges: for example Pumbedītha, unlike Sūra, denied the authority of the Palestinian Talmud. Difficulties also arose when both Geonim were consulted by a far-off community and gave different answers: for example the Gaon of Sūra once became very angry with the rabbis of Kairouan who had also addressed the same query to the Gaon of Pumbedītha as well as to himself:

We do not know what they write and they do not know what we write ... and the name of God may be disgraced because of it. (9.3)

However in the end, and despite occasional conflicts, the Geonim succeeded in impressing their own permanent stamp, as well as that of the Talmud, on the Jewish religion.

Appointments to the office of Exilarch and Gaon were decided within the community; but the successful candidate could only take up his position after confirmation by the Khalīf. Though Jews were allowed to run their own internal affairs, the Muslim authorities were always ready to intervene – especially in disputes between Exilarchs and Geonim or those arising from rivalry for office when the matter was usually settled in favour of the party that offered the highest bribe.

For example in 930 Sa'adia Gaon, who had refused to countersign a decree by Exilarch David ben Zakkai, was deposed by David in favour of another scholar; and Sa'adia responded by excommunicating the Exilarch and nominating his brother in his stead. It then required a bribe of 60,000 dirhams to persuade the Muslim government to settle the matter by forcing Sa'adia, the intellectual giant of his age, to retire as Gaon of Sūra. As his most important books date from this period of temporary retirement, Sa'adia did in fact put the time gained to very good use.

The academies began their long decline after the death of Sa'adia in 942. Sūra itself was closed for the forty years between 948 and 988 because of shortage of students and funds. That was when Ḥisdai ibn Shaprūt, then at the peak of his influence at the Andalusian court, bought up copies of the Talmud lying unused at Sūra and used his wealth to tempt foreign scholars and poets to settle in Córdoba.

Ḥisdai ibn Shaprūt ... was the first to open the gates of jurisprudence,
chronology and other subjects to the Jews of Andalusia. Previously they had
referred to the Jews of Baghdad to learn the laws of their faith and to set the
calendar for their religious holidays ... Al-Ḥakam 11 ... procured for him the
works of the Jews of the East ... They were able as the result of this to dispense
with the inconvenience which had burdened them. (9.4)

Thus, for a time, Córdoba became the Andalusian Sūra; and Spain replaced Baghdad as the focus of Jewish learning and culture. Relations between the two centres remained close however, as attested by the lament written by the Spanish/Hebrew poet Solomon ibn Gabirol in 1038 on hearing of the death of Rab Hai, Gaon of Pumbedītha:

Weep my people, put on cord and sackcloth,
Break all the instruments of music and song,
For Rab Hai our master ... has gone.
And for what shall we first grieve and mourn?
For the ark which now lies hidden in Zion,
Or for Rab Hai buried in Babylon? (9-5)

The Babylonian academies somehow managed to struggle on until late in the 13th century – but by then new centres of learning in Spain and elsewhere had long since overtaken them.

STATE BANKERS

And Israel lived in peace and without disturbance ... They wore black clothes like the Abbásid family. Muslims lived in good relations with them and enjoyed no superior status. Only some Sufi mystics treated them badly; but they were severely punished ... (9.6)

Even discounting the exaggeration of the contemporary chronicler, that statement certainly represents a very marked change in status for at least some of the Jews of Abbásid Baghdad. Evidence that such conditions were not confined to Iraq is provided by the later satirical verses of an Egyptian poet:

Today Jews ... have become aristocrats. They have power and riches; and councillors and princes are chosen from amongst them. Egyptians, I advise you to become Jews – for the very sky has become Jewish. (9.7)

All over the Islamic world – and nowhere more so than in Baghdad, its economic heart – a new Jewish mercantile aristocracy had arisen, often with close ties to government. According to a contemporary Arab geographer, Jewish merchants from around Baghdad (called Radhanites) had been trading extensively between Spain and Italy (the "land of the Franks") in the West and China in the East since the previous century (see Map 5). Spices from the East to conserve food and mask the taste of badly preserved food were becoming an essential commodity in Europe and commanded very high prices indeed. So too was Chinese silk a top luxury item for, though both Byzantines and Arabs had acquired the secret of its production, it was centuries before silk of comparable quality was made outside China and even longer before its production began in Europe. Slaves were in demand everywhere; and eunuchs, who for religious reasons had to be castrated in non-Muslim lands and then imported, were highly prized in the Islamic world. Furs of all sorts and manufactured items, such as metalwork, though far bulkier to transport over long distances were still of sufficient value to make trade in them worthwhile.

The rapid expansion of trade turned the 10th century into a time of economic boom throughout Islam. That expansion required, and in turn was sustained by increased sophistication in the management of financial resources. With a great variety of gold and silver coins in circulation, the regulation of their proper exchange became essential; and a special office headed by a prominent official of the public exchequer was established in Baghdad for the purpose in 928. That office was occupied in succession by a Christian, several Muslims and the two Jews described below.

By that time, the use of letters of credit – in effect cheques, often postdated – had also come into widespread use for the safe transmission of funds from one place to another:

The Vizier Ibn al-Furāt then took his ink-pot and wrote an order to his banker Aharon ibn Amram, telling him to pay 2,000 dinars from his account to ... (9.8)

We know that letters of credit were used by the Jews of Kairouan to pay contributions towards the maintenance of the academies of Sūra and Pumbedītha; and also that the same method was used by the Abbāsid government to collect taxes from the provinces of its empire – even bribes were sometimes paid in this form. All letters of credit had to be encashed on receipt, unless used as security for loans or other transactions; and no doubt a substantial commission was charged. That system, akin to modern banking techniques, was a remarkable advance on the old method of cash payments, which prevailed in Europe for many centuries after.

It seems that despite the Islamic prohibition on employing dhimmīs in the public service, the state could not do without their services. His vizier justified this policy to Khalīf al-Mu'tadid on the grounds that Christians and Jews were "more faithfully attached" to his dynasty than were Muslims – an extraordinary statement! His successor, Khalīf Muqtadir (908 – 932), was reported to have been rather unfriendly to non-believers and eager to stress their inferiority by making them work in menial occupations and use packsaddles rather than ordinary saddles when riding. However we read that:

being a man of sound sense and good judgement, and at the same time addicted to sensuality and drinking, and profuse in his expenditure ... (9.9)

he soon found he could not manage without them. He issued a decree in 908 specifically admitting Christians and Jews to the professions of physician and state banker; and as he did not at the same time forbid dhimmīs to follow particular occupations, it is assumed that his edict was intended to be permissive rather than restrictive.

The first mention of the two Jewish merchants Yosef ibn Pinhas and Aharon ibn Amram was in 877 when they were employed by the Vizier on important financial matters. In 892 Yosef's son-in-law Netira behaved so well in the matter of the detection of a high-ranking embezzler that he earned the genuine gratitude of the khalīf and his chief advisors. It was however at the court of Khalīf al-Muqtadir that Yosef and Aharon attained the high positions that they and their descendants maintained without a break for over sixty years.

Yosef and Aharon are repeatedly mentioned in surviving documents either as "the Jewish bankers" or as "the merchants". The two partners founded a firm that their children and grandchildren continued after them. Starting off as international merchants, their activities expanded to include money changing, tax farming and banking; and they were eventually honoured with the title of Court Bankers. It is clear that Yosef and Aharon occupied privileged positions at court and enjoyed close personal relations with the khalīf, visiting him regularly in his inner palace. The influence of the sons of Aharon and Netira (Yosef's son-in-law) was such that Sa'adia Gaon used it as an inducement to persuade his supporters in Egypt to intervene on his behalf in his quarrel with the Exilarch:

Whenever you have any request ... bring it to my attention so that I may inform the heads of the prominent houses in Baghdad among whom I live, such as the sons of Netira and the sons of Aharon. They will procure a response from the Ruler for you ... (9.10)

In the words of Walter Fischel, on whose research into economic conditions in early Islam we so much rely, Arab sources of the 10th century reveal a prodigious desire to accumulate money, a mad rush to get rich – just as in Mrs Thatcher's Britain! This appetite for money was equalled only by the fear of losing it to the state, which rarely scrupled to get its hands on private fortunes by simple confiscation.

Wealth, often dishonestly obtained, was hidden away by a variety of means, even by burying it in the back garden; but secret deposits with leading merchant-bankers was the way most favoured by top officials. The Jewish Court Bankers must have been considered particularly trustworthy as their services were used for this purpose by a succession of Viziers. Such deposits were never entered in the books and their security depended solely on trust. The sums involved were sometimes huge, with figures of 100,000 dinars and more being mentioned – at a time when the annual cost of maintaining a middle-class family was put at about 250 dinars.

At an inquiry held after his downfall, former Vizier Ibn al-Furāt admitted to having transmitted bribes and funds confiscated by the state to his personal account with the bankers, rather than to the exchequer; and he further confessed to having secretly deposited a total of 160,000 dinars with Aharon and his son. The bankers confirmed the fact and amount of the deposit to the khalīf and handed the money over to him on demand. It is significant that Aharon does not seem to have been blamed for his involvement in such shady transactions: it must have been considered normal practice.

Not only was Khalīf al-Muqtadir "addicted to sensuality and drinking, and profuse in his expenditure" but the financial requirements of the state were also growing. Always urgent was the need to pay the armies of Turkish mercenary soldiers increasingly employed to police what was left of the empire.

The Viziers did their best to raise the necessary cash by selling state land, confiscating private fortunes, farming out the taxes of the provinces and auctioning government posts to the highest bidder. Salaries, pensions and other expenses were also cut in repeated drives for economy. But this was not enough to balance the budget; and so, just as in modern times, the Viziers turned to the private sector for help. It was not long before the financial stability of the empire depended on the Jewish Court Bankers; and lending money to the Abbāsid state became their principal business activity.

In the following example, Vizier 'Ali ibn 'Isa threatened the bankers with dire consequences if they refused to provide the facility demanded:

I shall refrain from inflicting penalties on you that may affect you and your heirs forever in return for a service that will cause you no damage. I need 30,000 dinars at the beginning of every month to pay ... the infantry troops. However I am not in possession of such a sum on the first or second days of the month.

I want you therefore to advance a loan of 150,000 dirhams on the first of each month, an amount you will get back during the course of the month from the Ahwaz revenue ... I am going to add as security 20,000 dinars as compensation for the first instalment ... (9-11)

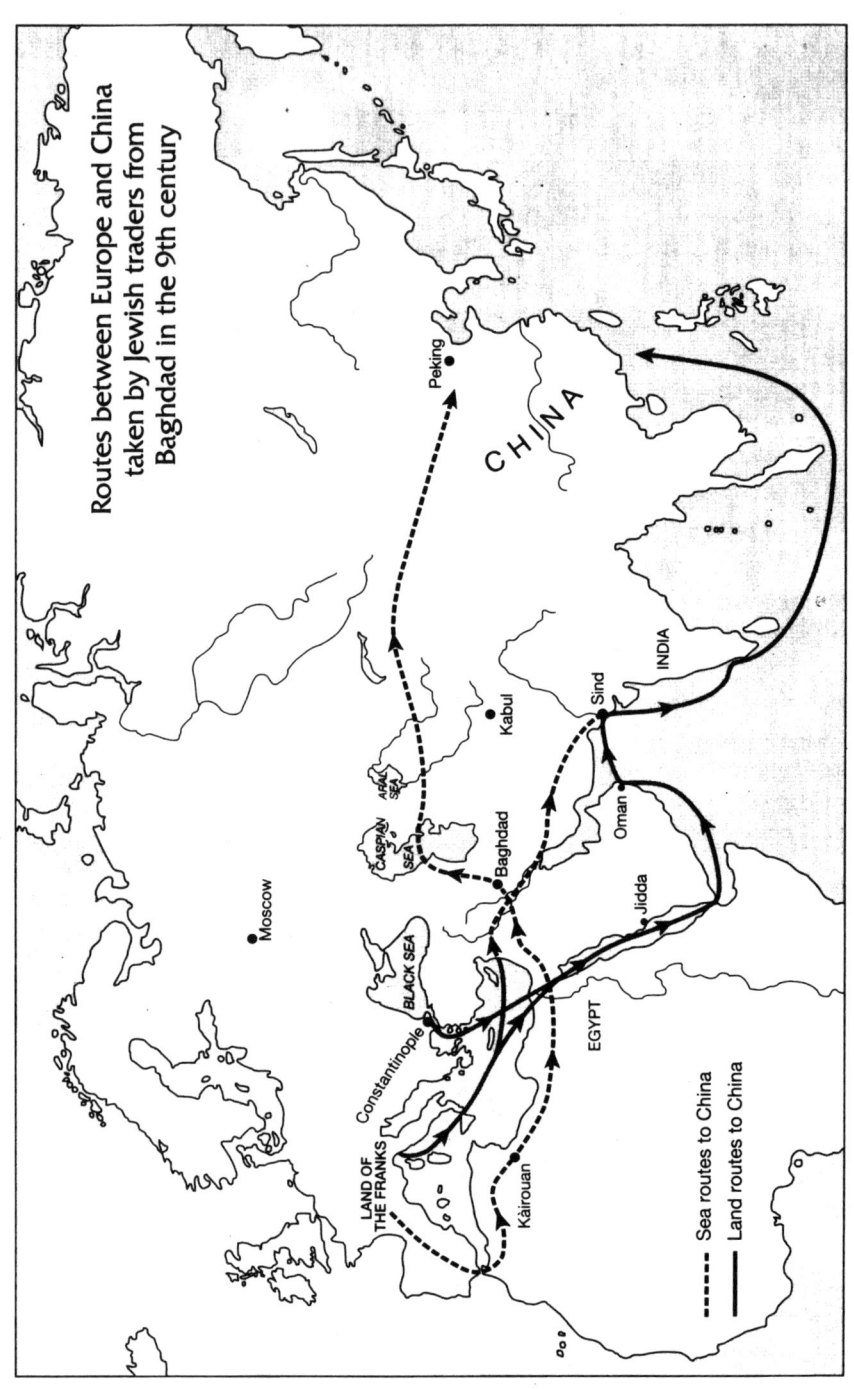

Yosef and Aharon "farmed" the taxes of the prosperous province of Ahwaz i.e. collected its taxes and remitted them, less commission, to the government in Baghdad. The bankers demurred at first before finally yielding to the Vizier's demands.

This type of transaction, possibly the first in history of a secured long-term government loan, is further illustrated by the following quotation:

When the Vizier 'Ali ibn 'Isa had to make payments for which he had no funds, he would take from the merchants Yosef and Aharon a loan of 10,000 dinars. The security consisted of letters of credit which had come in from the provinces but were not yet due for payment. Interest was paid at the rate of ... 2,500 dirhams a month (5% per month). This arrangement was made with Yosef ibn Pinhas and Aharon ibn Amram, and their representatives after their deaths, for a period of sixteen years. (9.12)

In those days, commerce took no account of the political boundaries of the rival Khalifates and kingdoms into which the Abbasid Empire had partly fragmented. Khalif al-Muqtadir was well aware that his Court Bankers relied on the trust of a network of prosperous merchant-bankers – Jewish, Christian and Muslim – throughout the entire Islamic world for the ready supply of money in the quantities he needed. It was thus very much in his interest to maintain the reputation of his Court Bankers, as can be seen from the following comment:

For they were never dismissed until their death ... in order to uphold the dignity of their office in the eyes of the merchants, so that the merchants might be prepared to lend their money through the Court Banker if necessary ... Were a Court Banker to be dismissed and another appointed in his place with whom the merchants had not yet had any dealings, the business of the Khalif would come to a standstill ... (9.13)

Despite frequent changes of administration – and there were no fewer than fifteen Viziers appointed during his reign – the fact that Khalif al-Muqtadir kept on his Jewish bankers for life showed just how much he must have trusted them as well as how indispensable they were to the workings of his government. The banking firm founded by Yosef and Aharon thrived during the rule of several khalifs and only came to an end in the 940s, when chaos brought the Khalifate to the brink of bankruptcy and the firm itself suffered irreparable losses in consequence. Such a history is highly unusual, perhaps even unique, in the Islamic Middle Ages.

It is clear from the above account that in the 10th century, ignoring political frontiers, a wealthy and influential Jewish mercantile class was already in existence throughout the Islamic world – sometimes, as in the case of the Court Bankers of Baghdad, wielding substantial influence in high places. In Egypt, Ya'qūb ibn Killis – who continued to patronise and protect Jews after his conversion to Islam in order to become Vizier – played a leading part in establishing the economic and political foundations of the new Fātimid Khalifate. And in Spain, Ḥisdai ibn Shaprūt occupied the important position of Director of Customs as well as representing his master the Ummayyad Khalīf on important diplomatic missions.

We know next to nothing about the lives of the humbler Jews of the period before the revelations of the Geniza documents first brought them to light; but it must be safe to assume that wealthy Jewish merchants and courtiers must have given employment to a host of dependants, and thus created a middle class far removed from the prevailing poverty of the general population.

CHAPTER 10

JEWISH-ARAB SYMBIOSIS

The period discussed in this chapter covers the three centuries roughly between 950 and 1250, described by historians as the High Middle Ages of Islam. At its beginning, the Abbāsid Khalifate of Baghdad was already in steep decline, eclipsed by the growth of the rival Fātimid Khalifate of Cairo, which at its peak commanded the allegiance of the whole of North Africa as well as of Egypt, Syria, Palestine and Arabia.

By 1150, the Fātimid Empire had dissolved and its area of control had shrunk back to the borders of Egypt. Tunisia and part of North Africa had been ravaged by wild Bedouin tribes unleashed by the Egyptians in revenge for its defection. In the far West, the fanatical Almohads had started on their destruction of the Jewish communities of Muslim Spain and Morocco.

At the end of the three hundred-year period, Baghdad was sacked by the Mongols and its Khalifate abolished. Also the Mamlūks, a cruel dynasty of Turkish slave-soldiers, seized the reigns of power in Egypt.

The years between saw the beginning of the rise of Christian Europe. Italian merchants were heavily engaged in lucrative trade with the Islamic lands across the Mediterranean, bringing new prosperity to their own city-states. The re-conquest of Sicily and northern Spain from the Muslims was proceeding; and successive waves of invading Crusaders from Europe were establishing short-lived Christian kingdoms in the Levant.

Those widespread changes in the Islamic world were reflected by mass migrations within it. Babylonian Jews first started to move westwards in appreciable numbers at the beginning of the 10th century because of the declining prosperity of Baghdad. Syrian and Egyptian Jews also moved west to Kairouān (Tunisia) and its dependencies in Sicily and North Africa because of economic opportunities created by the rise of its new Fātimid Khalifate. Later, after the Fātimids had conquered Egypt and made Cairo their capital, the flow was reversed – with Egypt becoming the magnet for migrants. This easterly migration of Jews increased towards the end of our period after the Bedouin devastation of Tunisia and when Jews from Spain and Morocco fled to Egypt and beyond to escape their Almohad persecutors.

It is only because of the treasure-trove of contemporary documents discovered in the Geniza of the Palestinian synagogue of Fustāt (Old Cairo), and S D Goitein's study of their social implications in his monumental book A Mediterranean Society, that we now have information on the everyday lives of some Jews of the period. Unfortunately we lack comparable material from a Babylonian source to enable us to extend our survey to cover the large Jewish communities of Iran and Central Asia in similar detail; and we can only assume that there was no great difference.

The most remarkable feature of the time was the almost complete freedom of travel, communications and trade throughout the wide expanse of the Islamic realm. It was as if political boundaries between the sometimes bitterly hostile Muslim states did not exist as men, books, money and goods flowed everywhere without restriction – except sometimes during major wars.

We can find no record of limits imposed on the movement of foreigners, even at times of international friction. Merchants from Sunni Tunisia, for example, had free access to remote areas of Fātimid Egypt when the two states were at loggerheads. Foreigners were free to buy land anywhere; and there is even mention in the Geniza of a Jew from Christian Europe buying a house in Cairo.

European shipping and merchants also participated in what was in effect a vast free-trade area, with Muslims, Christians and Jews ignoring all potential political obstacles to the easy flow of commerce. It was, for example, commonplace for Jews to travel on Italian ships; and Ibn Jubair, the Muslim geographer, journeyed from Morocco to Egypt, and then from Palestine to Sicily and on to Spain in Christian ships between the years 1183 and 1185, at the very height of the Crusader wars.

Ibn Jubair described how Muslim caravans passed safely through Crusader territory to seaports held by the Christians at times of heavy fighting. He added:

Likewise none of the Christian merchants is molested ... in Muslim territory. The Christians impose a tax on Muslims in their lands ... while the Christian merchants also pay customs for their goods in the land of the Muslims ... The warriors are engaged in their wars while the people are at ease. (10.1)

Ibn Jubair's last sentence quoted above, implying that the merchants of the Mediterranean area had created their own world of commerce that transcended all divisions of religion, race and politics, is particularly significant even if no doubt exaggerated. As described later, the Jews of

Islam enjoyed a very similar situation in their own internal affairs.

In the Fatimid empire at least, dhimmīs and (non-Muslim) foreigners never paid the double customs dues required by Islamic law. The power of the merchant class was such that when Saladin later tried to demand payment of this extra tax, he was forced to abandon the attempt because of the volume of protests.

Money in the form of coins issued by the various rulers also enjoyed free circulation and exchange. Gold dinars minted in Fatimid Egypt were an international currency within Islam – even in hostile Abbasid Baghdad. One example of this freedom of convertibility is the case of an 80-year-old Iranian Jew who left his home near the Caspian Sea to die in Jerusalem. He took 150 Fatimid dinars with him on his journey: these he exchanged in Baghdad for a draft on a well-known Cairo banker, which in turn he cashed on arrival.

Travel itself was slow, hazardous and costly, with journeys sometimes involving several years away from home. Sea voyages were always preferred to journeys overland; but even then, depending on where the ship called on route and the length of its stay there, it could take a very long time to reach its destination. Starting from Alexandria in Egypt, some typical journey times recorded in the Geniza were 65 days to Almería in Spain, 25 days to Marseilles in France, 72 days to Amalfi in Italy, 29 days and 50 days to Palermo in Sicily. No sea voyage was ever undertaken in winter, when the Mediterranean was too rough for the ships of the time.

Journeys by land, even short ones, were always made in organised caravans on regular routes for safety – either on foot or by donkey or mule. As it was inconceivable for a Jew to travel on the Sabbath, Jews either had to pay large sums to halt the entire caravan for the duration of each Sabbath, or else would have to ride on ahead in order to be able to observe their day of rest.

Travel by land took even longer than travel by sea. An illustration of this is the regular caravan that left Kairouan (Tunisia) at the end of January each year and did not reach Cairo until mid summer. In those circumstances it is hardly surprising that, for example, news of the death of a spiritual leader of Spanish Jewry did not reach the rabbis of Alexandria for seven months. The efficient mail service that linked all parts of the Muslim world depended on the regular caravans and so was equally slow.

The unity of the world of commerce was mirrored by that of Islam's many Jewish communities. Not only was each Jewish community self-governing within its own country, but it also formed part of the larger Jewish community that transcended the boundaries between individual states. Though a network of spies and secret police kept close watch on the minorities, Islam's treatment of Jews was remarkably liberal for most of the period. The loyalty of Jews to their own supreme authorities in Baghdad or Jerusalem was considered normal and not in any way threatening. This was primarily because, as argued by Goitein, the state itself possessed very little law of its own: law was not territorial, and each person was judged in accordance with the laws of his own religious community and sect.

Sūra and Pumbedītha, the two great academies of Jewish learning in Abāssid Baghdad were maintained by contributions from Jews all over the world, including from countries that were sworn enemies of the Abbāsid Khalīfs. In similar manner Jews from the hostile Sunni regions of North Africa supported the academy of Jerusalem under Fatimid rule: the academy also received regular donations from the Fātimid Khalīfs themselves. Even some Jewish communities in Christian Europe – Lucca in Italy, Narbonne and Montpellier in France, and Mainz in Germany – contributed to the upkeep of the academies of Baghdad and Jerusalem.

All Jews everywhere submitted their questions on religion, ritual and civil law to the academies; and thus it was not unusual for complex litigation originating in Kairouān (Tunisia) to be judged and settled in Baghdad. Furthermore most Jewish communal leaders and higher officials, such as judges, were appointed or at least confirmed in office by the Geonim of Baghdad – and sometimes, to make quite sure, also by the authorities in Jerusalem.

Baghdad took advantage of the freedom of communication to impress its permanent stamp on Judaism. Copies of the Talmud were sent out to distant communities, as were model prayer books and the beginnings of a legal code. Jewish scholars travelled to the academies in Baghdad and then on to other centres of learning to study or meet and confer with respected colleagues. We know from the Geniza that Hai Gaon in 10th century Baghdad was teaching students from (Christian) Constantinople and several towns in southern Italy as well as from all over the Muslim world. The main result of this centralisation of religious authority, knowledge and resources is that Jewish faith and practice became and has since largely remained remarkably uniform despite the wide dispersion of its adherents and the diversity of their cultural environments.

It is hardly surprising therefore that, by the end of the 12th century, the rite of the Babylonian Jews had superseded that of the Palestinians almost everywhere in the Islamic world. It was several centuries before the large increase in numbers of Europe's Ashkenazi Jews restored a mass following to the Palestinian tradition.

The wide circulation of people, books and ideas also gave rise to religious and intellectual conflict. The works of Maimonides were banned and burnt by the Jews of France, who were outraged by his borrowings from Greek philosophy. On the other hand French rabbis, who were much sought after in the Muslim East for their Jewish learning, sometimes earned the ridicule of the locals for their literal approach to the Bible and their lack of scholarly sophistication. Muslims too had similar difficulties, with the works of great Persian theologian al-Gazali (d. 1111) condemned and burnt in Almoravid Morocco.

Though the Islamic attitude to non-believers was unambiguously negative, religious toleration was accepted as the way of life, providing Muslims were on top. Anti-semitism was local and sporadic rather than endemic; and there was little sign of the deep-rooted emotional hostility to Jews found under Christian rule.

Coming now to more personal matters, Jews in all walks of life appear to have been well integrated with their neighbours. They lived and worked together with very little conflict; and this is confirmed by the many accounts in the Geniza of small loans, commercial partnerships and Jewish and Muslim doctors studying under each other. In the heartland of Islam, there were no restrictions on where Jews lived or the profession they followed – but Jews did tend to live together by choice, as did Christians. However Jews and Muslims were often neighbours; and members of one faith did not hesitate to rent rooms in the houses of the other. Islamic restrictions on the dress of dhimmīs, their eligibility to hold public office and their ability to convert slaves seem to have been mostly ignored during this period.

Jews were heavily engaged in professions such as trade and finance, disdained by the new military Turkish ruling class that displaced the former Arab rulers in country after country at the end of our period. Jews also specialised in other occupations shunned by observant Muslims, such as diplomacy and interpreting – which involved contact with non-believers – and the working of gold and silver. Only sometimes, and on the edges of the Islamic world – Morocco, Yemen and Central Asia – were Jews concentrated in "dirty" occupations such as cesspool cleaners, tanners, butchers and hangmen.

To the Arabs, peasants were beyond the pale of civilised life; and so the society portrayed in the Geniza was essentially urban and we know next to nothing about the lives of those who worked on the land. Townspeople were not completely cut off from the soil however; for even those of comparatively modest means often had a small plot or orchard which they tended themselves.

The very class-conscious population accepted social inequality without question. High officials such as chief judges, leading physicians and bankers – all close to the government – were the highest in rank. Next came members of the upper middle class of merchants and professionals. Below them, in order, followed the master craftsmen, ordinary urban craftsmen, artisans and labourers – with peasants at the very bottom. A man normally followed in the profession of his father; but the class structure was nowhere nearly as rigid as in feudal Europe and it was not unusual for someone with luck and ability to move up the ladder.

A man's social standing depended very much on the family from which he came, as well as on his occupation, wealth and general reputation. Piety and learning were important factors too, as was integrity – a quality rated highly in international business. Willingness to contribute generously to good causes and to help the community were also virtues commanding particular recognition and respect.

Paid employment of any kind was considered demeaning – almost a form of slavery – and a system of partnerships, sometimes very unequal, was substituted. A shipwrecked Tunisian merchant, who having lost everything at sea was forced to enter into employment on his arrival in Egypt, wrote movingly of his plight:

I eat bread in the service of others. Every minute of the day I gulp the cup of death because of my degradation and that of my children ... (10.2)

The rulers of most Islamic states employed armies of mercenary soldiers, many of whom were slaves. The army commanders too, sometimes occupying high positions in government, were often slaves, at least in the legal sense; and at the end of our period, the Mamlūks – a dynasty of Turkish military slaves – took control in Egypt.

Slavery as practised by the Jews of the period was as different from military slavery as it was from the mass agricultural slavery of the American plantations or the industrial slavery of other societies. Slaves were the personal possessions of the individuals who owned them and, as they were imported from distant countries and commanded high prices, they were much valued. The purchase of a male slave was an occasion for congratulation, almost as if the family had acquired a new son.

A slave was very much a full member of the household, with all the trust and affection that implied. The Geniza contains many references to slaves being freed by their masters, but very few indeed of their running away. In Jewish houses slaves were required to observe a modified form of Judaism, including keeping the Sabbath. According to law, they had to be sold if they had not agreed to convert to Judaism within a year of purchase; but once converted, they became full Jews in every respect.

The Biblical account of Abraham's slave Eliezer, who ran his master's household and travelled to Mesopotamia to choose a wife for his son Isaac, illustrates the best type of master-slave relationship in the Geniza period. The slave was often required to act as the trusted agent of his master, almost as a partner in his business; and the slave of a high-ranking man thus participated to some extent in status of his master and was treated with appropriate respect when engaged in business transactions. At the same time he was not above performing necessary menial tasks, especially when he and his master were travelling together.

Female slaves were in a different position as they were only used for domestic help and care of children. Unlike their counterparts in Muslim homes, who were at the absolute disposal of their masters, social and religious pressure ensured that female slaves belonging to Jewish families enjoyed substantial protection from sexual molestation.

In contrast to Muslim women, who were discouraged or even forbidden to pray in the mosque, Jewish women did attend synagogue where they sat in galleries with separate entrances: as today, there was general mingling in the synagogue courtyard after the end of the service. Though segregated in public, Jewish women were far freer than Muslims in the privacy of their own homes. There is an example in the Geniza of problems caused in a house shared by a Christian family and a Jewish family when the Christian woman converted to Islam and then had to be fully segregated.

All Jewish women, even the well to do, were expected to work in some way as well as run their households. Marriage contracts sometimes stipulated whether a wife's earnings belonged to her or to her husband; and if to her, whether they were reserved for clothing or could be spent at will. When a husband went abroad, sometimes for years at a time, he would usually deposit a sum of money on which his wife could draw for household expenses; and he might also declare that he had no claim on money earned by her "through work or spinning".

Working with textiles was the main occupation of women; but it is not clear whether this always took place at home or whether sometimes in small workshops: even upper class women sent their needlework products to the market for sale. Women also worked in occupations such as teaching, bride-combing (organising wedding preparations and celebrations), preparing for burials and professional mourning, as well as midwives and wet nurses. There is a query recorded in the Geniza from a Muslim family concerning the kasher meat required to enable their Jewish wet nurse to eat with them. Jewish women were often skilled in traditional (non-scientific) medicine; and there is even mention in the Geniza of a female oculist.

Female brokers visited houses to collect items of work for sale in the markets. There they appear to have acted in much the same manner as their male counterparts. One instance mentioned in a Geniza document is of a man who entrusted two Bibles to a woman broker for sale. Finding no buyer among the Elders of the community, she sold them to her own son for seven and a half dinars, from which she deducted her commission of one-third of a dinar. Six years later, the original owner discovered that the true value of each book was twenty dinars. He brought the case to court – and thus to our knowledge.

Free women were only very rarely employed as domestic help, partly because of their aversion to any form of paid employment and partly because only slaves performed such work. As few families could afford slaves, most women had to rely on their own extended family to run the household.

Polygamy, though allowed by Jewish law (it was only forbidden to Ashkenazim), was strongly discouraged by public opinion. However second wives were taken without much social disapproval in cases where the first wife had not produced children – or male children – within a ten-year period. The second wife usually fitted into the extended family structure without discord; and to the author's certain knowledge, this practice continued in Middle Eastern countries at least until the end of the 19th century, if not later.

CHAPTER 11

AL-ANDALUS

The Jews of al-Andalus, as Muslim Spain was called, were an integral part of the wider Mediterranean Jewish civilisation described in the preceding chapter; but there were differences between them and their brethren in North Africa and the Middle East. Situated as they were on the far western edge of the realm of Islam, their history had been continuous since Roman times and they had come to be regarded as one of the indigenous peoples of the land: Spanish Jews were very well integrated into the society around them. What Goitein described as the "bourgeois revolution", which had transformed Jews elsewhere into a nation of traders and artisans, largely passed them by; and Spanish Jews continued to own land and to cultivate it with their own hands. After the Arab conquest, conditions were such as to allow them to develop their own amalgam of religious and secular culture to a peak of excellence rarely experienced in other countries, and which eventually had significant influence outside Spain.

The earliest Jewish tombstones found in Spain date from the 1st to the 3rd centuries CE, which supports the view that Jews came to Spain with the Romans and not earlier as some traditions assert. Folk memories of pre-Roman Jewish settlements possibly confuse Jews with Phoenicians, whose language was closely akin to Hebrew and who did settle in Spain before the Romans: traces of Phoenician may still be found in the names of several Spanish cities.

The disintegration of Roman rule in the 5th century and its replacement by that of barbarian Visigothic invaders at first had little effect on Spain's Jews. That changed in the year 587 CE when the Visigothic king converted from the Arian to the Catholic form of Christianity: and it marked the end of traditional Roman acceptance of Judaism as a licit religion in Spain and the start of an era of increasing persecution by the Church.

In 613, King Sisebut's decreed that all Jews must accept baptism or quit the country. Thousands left for North Africa and the rest accepted Christianity; but most of the converts reverted to Judaism on the accession of Sisebut's more tolerant successor. That an appreciable number of Spain's Jews somehow managed to survive the ups and downs of subsequent royal policy is demonstrated by attempts in the later years of the century to attack their economic power which was based on agriculture and underpinned by slave labour. The Church's relentless anti-Jewish campaign culminated in 694 in the enslavement of all remaining Jews and the confiscation of their property: Jewish children were forcibly separated from their parents at the age of seven to be brought up as Christians. There were thus no openly professing Jews left in Spain by the time of the Arab conquest.

Tāriq ibn Ziyād, leader of the vanguard of the Muslim forces that had conquered Morocco, landed at Gibraltar in the year 711. His small army of Berbers and Arabs, augmented by local Christian malcontents, rapidly advanced into the heart of Spain, capturing Toledo and penetrating as far as Burgos before falling back. The conquest of Spain was completed by Mūsā ibn Nusair, supreme commander of the Muslim armies of North Africa, who landed in Spain the following year with a force of 18,000 Arab troops.

The intensity of their suffering over more than a century of Catholic rule caused all former Jews throughout the peninsula to welcome the Arab invaders as liberators. They promptly cast off their Christian guise and, assuming their true identity, offered the Arabs every assistance in their struggle against the Catholic Visigoths. The conquerors were few in number; and so the Jews were able to render them valuable service by supplying garrisons for the captured cities.

Mughīth entered Córdoba's municipal palace and occupied it ... He gathered the Jews of Córdoba together and made them into a garrison over the city ... They then proceeded to ... Elvira, which they besieged and captured. On that very day, they gathered its Jews together. It had become their custom to gather the Jews in each town and set them as a garrison over the place. They would leave them with a party of Muslims, while most of the soldiers would march on. They did this in Granada and Elvira ... (11.1)

Despite many years of the most severe persecution it seems that the Jews of Spain, still deeply rooted in the country, had remained a significant force. They were mobilised by the conquerors and concentrated into particular areas of the larger towns, where they occupied the empty houses of Visigoths who had fled before the Arab advance. Thus one Arab chronicler reported that:

When Jews were found in a district, they were concentrated within its principal city.

and another that:

This became the fixed method of the conquerors. They concentrated the Jews within the fortress of every city they took.

Though the conquest of Spain was accomplished with relatively little bloodshed, the consolidation of Muslim rule was not so easily achieved. There was a continual struggle for power between the Arab tribes, with repeated renewal of the old rivalry between tribesmen from the Yemen and those from the north of Arabia. Arabs from Medina and from Syria formed two more competing factions; and opposed to all Arabs were the Berbers, who hated their haughty ways and much resented what they considered to be grossly unfair treatment in the division of the spoils of conquest.

The inhabitants of al-Andalus stood by helplessly as their alien rulers engaged in a succession of civil wars that reduced the country to chaos. Most Christians simply accepted the fact of conquest, though some converted to Islam to share in the benefits of Muslim rule and a minority continued to maintain implacable hostility to the Muslims and their religion. The conquest had at a stroke transformed Spain's Jews into free men in alliance with the new rulers but the honeymoon did not last. The Arabs ignored the special relationship as soon as they no longer needed Jewish help and insisted that Jews like Christians had the status of dhimmīs, just as in the rest of the Abbāsid Empire. Though bitterly disappointed by this development, the Jews accepted that their conditions were still immeasurably better than before the coming of the Arabs; and they remained totally loyal to the conquerors throughout the many civil wars that followed.

One of the first effects of the Arab conquest was the return to Spain of many of the descendants of Jews who had fled to North Africa during the Visigothic persecutions. They were later joined by others attracted by the economic opportunities offered by this rich new land; and though small in scale compared with the parallel immigration of Arabs and Berbers, the number of Jews entering Spain was considerable. This flow of people reversed at times of insupportable levels of taxation or when recurring civil wars caused intolerable hardship, with Jews then leaving Spain for North Africa or the south of Italy. A regular ebb and flow of Jews into and out of the country, and from one part to another, was to remain a constant feature of Jewish life in al-Andalus.

Eventually a few Jews also made their way over the Pyrenees into the

Kingdom of the Franks, where they were made welcome because of their commercial expertise and their ability to supply the nobility with the jewels, spices and other exotic articles from the east that they craved. King Louis the Pious, son of Charlemagne, granted Abraham of Saragossa special permission to settle and trade in France; and it is of interest that he dealt in Christian slaves as well as in other commodities. Abraham was exempted from taxes and allowed to practise his religion unhindered. Other Jews were later able to perform valuable services in the Christian kingdoms that arose in the north and the east of Spain.

With al-Andalus now part of the great Abbāsid Empire stretching from India to the Atlantic Ocean, the isolation of its Jews was ended and they lost no time in establishing links with the Jewish world and especially with its centre in Baghdad. In the words of the historian Eliahu Ashtor, the Jewish settlement in Spain became a cultural colony of Babylonian Jewry, with Babylonian customs and pronunciation of Hebrew supplanting all others. Copies of the Talmud and other books were urgently sought and a steady stream of inquiries was addressed to the academies of Sūra and Pumbedītha, these being first sent to the academies' permanent representatives in Kairouān and then on to Fustāt (Old Cairo) for transmission to Baghdad. Amram Gaon in Baghdad specially composed a prayer book for use in Spain.

Natrōnai bar Ḥabibae is given much of the credit for re-uniting the Jews of al-Andalus with their religious heritage. Descended from the royal House of David, he left Iraq after the failure of his bid to become Exilarch. Natrōnai reached Spain in the year 771 and was received with much honour, becoming the religious teacher of its Jewish communities. It was even claimed that he performed the incredible feat of writing out a copy of the Talmud from memory.

It was 'Abd al-Raḥmān, the one-eyed grandson of one of the last of the Ummayad Khalifs of Damascus, who finally succeeded in uniting Muslim Spain. 'Abd al-Raḥmān, who had taken refuge with his mother's Berber tribe in Morocco after having escaped the massacre of his family by the victorious Abbāsids, was invited to Spain in 755 by other Ummayads who had found shelter there. He crossed over the straits of Gibraltar and, after a series of battles, was proclaimed Amir (prince) in the following year. His new Ummayad dynasty ruled Spain from Córdoba without a break for the next 250 years.

The Ummayads, well aware of how few Arabs there were in the country, treated their non-Muslim subjects with tolerance in an attempt to encourage loyalty to the dynasty and foster a sense of unity. Though governed by the Malikite school of Islamic law, which had the harshest attitude to dhimmīs, Jews were never oppressed by the Ummayads; and nor were Christians, despite extreme provocation from a handful of zealots who demanded and eventually obtained martyrdom at the hands of the reluctant Muslims.

It should not be supposed that the period of Muslim rule was tranquil at any time or that Spain's inhabitants were ever spared the suffering caused by incessant conflict. 'Abd al-Raḥmān I started the custom of launching armed raids or invasions in the spring of each year against the Christian kingdoms in the north, which produced a rich supply of booty and slaves but resulted in increased hatred between Christians and Muslims in al-Andalus itself. 'Abd al-Raḥmān and his successors also had many internal revolts to contend with; and these got worse and more frequent with time, eventually causing the almost complete disintegration of the Ummayad state in the early years of the 10th century.

In the year 929, 'Abd al-Raḥmān III took the decisive step of assuming the title of Khalīf, in opposition to the Abbāsid Khalīf of Baghdad, and managed to re-impose Ummayad rule over the whole of al-Andalus. His reign and that of his successor Hakam II (961-976) inaugurated what was later to be considered the golden age of Islam in Spain; and Córdoba, with its quarter of a million inhabitants, became for a time the largest and most cultivated city in Europe. The thriving economy was based on agriculture and high-quality manufacture – silk, linen and other textiles, leatherwork and metalwork (including silver and gold) – and boosted by a plentiful supply of plunder and slaves from the Christian north. This sustained the high culture of the Ummayad court and enabled it to survive the eventual overthrow of the dynasty and the fragmentation of the kingdom.

Ḥisdai ibn Shaprūt, or Abu Yusuf as he was known to Muslims, was born in Jaén in 910. His education in Arabic, Latin, Hebrew and rabbinics fitted him well for the role he was to play in the Muslim government of al-Andalus; but like so many Jews before and since, it was his reputation as a doctor that first brought him to the attention of the court. Ḥisdai's discovery of the composition of theriaca, the wonder drug of the age, gained him a place in the small group of court physicians; and in that post he was able to gain the confidence of 'Abd al-Raḥmān III and demonstrate his grasp of financial and administrative affairs. The khalīf appointed Ḥisdai Director of Customs, an important position because of the substantial revenue that duties on ships' cargoes provided for the royal exchequer – but not sufficiently prominent to attract the ire of too many of the Muslim theologians to whom the employment of any dhimmī in public office was repugnant. Totally loyal to the Muslim state, Ḥisdai rose to become one of the khalīf's favourites. He assisted the khalīf in his own personal management of the foreign affairs of the kingdom and was often called upon to undertake important diplomatic missions on his master's behalf: Ḥisdai's knowledge of Latin made him the obvious choice to handle negotiations with the Christian kings of Europe; and he managed such matters with conspicuous success.

The khalīf also gave Ḥisdai supreme authority over all the Jewish communities of Muslim Spain; and it was in that capacity that he stimulated the birth of an advanced Jewish culture, echoing the high Islamic civilisation of the new Khalifate centred on Córdoba. Acting in similar manner to that of a cultivated Muslim noble, Ḥisdai surrounded himself with Jewish scholars and poets: he attracted some to Spain by generous gifts and subsidised many others in their work. Under his patronage and influenced by the example of Arabic, a far more flexible and sensitive form of Hebrew poetry emerged, which became one of the glories of the Jewish achievement in Spain.

Again, learning from comparisons with Arabic, understanding of the Hebrew language made great strides in Ḥisdai's time and subsequently. The grammar of Hebrew, a language which had not been spoken for well over one thousand years, was almost unknown prior to contact with the Muslim Arabs who were obsessed with Arabic, the language of their holy Qur'ān. Crucial discoveries, such as the three-letter root of Hebrew verbs, enabled scholars to look again at ancient texts and correct traditional translations of many obscure passages. Grammar, which may seem an arid subject today, was then at the forefront of exciting new advances in knowledge.

It was during Ḥisdai's rule over the Jewish communities of Muslim Spain that their dependence on the Babylonian academies diminished.

Ḥisdai ibn Shaprūt ... was the first to open the gates of jurisprudence, chronology and other subjects to the Jews of Andalusia. Previously they had referred to the Jews of Baghdad to learn the laws of their faith and to set the calendar for their religious holidays ... (11.2)

In this task he was encouraged by 'Abd al-Raḥmān and his successor al-Ḥakam II who, having severed dependence on the Abbasid Khalīf of Baghdad and set up a rival khalifate of their own, cannot have been sorry to see their Jewish subjects also asserting independence of Baghdad.

Al-Ḥakam II had the highest regard for Ḥisdai's professional ability, talent and culture; and he procured for him the works of the Jews of the East which he desired. Then Ḥisdai taught the Jews of Spain that of which they had been ignorant. They were able as the result of this to dispense with the inconvenience (reliance on Baghdad) which had burdened them. (11-2)

The academies of Babylon were then in decline; and Ḥisdai's agents bought up unused copies of the Talmud and any other books they could find in Sūra and elsewhere for use in Córdoba.

... His wealth went to Sūra
Whence came the books
To teach them the laws
Sweet as honey
And righteous statutes
Clear and just. (11.3)

Ḥisdai was assisted in his task of founding an independent centre of Jewish learning in Spain by the coincidence of the capture at sea by Spanish pirates of Moshe ben Ḥanokh, an outstanding Jewish scholar from southern Italy. The rabbi was promptly ransomed by the Jews of Spain; and such was his learning that the incumbent rabbi made way to allow Ḥanokh to assume his own position as Chief Rabbi of the Jewish academy of Córdoba. Though contact with Baghdad was later renewed, the leadership of the Jewish world gradually shifted to Muslim Spain.

Ummayad rule faltered in the early years of the 11th century when the citizens of Córdoba, sickened by the excesses of the governing classes and led by discontented nobles, revolted and deposed the by then nominal ruler Khalīf Hisham II in favour of one of his kinsmen. Revolt followed revolt until an army of wild Berbers conquered and sacked Córdoba in 1013; and the Ummayad dynasty finally petered out some twenty years later. Al-Andalus then split up into independent states, each ruled by a Berber, Arab or Slav prince and often at war with each other. (The 'Slavs' were former military slaves, imported from Europe, who had themselves seized the reins of power.)

Freed from the necessity to maintain the Khalifate and enforce the rules of the strict Malikite school of Islamic law, the petty Berber, Arab and Slav princes welcomed the presence of talented Jews at their courts and freely employed their various skills to maximum advantage, particularly in financial matters. This was the golden age of the Jews of al-Andalus, a time when they managed to combine significant advances in religious learning with broad secular culture and real political power.

The most spectacular example of the success and prosperity of the Jews of al-Andalus in their golden age comes from the Berber Kingdom of Granada. Samuel ibn Nagrīla, a man of the highest learning and culture and a fine Hebrew poet, served as Vizier of Granada for twenty-six years until his death in 1056. Not only did he personally lead the king's army into battle, but he was also Nagīd (head) of the Jewish community and took pleasure in teaching Talmud in the academy whenever his official duties permitted. The Nagīd, himself a scholar with an international reputation who had even dared to write a critical treatise on the Qur'ān, lived in great state and acted as patron to the host of Jewish scholars, artists and students who flocked to live under his protection.

Samuel presided over a period of spectacular economic boom in the Kingdom of Granada. Increases in the production of cotton and sugar cane, and improved methods of mining base and precious metals brought prosperity to all. The kingdom's Jews, who mostly lived in the cities of Granada, Lucena and Jaén, also benefited from the improved economic conditions; and, attracted by Samuel's fame, many Jews migrated to Granada from Muslim Spain and from elsewhere in the Jewish world. Samuel and the Jewish officials who came to power as a result of his influence lived as the members of the Muslim nobility, with fine houses and life-styles appropriate to their rank.

Samuel was succeeded in office as Vizier and Nagīd by his twenty-year old son Joseph who, despite his youth, managed to fulfil many of the expectations of his royal master. Unfortunately Joseph, lacking the maturity and wisdom of his father, allowed his high office to go to his head: he and his fellow Jewish courtiers behaved with such arrogance that they aroused the deep resentment of the Muslim nobles and theologians and the hatred of the masses. An account of Joseph's murder in 1066 and the subsequent massacre of Granada's Jews is included in the following chapter. It should be noted though that the Granada massacre of 1066 was the first instance of persecution of Jews in Muslim Spain, which had enjoyed an almost unblemished record of tolerance for the preceding 350 years.

Muslim Spain was finally re-united by the Berber Almohads who invaded from North Africa in 1146, partly in response to the increasing pace of Christian re-conquest of the north of the peninsula. The fanatical Almohads, who brought their own schismatic form of Islam with them, put an end to the thriving Jewish communities of al-Andalus: Judaism was banned and its adherents either emigrated or accepted Islam – some sincerely but others continuing as secret Jews behind their Muslim guise. Despite its tragic end, the record of the Jewish presence in al-Andalus is one of the best in the history of Muslim-Jewish relations. The rules of the Dhimma were applied with leniency or hardly at all; and Jews as a whole fared no worse than the rest of the population during the many conflicts and wars that took place during the period.

The rich Jewish culture first developed under Islam continued to flourish in the expanding Christian kingdoms of Spain until a violent explosion of intolerance in 1391 ushered in a century of persecution that culminated in the expulsion of 1492. Though beyond the scope of this book, the fate of the heirs to the Jewish civilisation of Muslim Spain is of abiding interest; and the figures included in the following chart represent a reasonable compromise between widely differing estimates prepared by the historians of the period.

THE FATE OF THE JEWS OF CHRISTIAN SPAIN

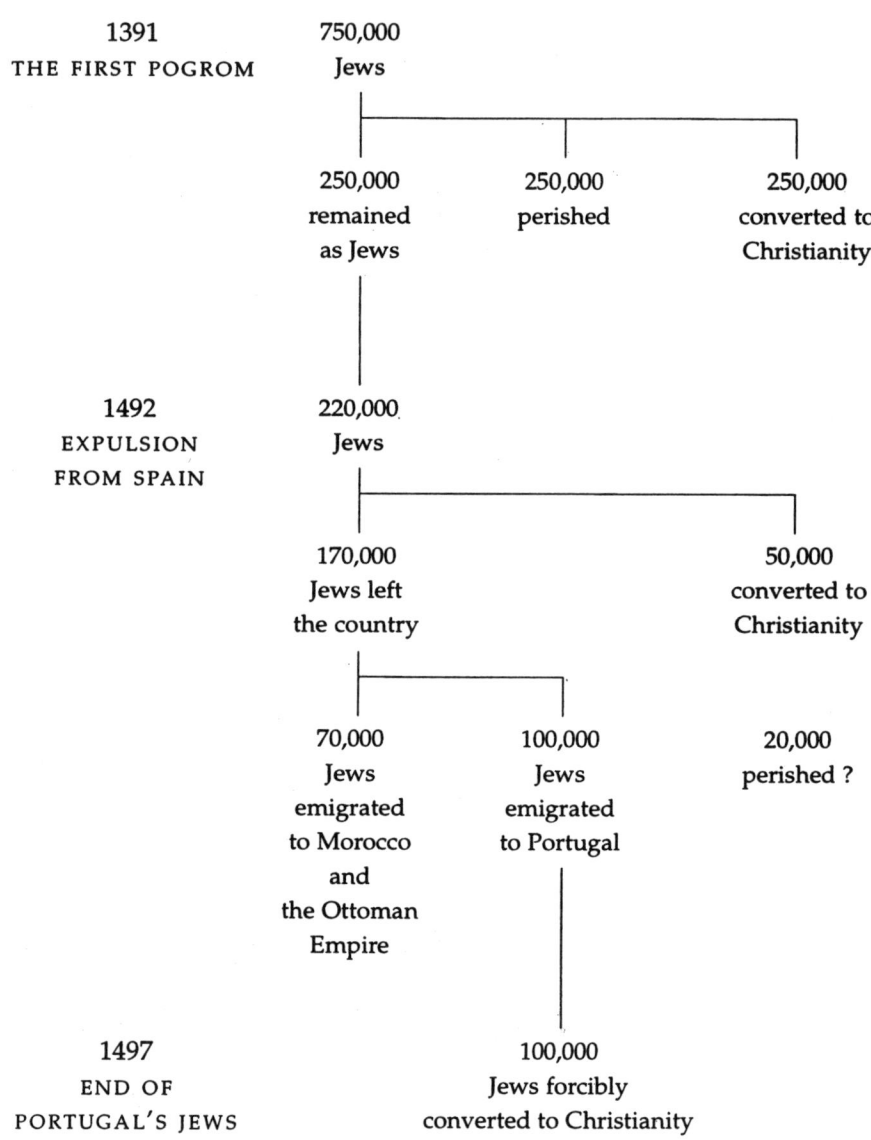

1391 THE FIRST POGROM	750,000 Jews		
	250,000 remained as Jews	250,000 perished	250,000 converted to Christianity
1492 EXPULSION FROM SPAIN	220,000 Jews		
	170,000 Jews left the country		50,000 converted to Christianity
	70,000 Jews emigrated to Morocco and the Ottoman Empire	100,000 Jews emigrated to Portugal	20,000 perished ?
1497 END OF PORTUGAL'S JEWS		100,000 Jews forcibly converted to Christianity	

CHAPTER 12

MASSACRES AND FORCED CONVERSIONS

There must have been many Jewish converts to Islam in its early years, both during the conquest itself and in the upheaval that followed; and Muslim historians recorded the names of several former Jews who played a prominent part in the development of the new religion. It is also supposed that large numbers of Jews converted later because of disappointment at the failure of prophesies predicting the coming of the Messiah as the result of the world convulsion caused by the victory of the Arabs. But this is mostly conjecture, as neither Jews nor Arabs thought such conversions worth recording – for Jews they were too shameful and for Arabs, just a matter of course.

Forced conversions of Jews were rare in mainstream (Sunni) Islam, though they did occur from time to time on the borders of the Muslim world and particularly in countries dominated by Shi'ites and other sectarians.

The Fātimid Khalīf al-Ḥakim of Egypt once earned the fulsome praise of Cairo's Jews for saving some two hundred of them who had been arrested in response to the actions of an angry mob:

When their cry was heard by our lord the Khalīf and he knew of their pain and suffering, he took pity on them in their misery ... The Khalīf ordered the prisoners to be released ... and they did as he commanded ... They gathered around the gates of the palace and blessed the Khalīf ... and they proceeded through the streets, blessing the Khalīf as they walked, until they reached the Great Synagogue. There they took out three Torah scrolls and gave thanks to God ... they blessed the Khalīf again and recited the great Hallel ... (12.1)

Al-Ḥakim fell ill in 1012 – went mad according to some sources – and then turned violently against Christians and, though to a lesser extent, against Jews. He ordered the destruction of all churches and synagogues and the compulsory conversion of Christians and Jews to Islam. It was reported that the Christian conversion office in Cairo was so besieged with applicants that many were trampled to death in the crush.

Christians suffered most from the persecution that accompanied the khalīf's decree; and even the Church of the Holy Sepulchre in Jerusalem was destroyed on his orders. According to legend, at the height of the persecution of the Christians, al-Ḥakim overheard a Haggadah (the traditional account of the exodus of the Children of Israel from Egypt) being recited by Jews at Passover. He assumed that the wicked Pharaoh in the story referred to him; and extended his persecution to include Jews.

Eight years later, al-Ḥakim returned to his senses and ordered the rebuilding of the ruined churches and synagogues. He also permitted all unwilling converts to return to their original faiths.

Two letters found in the Geniza, dated 1198 and 1202, tell of a somewhat similar situation in the Yemen, where fanatical Shi'ites had already forcibly converted many Jews to Islam. Al-Mu'izz, an imposter, proclaimed himself Khalīf and sought to complete the process – starting with the beheading of several Jews who had returned to their ancestral faith. He also tried to interfere with foreign Jewish traders visiting Aden, but fortunately changed his mind in time. The false khalīf was eventually killed by troops loyal to the legitimate Sultan and the position of the Jews was restored:

The affair ended happily ... the Holy One, blessed be he ... brought relief to the Jews in the entire country of Yemen ... Finally the Sultan came to us and relief became complete with the help of God ... (12.2)

A potentially more serious situation arose in early 12th century Spain when an Islamic jurist in Córdoba claimed to have found a tradition that Muḥammad's decree of toleration was intended to last for only five hundred years. In the year 1105, the Jews of Muslim Spain were warned to convert to Islam before the time limit expired two years thence. Fortunately heavy bribes and the moderating influence of the Quad'ī of Córdoba were sufficient to avert disaster.

That reprieve was not long lasting though, for in 1145 the fanatical Berber sect of Almohads overran Muslim Spain and much of North Africa. The Almohads were schismatic Muslims with strong messianic pretensions who refused to tolerate traditional Muslims indifferent to their new version of Islam, let alone dhimmī non-believers. The following year, 'Abd al-Mu'mim personally delivered the following ultimatum to an assembly of Christian and Jewish notables:

Have you not denied ... our prophet Muḥammad and refused to believe that he was the Messenger promised in your scripture? Your ancestors have asserted that the Messiah will come ... no later than five hundred years ... We must not allow you to persevere in your error ... You have only the choice of Islam or death. (12.3)

Fortunately the Almohads were at first satisfied with the recitation of the simple declaration "There is no god but God, and Muḥammad is his Messenger" and were not too concerned with subsequent behaviour. Some Jewish martyrs died for their faith but the majority acquiesced, being persuaded that such declaration, made to save life, did not amount to idolatry: many fled to more tolerant lands as soon as they found an opportunity to escape. The family of the great Jewish sage Maimonides left Córdoba for Fez in Morocco at this time, before finally finding refuge in Egypt.

The later Almohads were far more rigorous in their religious requirements and discriminated harshly against Christian and Jewish converts to Islam. The "new Muslims" were supervised strictly and brought to court on the slightest pretext: they had to wear distinctive clothing and were forbidden to engage in commerce, their principal occupation. The Almohads caused permanent damage to the Jewish communities of North Africa, which never fully recovered from the effects of the long-lasting flames of intolerance kindled by them. The Christians of Morocco did not survive Almohad persecution and disappeared completely.

The Jews of Iran and Central Asia also suffered from recurring bouts of intolerance, almost always instigated by the Shi'ite majority; but as the major periods of oppression occurred after the first 500 years of Islam, they will be described in Part Three of this book.

The contrast between the conditions in which most of Islam's Jews lived and those imposed on their brethren in Christian Europe could not have been greater – especially after Pope Urban 11 launched the first Crusade in his address to the assembled clergy and nobility of France in 1095. With few exceptions, the Jews of Islam were able to live full and satisfactory Jewish lives within their own communities. They suffered not so very much more than other sections of the population from the invasions, revolts, riots and other disturbances that were so prominent a feature of the period.

However the price for that relatively secure existence was acceptance by the Jews of special status as a people under the protection of Islam and acknowledgement of the supremacy of Muslims and their religion decreed by Islamic law. It was when Jews rose too high in the world and forgot their subordinate position, when they openly flaunted their wealth and power, that they provoked the fury of the often-oppressed Muslim masses. The inevitable backlashes that followed were second to none in their ferocity; and two of the worst episodes are described below.

The first occurred in Muslim Spain where Ḥisdai ibn Shaprūt (905 – 975) had served as trusted advisor to two khalīfs but who, in deference to Islamic law, had never been elevated to one of the top offices of state. Following the end of the Ummayad Khalifate and the division of Muslim Spain into many petty kingdoms, Jews rose to high office in several of the newly established courts. This encroachment on what should have been the exclusively Muslim preserve of government reached its peak with the career of Samuel ha-Nagīd, who served as Vizier in the Berber Kingdom of Granada for twenty-six years until his death in 1056. Samuel, though himself a scholar rather than a soldier, even commanded his master's armies on the battlefield. The Jewish Vizier's success was deeply resented by the Muslim courtiers, whose feelings must have been particularly inflamed by a fawning poem written in his honour by a local poet Muntafil, himself a Muslim:

... If only men could distinguish truth from error, they would apply their lips only to your fingers. Instead of trying to please the Lord by kissing the black stone at Mecca, they would kiss your hands ... (12-4)

Samuel was succeeded in office by his son Joseph who, lacking the skill and wisdom of his father, aroused even more jealousy by his arrogant behaviour. The proud bearing of Joseph and the other Jewish patricians of Granada became more and more resented as a deep affront to Islam, as is shown in the following extract from a long poem addressed to the king. The poem lists the many misdeeds of Joseph and his fellow Jews, and in particular laments the fact of their wealth and superior position in society.

... Through him the Jews have become great and proud and arrogant – they who were among the most abject ... How many a worthy Muslim humbly obeys the vilest ape among these miscreants ... How can you love this bastard brood when they have made you hateful to all the world ... They divided up the city and the provinces, with one of their accursed men everywhere. They collect all the revenues, they munch and they crunch. They dress in the finest clothes ... Do not consider it a breach of faith to kill them ... (12-5)

Joseph was assassinated during a popular uprising against him in 1066

– the very year in which the Normans invaded Britain – and his body was paraded through the streets before being nailed to a wooded cross and displayed on the city's main gate. On the following morning a mob rampaged through the Jewish quarter of Granada, pillaging its houses and slaughtering many of its inhabitants.

Another instance of violent Muslim backlash against Jewish success is described in the following chapter. It occurred in the late 13th century and involved the downfall of Sa'd ad-Daula, Jewish Vizier to the pagan Mongol court. This event is particularly instructive because of its parallel with modern times when Jews, who flourished during the European colonial period between the two world wars, also suffered from a violent backlash when the Arab countries achieved their independence.

History contains many other examples of retribution overtaking Jewish communities which so forgot themselves as to rejoice in positions of power over Muslims; but the instances quoted above are the most spectacular. A very similar episode took place in Christian Spain in June 1391, when envious mobs – whipped up by fanatical priests – launched the first of the series of savage pogroms which ended one hundred years later in the total destruction of what was then the largest, most prosperous and best-established Jewish community in the world.

Part 3

Jews in the world of Islam
The later period

CHAPTER 13

TURKISH AND MONGOL INVASIONS

It was early in the 8th century that Islamic warriors crossed over the river Oxus and first encountered the Turkish-speaking peoples of Central Asia. The province of Transoxiana, between the rivers Oxus (Amu Darya) and Jaxartes (Sir Darya) – formerly under pagan, Buddhist and Zoroastrian influences – was firmly incorporated into the Muslim world; and its main cities, Bukhara and Samarkand, became vibrant centres of Muslim religion and culture in Asia.

The Turks and their cousins the Mongols were eventually destined to rule over almost the entire realm of Islam; but at first it was only as individual soldiers, and as bands of soldiers, that they made their mark. Imported into the Muslim world as slaves, usually in childhood, they were converted to Islam and trained as élite soldiers, loyal only to the persons of their masters.

Khalīf al-Mu'tasim (833-842), whose own mother was a Turkish slave, first employed Turkish soldiers from Transoxiana to form his own personal bodyguard. He enlisted some 4,000 of them to counter the influence of his dangerously ambitious officer corps, little realising that they would eventually become a far greater menace to his independence. From that time on, Turkish slave-soldiers were increasingly employed by Islamic rulers in preference to Arabs and Iranians, with the result that native officers were gradually ousted from their position of military influence and political power.

Later to be called Mamlūks, to distinguish them from ordinary slaves, members of this elite Turkish military caste gradually usurped the

1 Timūr's tomb in Samarkand

2 Mehmet the Conqueror
from a contempory portrait by Sinan Bey

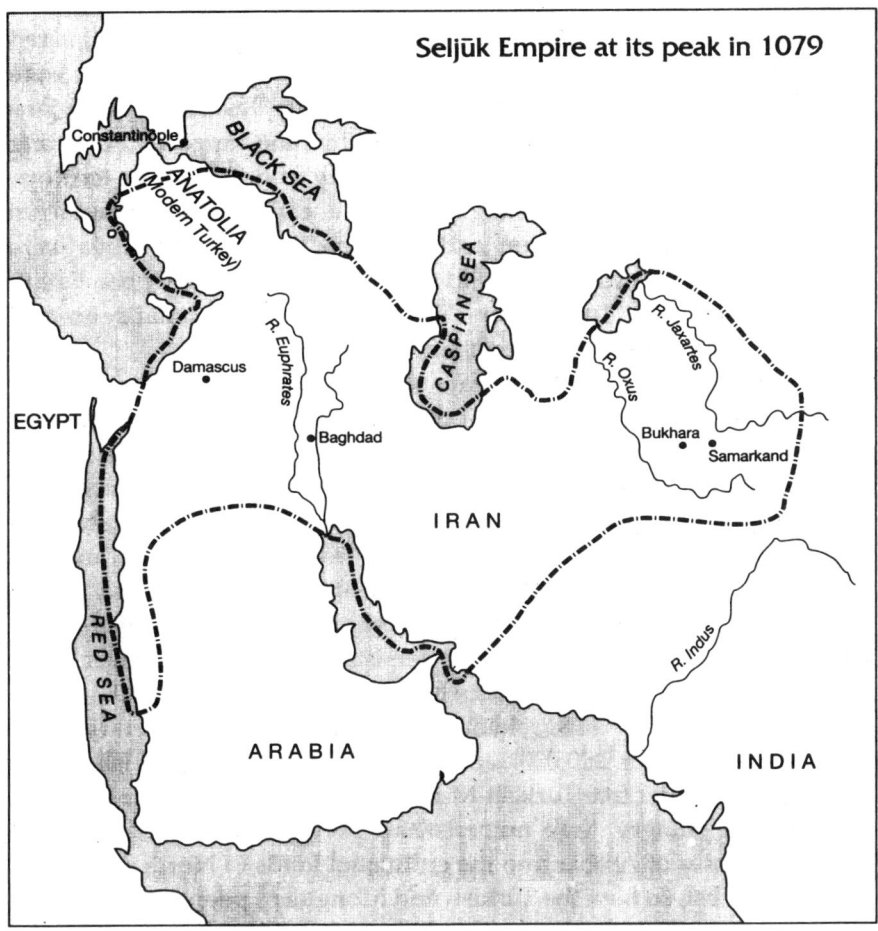

power of the khalīfs and the other rulers of the Islamic world. As one commentator gloomily observed:

The bondsmen of yesterday become the army commanders of today and the sultans of tomorrow.

During the course of the 11th, 12th and 13th centuries, Turkish slave-soldiers seized power for themselves in country after country, ruling as military despots. Mamlūks, for example, governed Egypt for over 250 years before the Ottoman Turks ousted them in 1517.

This period coincided with simultaneous threats from all sides to the once serenely self-confident world of Islam. Christians re-conquered Sicily and were advancing through northern Spain. Crusader states were established as Christian footholds in the Middle East itself. Georgians succeeded in setting up an independent Christian kingdom bordering on the Black Sea, from which they constantly raided Muslim territory. North African Berbers, preaching a deviant and fiercely intolerant form of Islam seized Muslim Spain and Morocco. Tunisia and Libya were devastated by an invasion of wild Bedouin tribes from Upper Egypt. And in Asia, first Turkish and then Mongolian nomads exerted increasing pressure on the settled lands of Islam.

Good government and the welfare of the native peoples were far from the thoughts of this new breed of military rulers. Economic boom and expansion gave way to stagnation and decline, bringing hardship and oppression in their wake. As living conditions worsened, the increasingly desperate masses lashed out in their frustration at the only target weaker than themselves – minorities such as Jews; and the authorities responded with even harsher policies. For the Jewish people as a whole the centuries of ease and prosperity under Islam were over: hard times had returned and would persist until the rise to power of the Ottoman Turks in the 15th century brought much needed relief.

In the year 960 the Karakhanids, said by a contemporary Arab historian to number 200,000 tents, converted en-masse to Islam and established the first free Turkish-Muslim kingdom beyond the Jaxartes.

Just as the hungry Arab nomads had previously erupted from the barren expanses of Arabia into the cultivated lands of North Africa and the Middle East, so now the Turkish and Mongolian peoples of the Asian steppes were also on the move. It was not many years after the conversion of the Karakhanids that the Kipchaks, from beyond the river Irtish (see map 7), surged westwards to the Jaxartes and into the territory of the Oghuz (or Ghuzz) people: they then swept on, across Russia into Eastern Europe. In turn, the pagan Oghuz, displaced from their ancestral lands by the Kipchaks, moved into Muslim territory.

One of the first waves of Oghuz invaders, led by Seljūk, settled in Bukhàra in 956 and embraced Islam. In traditional manner, Seljūk's armies first served the existing Muslim dynasties of the region as mercenaries before later supplanting them and seizing power for themselves. As increasing numbers of Turkish tribesmen moved in to swell their armies, the area of Seljūk conquest expanded in all directions. Tugrul, a grandson of Seljūk, captured Baghdad in 1055, restored the Sunni Khalīf as the titular head of Islam and himself assumed the title of

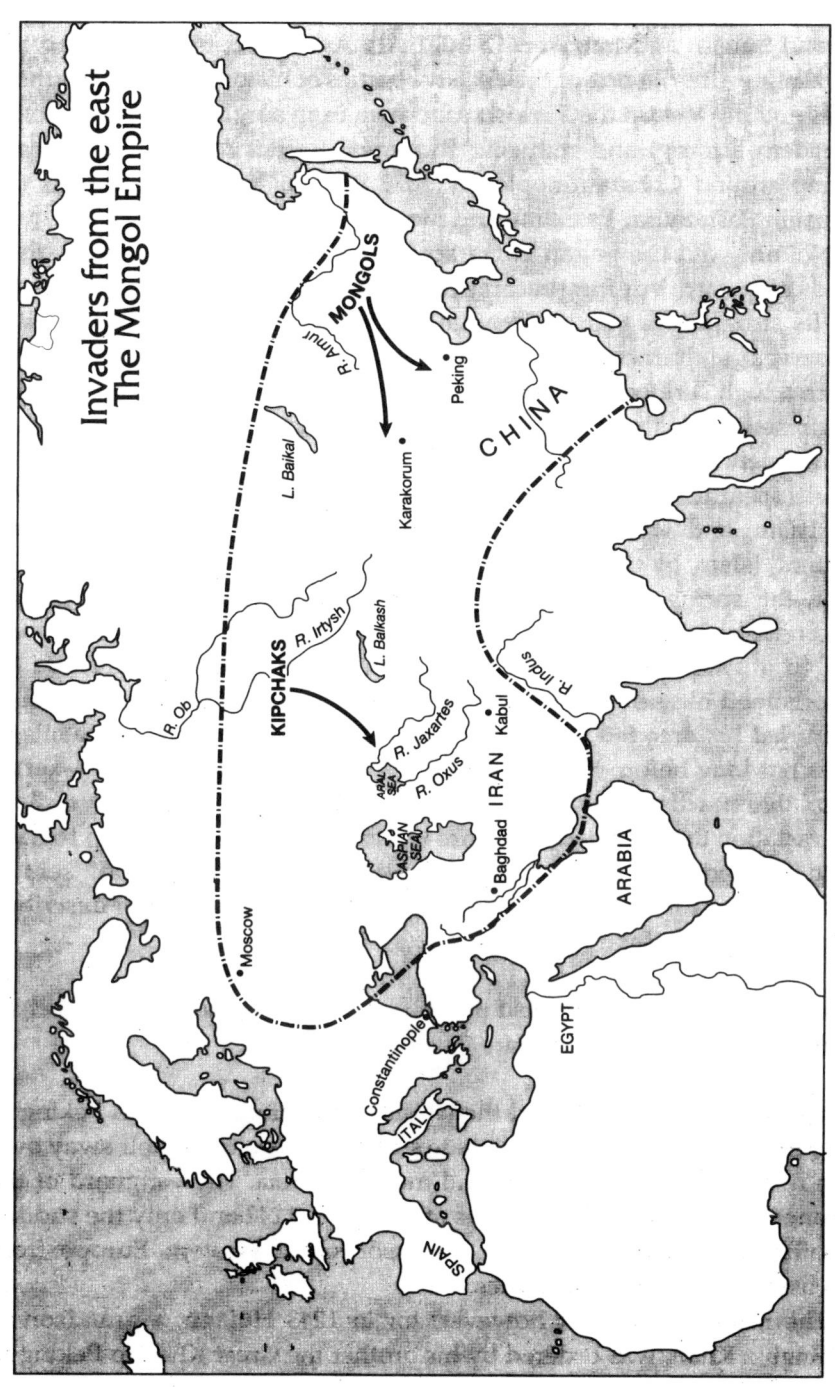

Grand Sultān. At Manzikert in 1071 Alp Aslan decisively defeated the Byzantine army in one of the decisive battles of history, after which there was nothing to stop the Turkish tribesmen from surging on into Anatolia (modern Turkey) and reducing Byzantine territory in Asia to a mere rump around Constantinople. By 1079 the Seljūks had conquered the Muslim East, Syria, Palestine and most of Anatolia.

Not only did the pagan Turks accept the religion of the peoples they had conquered, but they became its ardent champions and took the lead in its struggle for world domination. As the historian Bernard Lewis observed, a characteristic of the Turks was that they embraced Islam with a high seriousness second to none. They so totally identified with their new faith that, unlike the Arabs and Iranians before them, they completely forgot their own pre-Islamic past. Being a warlike people, the Turks spearheaded the perpetual struggle against infidels on the borders of Islam; and were responsible for a general revival of mainstream (Sunni) Islam, by then much weakened by dissension and schism.

In the spring of 1206 Temujin, a petty chieftain who had gained ascendancy over many of the pagan Mongolian tribes, summoned them all to a great assembly on the banks of the river Onon. There he proclaimed himself their leader, with the title Chinghiz Khan, and first unfurled his dreaded white banner emblazoned with nine horsetails. It was not long before he found a pretext to cross over the river Jaxartes into the heartland of Islam. Sweeping all before him in a trail of devastation that terrified the entire world, Chinghiz Khan is said to have told the people of Bukhāra that he was "the scourge of God" sent to punish them for their sins. A 13th century European chronicler described the Mongols, or Tatars, as a

...detestable nation of Satan that poured out like devils from Tartarus (hell) so that they are rightly called Tartars (Tatars).

Chinghiz himself conquered the whole of the land mass from Peking to the Caspian Sea; and his immediate successors extended their sway over the rest of China, Persia, Iraq and most of Russia. The vanguard of the Mongol armies reached the gates of Vienna in 1242 and only the sudden death of Chinghiz's son and successor saved Western Europe from invasion by the Mongol hordes.

The respite was short however; for in 1243 Hūlāgū, a grandson of Chinghiz Khan, was ordered by his brother the Great Khan in Peking to conquer all the lands of Islam as far as Egypt. Within a few months the long-haired Mongolian horsemen had once again thundered across Iran. Baghdad was taken in 1258 and most of its population, including the khalīf, was massacred. Egypt alone was saved when Hūlāgū suddenly lifted the siege of Damascus to hurry back east on hearing of the death of the Great Khan. From that time on Egypt, spared from devastation, assumed a central role in Muslim affairs.

Following the fall of Baghdad and the end of the Abbāsid Khalifate in 1258, the pagan Mongols established a state in which Islam lost its dominant status and became just one religion among several. The Mongol rulers, who tolerated all faiths equally, formally abolished the Dhimma.

With the Mongols there is neither slave nor free man, neither believer nor pagan, neither Christian nor Jew but they regard all men as belonging to one and the same stock. (13.1)

Thus under the early Il-Khans, as the Mongol rulers of Iran were known, both Jews and Christians advanced in status at the expense of Muslims. In fact a decree was issued by Il-Khan Arghūn, forbidding Muslims from occupying positions in the administration of Iraq and Iran.

Sa'd ad-Daula, a Jewish physician and scholar who was said to have spoken the Turkish and Mongolian languages perfectly, performed valuable services to the state in the field of financial administration and the rooting out of corruption. He first became the trusted adviser and then the close personal friend of the Il-Khan. In 1289, in recognition of his worth, Arghūn appointed him "Chief of the Entire Administration, First Minister and Vizier over all the countries of the Empire". Contemporary accounts praise the Vizier's achievements in the administration of financial affairs, law and justice. It was said that:

His reforms led to the disappearance of oppression, robbery and thieving, that the finances of the state were consolidated and that all inhabitants benefited from his successful efforts. (13.2)

Sa'd ad-Daula, who seems to have had a positive attitude towards his religion, filled his administration with members of his own family and with other Jews. One Christian commentator of the time reported that Jews interpreted his singular rise to supreme power as a sign of the dawning Messianic Age; but there is no confirmation of this in other sources.

Sa'd's advancement and the subsequent enhancement of the status of many Jews were much resented by Muslims displaced from their positions of supremacy:

Behold at the present day there is a Jewish governor ... on the throne of the House of Abbas. Observe how Islam is brought low ... (13.3)

The Jewish Vizier also had many personal enemies among the Amirs of the court and survived a succession of conspiracies directed against him. His downfall finally came with the serious illness of his patron Il-Khan Arghūn. Only two years after his assumption of supreme power, Sa'd and a host of his supporters were killed in a sudden coup. The Il-Khan, who himself died a fortnight later, was never told of the murder though he did inquire about the absence of his Vizier and friend from his bedside.

The murder of Sa'd ad-Daula was the signal for the outbreak of a series of attacks on the Jews of the Empire. First, his brothers and relatives, serving as governors of the various provinces, met a similar fate. Then the Arabs turned against all other Jews. The following account is of what befell the Jews of Baghdad:

Then in Babel ... the Arabs armed themselves and went to the quarter of the Jews ... And when they wanted to go in and plunder them, the Jews rose up against them in great strength and they fought against the Arabs and killed and were killed. (13.4)

Casualties appear to have been small on the Jewish side that time because of their determined resistance. All the same, we read that:

... in Baghdad more than a hundred wealthy and noble Jews were slain and their property plundered ... This lasted for three days ... (13.4)

It seems that a wave of persecution must have overtaken all the Jewish communities of Iraq and Iran – for even the Christian commentator here quoted recorded that:

God stirred up his wrath against the Jews in every place ... There was no town left in Iraq in which Jews were not treated as the Jews of Baghdad, until some of them embraced Islam – although they later turned back again. (13.4)

And again:

The trials and wrath which were stirred up against the Jews at this time neither the tongue can utter nor the pen write down. (13.6)

Pagan rule did not last long as more and more Mongols converted to Islam. It was Il-Khan Ghazān Maḥmūd (1295-1303), Hūlāgū's seventh successor, who finally recognised (Sunni) Islam as the religion of the Mongol state.

The history of Sa'd ad-Daula is another prime example of what happened to the Jews when some of them went so far as to forget their subordinate status in the Islamic order and rose too high in wealth and authority. Apart from that lesson, we also learn from the chroniclers of the time that the Jewish communities of Iraq and Iran contained many "wealthy and noble" people; and that far from being cowed when attacked by the Baghdad mob, they gave as good as they got, fighting back against the Arabs with vigour, killing as well as being killed.

Something of a cultural renaissance followed the Mongol conquest. The first history of the world was commissioned from Rashīd-al-Dīn (1247-1318), a Jewish convert to Islam. It is significant that Rashīd, who was both physician and Vizier, recruited Chinese and Persian scholars, a Buddhist hermit, a Mongol tribal specialist and a Frankish monk to help him in his task. By then almost the whole Muslim world, from the Mediterranean to Central Asia and India, was ruled either by Turkish or by Mongol dynasties: Arab rule had disappeared without trace.

The last of the great invasions from the Asian steppes was led by Tīmūr Lang (Tamberlane), nominally a Sunni Muslim. Starting in 1380, Tīmūr conquered and devastated the whole of the Muslim East, literally creating huge pyramids of severed human heads wherever he passed. It was only Tīmūr's death in China in 1404 that saved Egypt from the Mongols and again confirmed its dominant position in the Muslim world.

As mentioned before, the condition of Islam's Jews was low during those turbulent times and remained low until the rise to power of the Ottoman Turks.

CHAPTER 14

THE OTTOMAN TURKS AND THE JEWS

The Ottomans were descended from one of the many clans of Turkish nomads that swept westwards from the steppes of Central Asia and decisively defeated the enfeebled Byzantine Empire at the battle of Manzikert in 1071. The tribesmen converted to Islam and then slowly expanded their grip on Byzantine territory: by the end of the 12th century they had established the Seljūk sultanate of Rūm (Rome) in eastern and central Anatolia (see map 6) and imposed traditional Islamic urban culture there. The Seljūk state finally collapsed as a direct result of the Mongol invasion; and this was followed by the entry into Anatolia of fresh waves of Turkish nomads, fleeing the Mongols and eager to join in the continuing struggle against the Byzantines.

Utmān (Osman), who died in about 1324, emerged as prince of one of the Anatolian provinces on the border of territory still held by Constantinople. He and his descendants – called the Ottomans – led the Muslim warriors in their holy war against the Christians, while enlarging their own territory in Anatolia.

Ottoman forces crossed the Dardanelles in 1354 and started to advance through the Balkans. Bāyazīd 1 (1389-1401) so impressed the Muslim world by his victories in Christian Europe and by his further success in incorporating the remaining Turkish principalities of Anatolia under his own rule that he was awarded the title Sultān of Rūm by the Abbāsid Khalīf – thus confirming his claim to the leadership of the Muslim East.

The decisive defeat of the Turks by Tīmūr the Mongol in 1402 led to the death of Bāyazīd 1, who took his own life, and to a sharp reversal of Ottoman fortunes.

By the time of Murād II (1444 – 1451) however, Ottoman control over the whole of Turkish Anatolia had been fully restored, enabling Murād to establish a fully-fledged Islamic court with a generous complement of poets, writers and scholars. Many of the features then introduced by Murād served as a pattern for the structure of the later Ottoman state.

A supreme religious and legal authority was created for the first time, with a graded hierarchy of professional scholars, each with a well-defined area of responsibility. Another important innovation was the establishment by Murād of the "devshirme" system under which Christian youths, mostly from the Balkans, were "gathered" by the

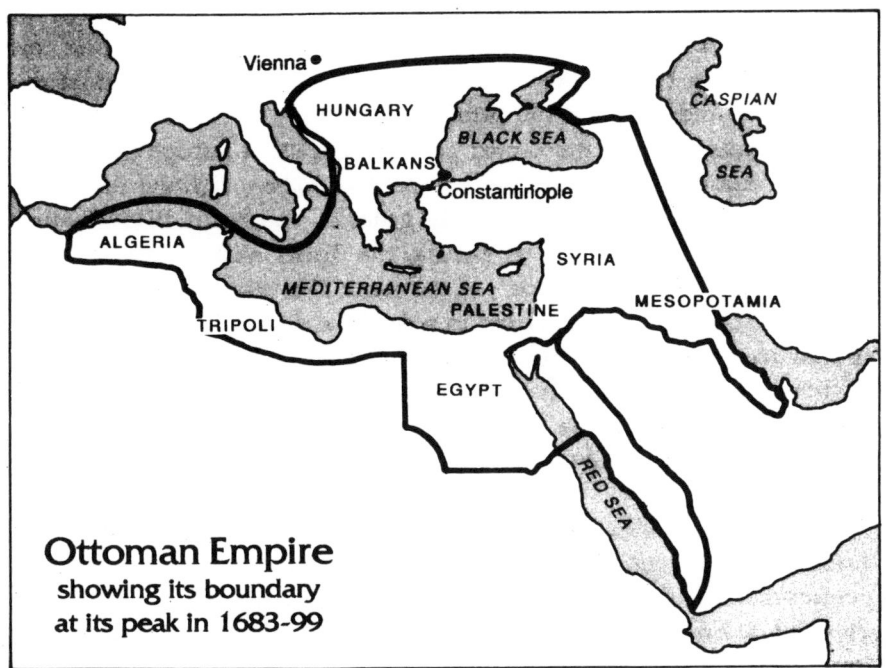

Ottoman Empire showing its boundary at its peak in 1683-99

Ottomans, enslaved, converted to Islam and trained as soldiers and administrators. This resulted in the gradual creation of a new ruling class of government officials and Janissaries (élite soldiers), all personal slaves of the Sultan and totally obedient to his rule. This process was bitterly opposed by the Turkish nobility who steadily lost influence and power as a result.

Murãd was the first sultan to execute all his brothers and half-brothers at the start of his reign to prevent risk of future challenge; and no fewer than eighty Ottoman princes were strangled for that purpose before the practice was discontinued in the 17th century. Infants were torn from their mothers' breasts on such occasions and a contemporary observer's description of the procession of nineteen coffins, including many tiny ones, that followed the body of the deceased sultan out of the palace in 1597 is particularly poignant. A luxurious form of life-imprisonment for such princes, consoled by a bevy of sterile concubines, eventually took the place of execution.

Murãd was succeeded by his son Mehmet II, soon to become known as Mehmet the Conqueror. On 29th May 1453, the European and the Anatolian parts of the empire were finally joined when Mehmet personally directed his Janissaries in their final assault on Constantinople, the eastern Rome. The city fell; and its fall marked the start of the Golden Age of the Ottoman Empire.

The Ottoman Turks caused near panic in Christian Europe when their armies conquered Constantinople in 1453 and then, fighting their way up through the Balkans, reached the gates of Vienna in 1529. Though unsuccessful in their siege of Vienna, the Turks remained a constant threat to the heart of Europe for the next 150 years until their final attempt to capture Vienna ended in a decisive defeat. During that time, special taxes to repel the Turks were collected all over Europe, including the north. Christian commentators of the day were pessimistic about the outcome of the struggle and many thought it inevitable that the invincible Turkish armies would in the end bring about total victory for Islam.

The existing Jewish communities of lands so far conquered by the Turks had for centuries suffered only humiliation, harassment and persecution at the hands of their Christian rulers. The Ottomans changed all that. They trusted the Jews, and valued the contribution they could make to the economic development of the Empire. Within the bounds of Islamic law, they treated the Jews with fairness and justice; and the Jews responded with gratitude and loyalty.

Bursa, the first town with a Jewish population to be captured by the Ottomans, fell to them in 1324. The Jewish inhabitants were Greek-speaking, called Romaniotes (or Gregos): they welcomed the Turks as liberators and actively helped them to conquer the city. As a reward, the Jews were invited to return to the town after its capture; and the Turks also brought in Jewish artisans and money-changers from Damascus and Adrianople to help re-populate Bursa, develop its economy and establish it as the first Ottoman capital.

The Jews of Bursa settled in a new Jewish quarter, where they built a grand synagogue, the Etz Hayim (Tree of Life), which remained in use until about 50 years ago. For the first time in almost a thousand years, they were allowed to work and trade without restriction, and to buy houses and land. In return, they had to demonstrate their submission to Muslim rule by paying the poll tax which was administered by the Jewish Elders, who took an oath on the numbers involved holding a Sepher Torah in their arms. In a revival of the position enjoyed by Jews in the earlier years of Islam, the Jewish community of Bursa was granted autonomy in most internal matters; and this served as a model for future Jewish life in the Ottoman Empire.

Ashkenazi Jews also found a haven in the Ottoman Empire. These included Jews expelled from Hungary in 1376, from France in 1394, from Sicily in the early 15th century, from Venetian-ruled Salonika and, in 1470, from Bavaria. In fact, shortly before the fall of Constantinople, the Turks seem to have actively encouraged Jewish immigration from Europe by offering the same conditions of tolerance and relative freedom that Jews had formerly enjoyed in the Abbāsid Empire of Baghdad, in Fātimid Egypt and in Muslim Spain.

The best known example of this propaganda is the famous letter from Rabbi Sarfati, Chief Rabbi of Edirne (formerly Adrianople), written in the first half of the 14th century and circulated in Central Europe, Northern France, the Rhineland and Hungary. Several versions of the letter exist. The shortest and most emotional version reads as follows:

Your cries and sobs have reached us. We have been told of all the troubles and persecutions which you have to suffer in German lands ... They wish to root out the memory of Jacob and erase the name of Israel. They always devise new persecutions. They wish to bring you to the stake ... I too was born in Germany and studied Torah with the German rabbis. I was driven out of my native country and came to the Turkish land, which is blessed by God and filled with all good things ... Here in the land of the Turks we have nothing of which to complain. We possess great fortunes: much gold and silver are in our hands. We are not oppressed with heavy taxes and our commerce is free and unhindered. Everything is cheap and every one of us lives in peace and freedom. Here the Jew is not compelled to wear a yellow hat as a badge of shame, as is the case in Germany ... Arise my brothers, gird up your loins, collect your forces and come to us. Here you will be free of your enemies. Here you will find rest ... (14.1)

Mehmed II, conqueror of Constantinople, pursued a similar policy towards the Jews as that of his ancestors who conquered Bursa and Edirne. He is reported to have issued a proclamation to all Jews:

Let those of my people who support me be rewarded by their God. Let them dwell in the best of the land, each beneath his vine and beneath his fig tree, with silver and with gold, with wealth and with cattle. Let him dwell in the land, trade in it and take possession of it. (14.2)

By those means and by transferring Jewish communities from other conquered cities, usually voluntarily but sometimes by force, Mehmed was able to enlarge the Jewish population of Constantinople and so help transform it into the new capital city of his empire. The 16th century Jewish historian Rabbi Eliyahu Capsali wrote of Mehmed as follows:

... In the first year of Sultan Mehmet, King of Turkey ... the Jews gathered together from all the cities of Turkey, both near and far ... and God assisted them from heaven while the king gave them good properties and houses full of goods. The Jews dwelt there according to their families and they multiplied exceedingly. From that day hence, from every place the king conquered that contained Jews, he immediately forced them to emigrate, taking them and sending them to Istanbul, the seat of his kingdom ... He gave them prosperity and where once there were only two or three congregations, the Jews multiplied in number to form more than forty congregations ... (14.3)

As at Bursa and Constantinople, Jews helped the Turks to liberate them from their Greek Christian oppressors in many other places – including Buda and Pest in 1526, Rhodes in 1522 and Belgrade in 1526. In most cases they were rewarded with tax exemptions, trade concessions, mineral rights, and even with free housing and shops.

From the 16th century onwards, Ottoman rule spread to Arab and other Muslim lands, where the resident Jewish communities also welcomed the victorious Turkish armies – first the Holy Land, Syria and Egypt, then Azerbaijan in 1524, Iraq in 1534, North Africa as far as the borders of Morocco, Yemen in 1628 and Iran in 1648. Indeed, Suleiman the Magnificent was accompanied by his Jewish physician and confidant, as well as by other Jewish scholars, when he first entered Baghdad in triumph. Local Jews could hardly fail to rejoice at that visible demonstration of the improvement in their status.

Rabbi Capsali claimed that Sultan Bàyazīd 11 (1481 – 1512), who ruled at the time of the expulsion of the Jews from Spain, made even more urgent efforts to attract Sephardi Jews into his domains. He wrote:

Sultan Bàyazīd, monarch of Turkey, heard of all the evil that the King of Spain inflicted on the Jews and he heard that they were seeking a refuge and a resting place. He took pity on them, wrote letters, sent messengers to proclaim throughout his kingdom that none of his city governors be wicked enough to refuse entry to Jews or to expel them. Instead they were to be given a gracious welcome, and anyone who did not behave in this manner would be put to death ... Thousands and tens of thousands of deported Jews came to the lands of the Turks and filled it... (14.4)

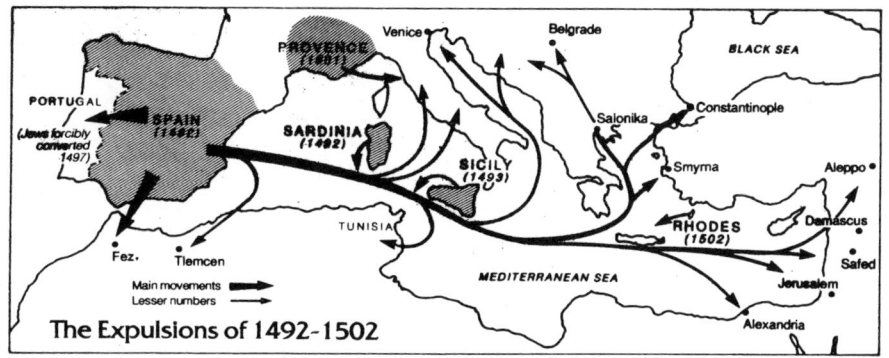

The Expulsions of 1492-1502

The Sultan is said to have remarked in conversation:

You call Ferdinand a wise king, he who impoverishes his country and enriches our own ... by expelling the Jews. (14.5)

The Turks found it hard to believe their good fortune in being able to acquire so many talented, cultivated, useful and grateful subjects. Not only did the Ottomans admit Jewish refugees but they actively encouraged them to come, often providing transport and directing where they should settle.

On the other hand, Bâyazîd II was a conservative Muslim in his attitude to non-believers, giving orders on several occasions to curb the activities of Jews and Christians at court and to close synagogues and churches built contrary to Islamic regulations. However, here as elsewhere, the paradox was more apparent than real – as we will see later.

The Jewish population of the Ottoman Empire was also enriched by a steady stream of Marranos (forced converts to Christianity who had remained secret Jews) who fled east from the 15th century onwards, sometimes bringing considerable capital with them. Rhodes, conquered by the Turks in 1522, became a main transit destination for New Christians seeking to return openly to Judaism. A special escape route was established for Marranos wealthy enough to obtain permission to leave Portugal for Antwerp. From there they travelled overland across Central Europe to Italy or the Balkans, where they took ship for the Ottoman Empire and freedom (see map 10). We know that one boatload of such refugees arrived in Ragusa (Dubrovnik) in 1544. Other New Christians, including some very wealthy individuals who later

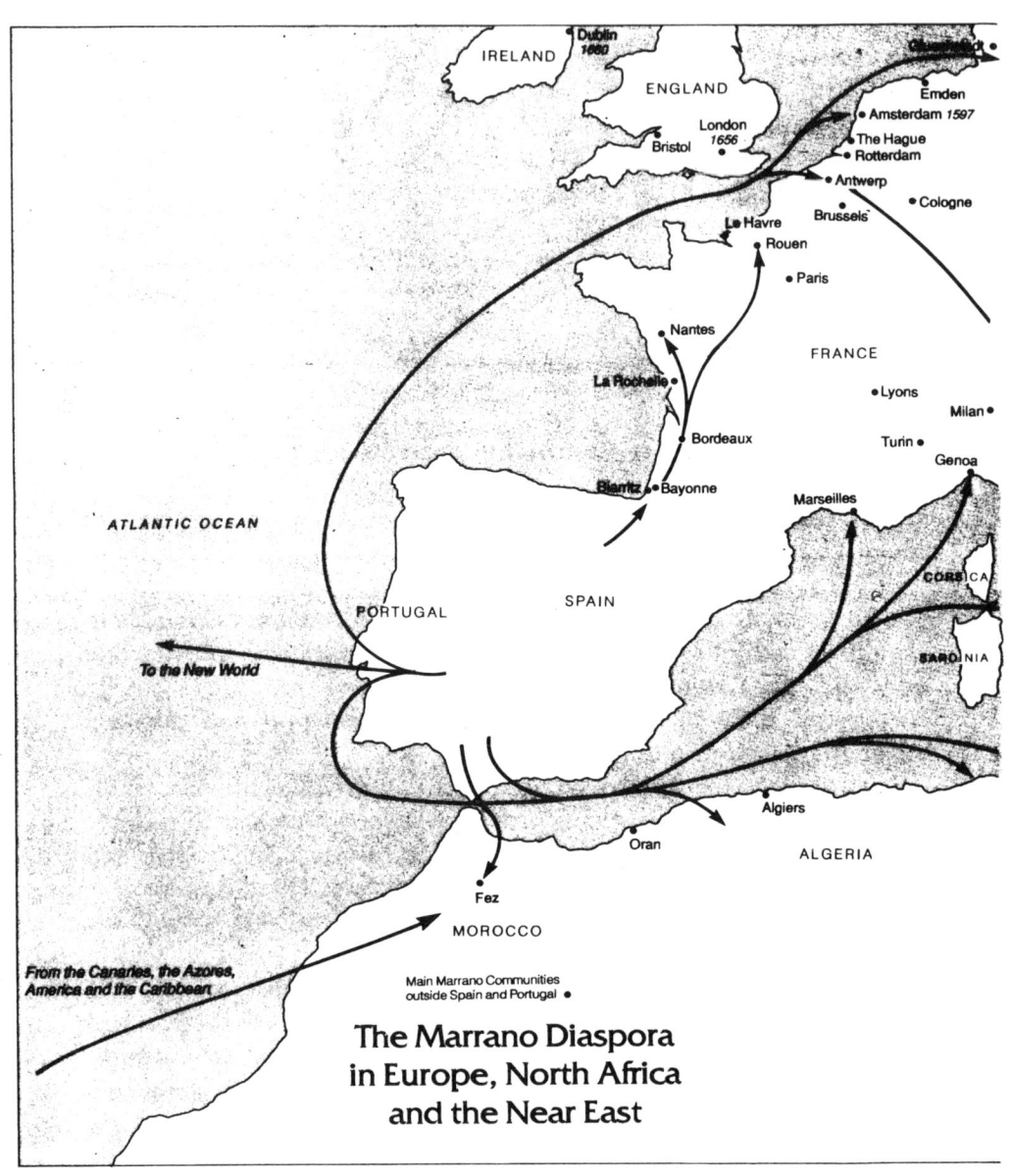

The Marrano Diaspora in Europe, North Africa and the Near East

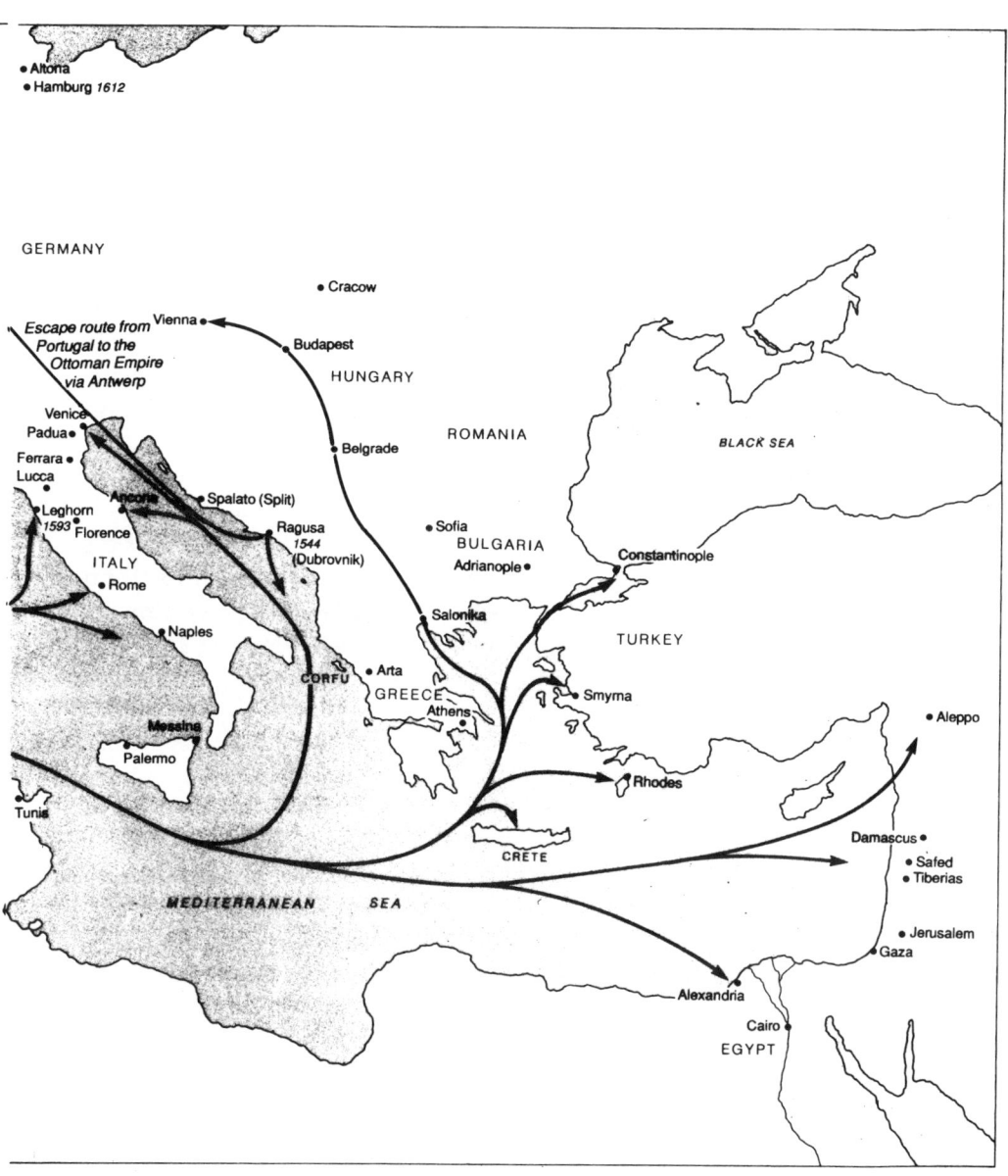

commanded much influence at the Sultan's court, came more directly, usually via Italy.

It is estimated that well over 100,000 Jews, and possibly more, found refuge in Ottoman territory at the end of the 15th century; but the exact figure will never be known. In the 16th century, considered the Golden Age of Ottoman Jewry, the total Jewish population of the Empire is estimated at between 150,000 and 200,000 souls – that is about 3% of the population. (The present proportion of Jews in the United Kingdom is about 0.5%.) It is even more interesting to compare the 150,000 to 200,000 Ottoman Jews to the estimated Jewish population of 75,000 for the whole of Poland and Lithuania in the same period. Clearly the Ottoman Jewish community was then the largest as well as the most free, prosperous and productive in the world.

It should not be forgotten that populations were small everywhere in those days: that of London was only 75,000 in 1530. The vast increase in the number of human beings came in later centuries, with the world's population multiplying over 10 times in the 300 years between 1650 and 1950; and the world's Jewish population increasing over five times – from 3 million to over 16 million – in the 100 years between 1820 and 1920.

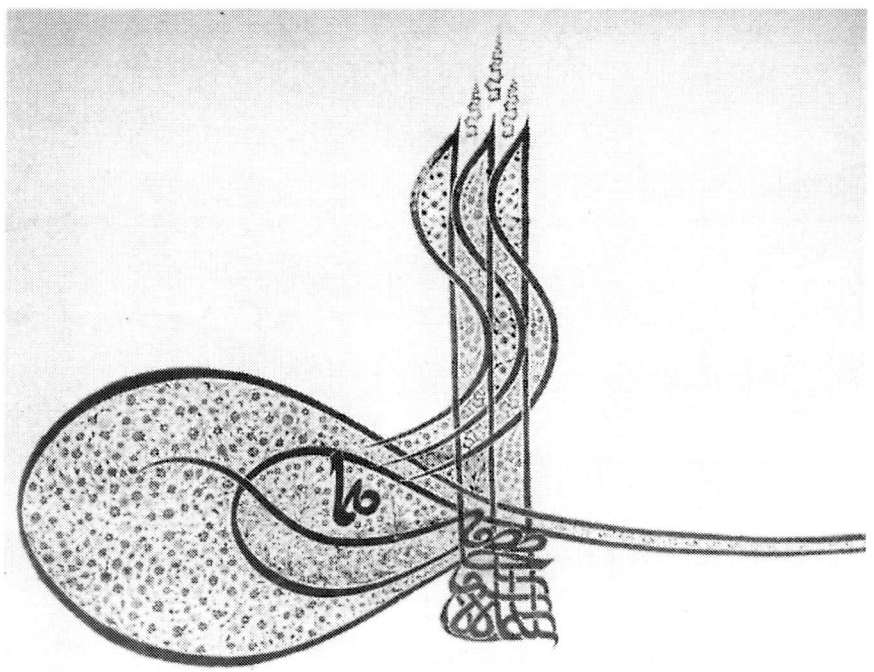

3 The 'tugra (ceremonial signature) of Suleiman the Magnificent

4 Moses Hamon
from a contemporary print

CHAPTER 15

THE JEWS IN OTTOMAN SOCIETY

The Turks, comparatively few in number, were faced with the formidable task of stabilising and then governing the vast empire conquered by the brilliance of their armies. In many places they took over towns and a countryside partly emptied by the ravages of war. In the Balkans, the Mediterranean islands and Anatolia they also took over a resentful and potentially untrustworthy Christian population.

The Turks were not colonists and made no attempt to cultivate the conquered lands and put down roots there: their Empire existed primarily as a source of wealth for the Sultan and the ruling class surrounding him. As a nation of Islamic warriors, it was beneath Turkish dignity to engage in occupations other than the army, the government or the mosque. They actively despised commerce, manufacture and the crafts. Furthermore, as strict Muslims they avoided contact with unbelievers, which effectively debarred them from diplomacy, money-changing, banking and international trade. They therefore welcomed the services of Jews, adept in occupations they disdained, and much preferred them to Christians – for Jews had no love for the Sultan's enemies in Europe and in the Byzantine Empire and were totally loyal to the Ottoman state.

The Jews provided the Ottoman Empire with the nucleus of a new middle class, one that was free from political ambition and on which the Turks could rely for a degree of loyalty they could not expect from their other subject peoples. To the Turks, the Jews were by far the most productive and stable minority in their domains. They were valued for their loyalty as well and for the personal contacts and skills they had brought with them from their countries of origin – including knowledge of European languages and ways.

Consequently the Turks maintained the Jews in a superior position to that of their Christian subjects and repeatedly protected them from Christian attack. The Turks kindly treatment of their own Jewish populations, and their warm welcome to Jewish refugees from Spain and elsewhere in Europe, ensured that the fate of Ottoman Jews would be closely bound to that of their Muslim hosts. As Turkey prospered, so did its Jews; and they became the leading doctors, tax officials, financiers, traders, interpreters and diplomats of the Empire.

The Jews introduced European medicine to Turkey – by then far superior to Arab medicine – which had huge significance in its effect on successive Sultans. An Italian Jew became personal physician to Mehmed the Conqueror and rose to a position of great influence at Court: he was followed in office by other Jews who also became the friends and confidants of successive Sultans.

Their knowledge of European languages and customs enabled Jews to act as interpreters, foreign-policy advisors and even sometimes as diplomatic envoys to European countries.

The great Jewish commercial houses and banks, run as close family businesses with networks of trusted contacts throughout the world, dominated the international trade of the Empire to an extent hard to visualise today. Nor did Jews neglect industry and crafts: textiles, in all their aspects from raw materials to the making of garments, became a Jewish speciality and in some places a monopoly. The Christians of Europe bitterly complained that it was Spanish Jews who had introduced the manufacture of gunpowder and cannons into Turkey and taught the Turks the art of modern warfare.

Jews were widely employed in the technical and financial administration of the Imperial Mint. Even before the arrival of mass immigration from Europe, Jews were active as tax inspectors, tax collectors and even as tax farmers. Most employees of the Ottoman Customs Service, from the highest rank to the lowest, were Jews; and many Ottoman Customs receipts to Venetian merchants, now stored in Venetian archives, were actually written in Hebrew characters.

Jews served as middlemen or local representatives in the transactions of European merchants, for few foreigners ever bothered to learn Arabic or Turkish; but their role was later reduced when Europeans, including the English Levant Company, barred Jews from their employment. More often than not, local Christians served the Europeans and local Jews served the Turks in such transactions.

A French monk, visiting Turkey in 1681, wrote revealingly of the place of the Jews in Ottoman society. Note the strongly anti-semitic remark with which he felt compelled to end his letter:

They are so skilled and hardworking that they make themselves necessary to everybody. There is no considerable family among the Turks and foreign merchants which does not have a Jew in its service, whether to value merchandise and assess its quality, to serve as interpreter, or to give advice on everything that happens ... it is only from them (the Jews) that one can obtain knowledge in trading matters ... this forces the merchants to make use of them, however great their aversion to them. (15.1)

Jews were also prominent in the economic affairs of the provinces. When a pasha left Istanbul to take up appointment as the governor of a province, for example, he usually took "a man of business" with him to handle affairs that were beneath his dignity or beyond his competence to deal with himself; and that person was often a Sephardi Jew. When, in later years, the provinces became semi-autonomous and their rulers hereditary, Jewish merchants or financiers fulfilled similar functions for those rulers as their "men of business".

As already explained, many of the restrictive regulations on dhimmīs prescribed by Muslim law were ignored by the rulers of Islam in times of prosperity and confidence. This is illustrated by Rabbi Sarfati's letter to the Jews of Europe quoted in the last chapter, boasting that Jews can wear whatever clothes they wish in the Ottoman Empire – unlike the Jews of Christian Germany, obliged to wear a yellow hat as a mark of shame. At the peak of Ottoman power, the enforcement of most of the restrictions of the Dhimma (the so-called treaty of "protection") on Jews could be avoided merely by the payment of a special fee – in effect by buying a license. Furthermore, some sultans took care to stress the positive side of the Dhimma rather than its negative aspects. Thus the firman issued by Mehmed III in 1602 stated:

Since in accordance with what almighty God commanded in the Qur'an concerning the communities of Jews and Christians, who are people of the Dhimma, their protection and the preservation and safeguarding of their lives and possessions are a perpetual and collective duty of Muslims and a necessary obligation on all the sovereigns of Islam and honourable rulers ... Every one of these communities that pays (poll) tax to me ... shall live in tranquillity and peace of mind ... (15.2)

Christians, in those days perceived as a potential fifth column, usually fared worse than Jews. Placed by Mehmed the Conqueror in a more privileged position, Jews were in fact, though never in law, relieved of many of the restrictions imposed on dhimmīs in general and on Christians in particular. And Jews were able to maintain that advantage until conditions began to change in the middle of the 17th century as a result of European pressure on the weakening Ottoman Empire.

The Turks did not seek to interfere with the personal lives of their subject peoples: they required from them only submission, loyalty, tranquillity and revenue. The Empire existed primarily for the promotion of Islam and for the taxes that poured into their coffers. As in the great Islamic empires of the past, the Turks allowed their minority communities a large measure of internal self-government, including full religious freedom. Each community ruled itself under its own leaders, directly responsible to the Sultan for keeping the peace and collecting the taxes. If all went well, ordinary people had little contact with the government, which only intervened when taxes were not paid or other things went badly wrong.

Each religious community had its own language, laws, courts of justice and means of enforcement: a small prison was sometimes housed in the basement of the synagogue. The community levied and collected its own taxes, both for internal use and to pay the demands of the state. It dealt with religious affairs, economic regulation, education, social security and everyday matters such as cleaning and lighting the streets and fighting fires. Its members mostly lived in their own quarter of the city, grouped around their particular church or synagogue – but this by choice and not by coercion as in European ghettos.

The intellectual and cultural stimulus provided by European Sephardim created a Golden Age for Jewish scholarship and intellectual achievement. Many famous Spanish rabbis settled in the Ottoman Empire, particularly in Istanbul and Salonika: some brought their libraries with them, including rare manuscripts. From Spain and Italy came masters of the new art of printing: freed at last from Christian censorship, they produced Hebrew books of the finest quality. Jews, who had introduced printing to Turkey at the end of the 15th century, were only allowed to print Hebrew texts; but they also contributed their skills when the first Turkish printing presses were established in the 18th century.

New institutions of Jewish learning were set up to augment those already existing. Salonika and Istanbul became leading centres of scholarship. Knowledge of Hebrew, the language of instruction in the schools and colleges to which students came from far and near, was widespread. The galaxy of famous names of the period includes Isaac Adarbi, Solomon Alkabetz, Moses Asmonino, Jacob and Levi Habib, Joseph Caro and Samuel de Medina. Salonika, Sefad and Tiberias were homes to influential communities of mystical scholars; and from Safed, Isaac Luria's new Kabbalah (mystical interpretation of the secrets of creation and the purpose of human life) swept the Jewish world. Nor was secular learning ignored. The Sephardim, with their knowledge of Spanish, Latin and Arabic, maintained contact with the outside world and engaged in all kinds of literary and musical activity. Jews also brought the art of theatre with them from Europe, never before seen in Turkish lands.

Salonika's Talmud Torah was a particular source of pride and, most unusually, the many rival Jewish communities of the town all united to support it. It housed elementary schools, which provided each poor child with a new set of clothes at Ḥanukah, institutions of higher Jewish learning, a fine reference library and a lending library. The famous physician Amatus Lusitanus taught for a time in its secular college, whose curriculum included subjects as diverse as Latin, Arabic, philosophy, astronomy, the natural sciences and medicine.

Unlike the Greek and Armenian Christian communities which were centrally organised under Patriarchs appointed by the sultan, the Jews of the Empire refused to accept unified authority and were divided into the following main groups:

1. Greek-speaking Romaniotes, survivors of Roman and Byzantine rule, who regarded themselves as the aristocracy and looked down on the newcomers from Europe.

2. Arabic-speaking (Musta'rab) Jews, who thought themselves heirs to the cultures of the Umayyad Empire of Damascus and the Abbasid Empire of Baghdad. Though themselves divided into easterners from Iraq and westerners from Aleppo, Damascus and Cairo, they considered themselves superior to both Romaniote and European Jews.

3. Yiddish-speaking Ashkenazi Jews, refugees from relentless Christian persecution and segregation, who had stricter religious standards than other Jews, whom they regarded as irreligious. In turn, they were thought uneducated and uncouth.

4. The Sephardim, some but by no means all of whom were descended from wealthy nobles, businessmen and intellectuals who had mixed freely with their social equals in Europe, regarded the other Jewish groups as backward – which of course they were by their Western standards. Despite the glamour of their name, it must not be forgotten that most Sephardim were humble craftsmen and artisans. Moreover, they were far from united themselves, being split into separate communities deriving from their countries and even from their cities of origin.

5. Last of all came the Karaites, who differed from everyone else in

their rejection of rabbinic (as opposed to Biblical) law. They kept to themselves and were shunned by the others: intermarriage was forbidden by both sides.

There were at least 40 independent communities in Istanbul and no fewer than eighteen in the smaller city of Salonika. Those of Salonika included two Romaniote communities, one Ashkenazi community of Jews from Germany and Hungary, five from Spain (Castille, Aragon, Catalonia, The Expulsion and Majorca) three from Portugal (Lisbon, Evora and Portugal), five from Italy (Apulia, Otranto, Calabria and Italia), one from Sicily and one from Provence.

Bitter quarrels plagued these communities for they disagreed on almost everything – whether in ritual matters, religious observance, marriage laws, shechita (ritual slaughter of cattle for food) and in the treatment of Marranos seeking to return to Judaism. As a result, many of them split even further – one into no fewer than five smaller kehillot. They came together only to distribute the tax burdens between them, to support large-scale institutions such as the renowned Talmud Torah of Salonika, and in the face of serious danger from the outside. Eventually, with the exception of some Ashkenazi groups, the Sephardim either absorbed the others or, in places where they were a tiny minority, they merged with the Arabic-speaking Jews.

Though tradition maintains that the Romaniote Grand Rabbis of Istanbul, Moses Capsali (1420-95) and his successor Eliyahu Mizrahi, were each appointed as Haḥambashi (Chief Rabbi) in charge of all the Jews of the Empire, it seems that they exercised little or no authority outside the capital city. After the death of Grand Rabbi Mizrahi, the Jews of Istanbul were unable to agree on the choice of a successor to represent them, even within the city; and the office of Grand Rabbi of Istanbul lapsed until the mid 19th century, when the post of Haḥambashi (Chief Rabbi and head of all the Jews of the Empire) was established as part of the Ottoman government's programme of reforms.

With no Grand Rabbi or central authority to handle their affairs and represent their interests in Istanbul, the Jews of the Empire had to rely on the personal influence of prominent Jewish courtiers close to the sultan. This worked well enough in the heyday of the Empire, but not during its decline when there were very few Jews left in high places.

An Italian Jew, Yakūb, was appointed physician to Mehmed the Conqueror; and it was not long before he became the Sultan's principal financial adviser. He eventually converted to Islam and so pleased his royal master that he and his family were granted exemption from paying taxes. Moses Capsali and Eliyahu Mizrahi, as leaders of the Jewish community, both had access to the court. Joseph Hamon from Granada was appointed physician to Sultan Bâyazîd II shortly after his arrival in Istanbul and became the sultan's trusted adviser: he first served Bâyazîd and then his son Sultan Selim 1. On Joseph's death, his position passed to his son Moses and then on to his grandson. Moses enjoyed the special confidence of Sultan Suleiman the Magnificent, who issued a firmân at his behest, in effect forbidding the bringing of ritual murder charges against Jews: such charges were frequently brought by the Christians, who maintained their hatred of the Jews throughout the entire period of Ottoman occupation.

The great Jewish merchants, industrialists and bankers of the capital also had much influence at court. It was they who persuaded the sultan to intervene with the Doge of Venice and King Henri II of France to rescue the vast family fortune of the former Marrano, Doña Gracia Mendes, who settled in Istanbul in 1553. Doña Gracia's nephew and son-in-law, Don Joseph Nasî, was created Duke of Naxos for his services to the state: it was he who persuaded the sultan to intervene with the Pope on behalf of persecuted Marranos in Ancona (Italy) and who organised a trade boycott on their behalf. Don Joseph also obtained the Sultan's licence to rebuild Tiberias in the Holy Land as a haven for persecuted Jews. Another Jewish notable, the Duke of Mitelene, continued that work after him, before the settlement finally petered out.

Jewish women too made their mark on the affairs of state. A series of remarkable women – called "kiras" (ladies) – who acted as purveyors to the Imperial harem, were able to bring considerable, if indirect, influence to bear on some of the sultans.

The first shadow fell across the golden age of Ottoman Jewry in 1574 when Sultan Murâd III, in a sudden fit of temper caused by a report that a Jewish woman had flaunted a valuable necklace on the streets of the capital, decreed the destruction of the Jews – though in reality this may not have been intended too seriously, but rather as the means of exacting a heavy payment for his treasury. Murâd was soon persuaded to change his mind by a Jewish courtier, Solomon Ashkenazi, who intervened with the sultan's mother and the Grand Vizier to prevent catastrophe. By 1636 there was no longer a Jewish courtier persuasive enough to move the sultan; and the Jews were unable to prevent the unjust execution of a Jewish delegate from Salonika who had fallen foul of the Janissaries. The Golden Age was finally drawing to its close.

CHAPTER 16

OTTOMAN AND JEWISH DECLINE

Turkey began to decay from within after the death of Suleiman the Magnificent in 1566. The sultans who succeeded him lacked the ability of their ten brilliant predecessors. Spoilt by the wealth that flowed so effortlessly into their coffers, they grew increasingly decadent and devoted far more time to court intrigue and the affairs of the harem than to government.

The sultans bred their own successors from the dependent female slave-concubines of the harem rather than from free Muslim women with well defined legal rights: very few indeed ever attained the rank of queen. Each concubine was restricted to a single son, after which sexual relations with the sultan usually ended and the fortunate mother was left with a potential claimant to the throne to whose interests she could devote the rest of her life.

With sultans increasingly unwilling to leave the precincts of the palace, let alone lead their armies in battle outside the city, the harem became the focus of their lives. Its number of women increased sixfold to over 950 in the hundred years up to 1650, whilst household expenditure rose fourteenfold in the same period. Consumption of food and drink was wildly extravagant, with records showing 168 kilos of almonds and 224 kilos of musk-scented rosewater used in a single day.

The harem itself was administered by a cadre of black eunuchs, castrated outside the Muslim Empire and then sent to Istanbul for sale in the slave market. The Chief Black Eunuch became a powerful person at court, whose influence in later years sometimes came near to that of the Grand Vizier. The sultan's mother, the Valide, also assumed increasing authority to fill the vacuum left by her son languishing in the harem.

The balance of power so carefully maintained by previous sultans between the old Turkish nobility and the corps of slaves groomed for the army and administration under the old devshirme system broke down completely. The devshirme men – originally Christian converts and their descendants – in effect seized power and drove the Turkish nobles back to their country estates. They dominated the sultans and the government, manipulating both for their own benefit.

The sultans' élite army corps of Janissaries deteriorated in quality as the devshirme system of gathering the best of the Christian youths of the

Empire for training as privileged slaves of the sultan declined after the middle of the 16th century: the last levy of such children took place in 1703. The devshirme men were progressively replaced by the sons of former Janissaries, by local craftsmen – butchers and bakers, boatmen and slave-dealers – and even by the servants of Pashas who wished to shift the expense of their maintenance to the public purse. In 1582 Murad III enlisted thousands of entertainers, acrobats and wrestlers into the corps of Janissaries to reward them for the success of the elaborate celebrations staged to mark his son's circumcision.

The balance of power and weakness between the sultans and their crack corps shifted decisively in the Janissaries' favour as their dependence on the sultans decreased and they degenerated into a greedy and undisciplined power group, constantly fomenting revolt. They did of course have a vested interest in unrest as they stood to gain huge gifts on each new accesssion to the throne.

Corruption increased as the sultans' grip on government relaxed. Nepotism became the rule rather than the exception, with many important offices of state becoming hereditary and other government posts openly auctioned to the highest bidder. As a consequence the huge bureaucracy became increasingly inefficient; and as control over the far-flung provinces of the Empire weakened, their governors started to behave as independent autocrats and paid no more than lip-service to the government in Istanbul. Local governors proved lazy, greedy and corrupt, abusing their positions for personal gain and allowing the Janissaries to run amok and oppress the local populations.

Lawlessness and chaos multiplied and it became almost impossible to travel along main roads without danger of being robbed: merchants, ordinary travellers, and even farmers going to market had to hire armed guards to have a reasonable chance of reaching their destinations unharmed. Large-scale brigandage was rife in the Balkans and Anatolia, with armed bands roaming freely and driving peasants off their land. Janissaries and ordinary Ottoman soldiers, stationed throughout the Empire to enforce law and order, added to the anarchy by themselves looting at will. Mamlūk slaves of the Ottoman governors of the Arab provinces of the Empire seized power and oppressed the ordinary people, Muslims and non-Muslims alike, reducing their masters to little more than puppets. Even Istanbul itself was subjected to a series of Janissary revolts as rival factions jockeyed for power.

When a sultan died or was deposed, the chances of any candidate for succession depended on the power of his mother in the harem and on the strength of her supporting faction. Such a system certainly favoured the most able mothers; but it often allowed markedly inferior princes to gain the throne to the detriment of firm government.

The army suffered from similar malaise as the borders of the Empire crumbled, at first gradually and then more rapidly. The long Ottoman struggle with the Hapsburg Empire for control of Central Europe was lost with the abandonment of the second siege of Vienna in 1683; and that reverse was followed only three years later by the loss of Buda which had been in Turkish hands since 1541. At the end of the 17th century the Ottomans, themselves a defeated power for the first time, found themselves in the unusual position of being compelled to sign a peace treaty with the Austrians – so unlike former days when the Turks had simply dictated terms. The Russians too, having freed Moscow from the Muslim Tatars, pushed on rapidly towards the south, seizing the Crimea and then proceeding to occupy all the territory along the northern shore of the Black Sea.

Christian pressure on the Ottoman Empire was not limited to the successes of the Austrian and Russian armies against the previously invincible Turks, for Christians were advancing everywhere – in Spain, on the Mediterranean sea and even on the coast of North Africa. However it was the rise of Western sea power and advanced technology that proved the decisive element in the long struggle between Christendom and the Islamic world. The ships built by the once comparatively backward and uncivilised countries of Western Europe, though tiny by our standards today, were revolutionary at the time: they braved the ocean storms to round the Cape of Good Hope and reach the fabulous markets of India and the Far East, previously the exclusive preserve of Muslim merchants. Other ships crossed the Atlantic to discover the New World of the Americas and then milk its rich resources. Ottoman trading superiority was progressively undermined and then destroyed by the West. Turkish manufacture too, including the all-important textile industry, also suffered grievously from European competition as Europeans came to dominate both local and world markets. The Christian West outflanked the land-bound world of Islam, imposed its mastery on the globe and stamped its own values on it. That situation continues to this day and still provokes strong Muslim resentment.

The developing nation states of Europe soon realised what was happening in the Ottoman Empire and took full advantage of its decline in their scramble for the spoils. As early as 1455, Mehmed the Conqueror had confirmed the pre-conquest privileges of two small colonies of Genovese and Venetian merchants in Istanbul: he permitted them to continue to live in their own quarters of the capital, governed by their own national laws and administered by their own consuls. In 1535 the first Capitulation Agreement was signed by Suleiman the Magnificent as a sweetener to the King of France, who had joined him in a military alliance against the Hapsburg Empire. By its terms, French subjects and their local employees were enabled to live in the Ottoman Empire under French law administered by French consuls: they were exempted from all Ottoman laws and controls, and paid no taxes other than a reduced customs levy of 3% as opposed to the normal 5%. France was also given the exclusive right to control and protect other Europeans wishing to travel, live or trade in the Empire. That protection was later extended to include all Catholics together with their monasteries and charitable institutions, with the result that French language and culture predominated in most of the Levant until modern times. It was not long before Great Britain, Holland and other European powers sought and were granted similar privileges.

All this mattered little while Turkey was still a great power but during the years of its long decline Europeans exploited Ottoman weakness to the full and abused the rights granted to them. Hundreds if not thousands of Europeans entered Ottoman territory and transformed the tiny protected communities of foreign merchants into large and wealthy colonies – virtually independent states within Turkish territory. The consuls granted or sold their protection to large numbers of Ottoman subjects in defiance of the terms of the Capitulation agreements. In this they were prompted by personal greed as well as by a deliberate attempt to increase their influence on the faltering Ottoman government by multiplying their opportunities to intervene on behalf of protégés. It was also alleged by the Turks that less scrupulous consuls sold their protection to land and sea pirates and acted as "fences" in return for a share of the proceeds.

The insatiable need of the Turks for more and more revenue resulted in ruinous increases in taxation. The consequence was inflation, accompanied by the usual economic ills: the coinage was debased time and again, further fanning the inflation. Economic misery was exacerbated by successful European competition in trade and industry, the effects of which added to the general decline. The vast forests of Anatolia and the Balkans were cut down. Extreme hardship emptied the countryside as peasants fled to the towns: crop yields slumped and sporadic shortages of food increased the misery of the urban poor. Roads decayed and organised piracy made travel by sea even more hazardous. And the great Roman aqueducts which had brought water to Istanbul and other cities fell into ruins, leaving the urban population with polluted water.

All that and the general overcrowding and lack of sanitation led to devastating epidemics of plague, cholera and typhoid. Fire-fighting arrangements proved inadequate and there were no fewer than sixty major fires in Istanbul alone during the 18th century, each destroying a large part of the city. It just never occurred to the government to do anything to prevent the disasters or mitigate their effects. As described by European travellers in the 18th and early 19th centuries, many Ottoman cities had by then become overcrowded, filthy and poverty-stricken. To some extent those reports mirrored the changed expectations of the Europeans whose own standards had caught up and overtaken those of the Turks, but there was still much truth in them.

The Jews, who depended on trade, industry and commerce for their livelihood, suffered disproportionately from the worsening economic conditions and the deterioration of law and order. Their role as international traders was also much affected by the shrinking of markets that accompanied the contraction of the Empire and the emergence of European imperialism. The Jews, who had so closely identified with the Empire in its rise to power, shared fully in its decline. As the fortunes of the Empire worsened, so too did that of its Jewish communities – but to an even greater extent. The relatively privileged position of Jews in Ottoman society was eroded and Jews sank in status to one of the least useful of the minority groups of the Empire.

As the wealth and influence of the Jewish community declined, so too did its skills. Educational standards, formerly so high, were particularly affected as Jews lost the will to rise above the torpor that paralysed a Muslim world fast losing confidence in its own worth. Their knowledge of European languages and the Latin script, on which the Turks had so much depended, died out. Even Spanish – preserved in its Ladino form as the day-to-day language of the masses – was written in Hebrew characters, making it useless for the purposes of international communication and diplomacy. Religious education also suffered, particularly knowledge of Hebrew; and the rabbis were forced to respond by writing and publishing in Ladino.

The emerging Christian powers of Europe loomed ever larger in Ottoman consciousness; and the Jews, who had lost their familiarity with Europe and even forgotten its languages, became less useful than native Greek and Armenian Christians who spoke the right languages and were in touch with fellow Christians abroad. Jewish doctors, who had once brought the latest medical knowledge to Turkey and had risen to positions of trust in the courts of the greatest Ottoman Sultans, were ousted by Christian competitors: isolated from what was going on in Europe, Jewish doctors were no longer a match for Greek Christians returning home from European universities with superior knowledge and skills.

The influx of talented European Jews, once so welcomed by the Turks, dried up. Most Marrano refugees went to places like Amsterdam, Venice, Livorno and Bordeaux instead of to Salonika or Istanbul as before. Once there, their activities benefited their new homes, which were in direct competition with the trading centres of the Empire. Those Jews who continued to find sanctuary in Ottoman lands came as penniless refugees from Poland, Hungary and Central Europe; and as they had neither the ability nor the education of the Sephardim, the effort of supporting them added yet another burden to the already impoverished Jewish communities.

Many of the devshirme men, who now virtually ruled the Empire, had started their careers as Christian slaves or their descendants and had carried traces of virulent Greek Christian anti-semitism with them into the government and into the army corps of Janissaries. The unruly Janissaries preyed on Jews more than on Christians or Muslims; for unlike Christians who could rely on powerful European states for protection, Jews had no one to turn to for help. Influenced by European merchants and diplomats, the devshirme men drove the Jews from their favoured positions in the administration and replaced them with Christians.

European merchants, protected by the Capitulation treaties, also helped to topple Jews from their positions of commercial supremacy in favour of native Christian protégés. Jews at first derived little benefit from the Capitulations for in the early part of the 18th century, the French, British and Dutch consuls refused to extend their protection to Jews in order to favour Christians. That was greatly to the detriment of Jewish trade as the Jews were denied the opportunity to compete on anything like equal terms with their rivals. But a few Ottoman Jews did succeed in acting as agents for European merchants, especially when those merchants were themselves Jewish – usually from Livorno in Italy – and were thus able to enjoy the fruits of the protection and tax exemption provided by the Capitulations.

With no leader in a position to bend the Sultan's ear, Jews became increasingly exposed to the tyranny and arbitrary exactions of greedy government officials. But it is important to remember that they were never actually persecuted as in Christian Europe. The weakening of central control of the Empire and its fragmentation into semi-autonomous provinces also had a bad effect on Jewish life. Greedy local rulers oppressed their populations without restraint and Jewish communities, being the most vulnerable, suffered the most. The sultans, who acted fairly to the Jews and protected them whenever they could, were too weak and too far away to be of much help.

The Turks' own attitude to minorities became more negative, and even hostile on occasion, during the years of weakness and decline. As the Muslim masses suffered, so too did their tolerance of dhimmīs diminish; and both local and central governments responded by tightening up the enforcement of humiliating Islamic restrictions on dhimmīs. The old days when such regulations, especially as applied to Jews, were more notional than real were gone. This time it was the Jews, denied the protection of the ever more powerful Christians of Europe, who fared the worst. Individual Jews, displaced from the government posts which had once been their preserve, were forced to wear modest, distinctive dress in public: no longer could they ride through the streets in gorgeous attire. However, open persecution or violence were rare; and when they did occur, such attacks were almost always instigated by Christians and prompted by commercial rivalry or simple anti-semitism.

Christian anti-semitism, often encouraged by European consuls, increased within the Empire. The allegation that Jews murdered Christian children in order to use their blood to bake unleavened bread for Passover, known as the "blood libel", was one of the most destructive accusations made against Jews in medieval times and usually resulted in riot and massacre. Such accusations against Jewish communities were rare during the period of Ottoman strength and then had been promptly suppressed by the sultans: these rose to epidemic proportions in the 19th century, when there were over 35 reported cases in the Middle East alone and many more in the Greek and Balkan provinces of the Empire. The accusations were invariably made by members of the Greek-Christian population and then inflamed by their newspapers: they were supported and sometimes even instigated by foreign diplomatic representatives, especially by the French. Jews could usually enlist the goodwill of the Turks for their protection and later in the century, the help of British,

Austrian and Prussian representatives.

Of course Jews were given short shift in those European lands re-conquered by the Christians: rightly perceived as the friends and allies of the Turks and hated anyhow as Jews, they were massacred and driven-out without mercy.

The one positive result of the increasing poverty and vulnerability of the Jewish communities was that at last they began to combine together in self-defence, electing a single rabbi in each city (a triumvirate in Salonika) to represent and rule over them. The condition of the mass of the Jews of the Ottoman Empire declined steadily until its lowest point was reached in the first half of the nineteenth century, when European travellers to the Middle East described their poverty and obscurity with some relish. Though the European view was partly influenced by other factors, the misery of Ottoman Jewry was real enough.

CHAPTER 17

REDEMPTION

One event above all others marked the irreversible decline of Ottoman Jewry and the erosion of its self-confidence and hope for the future. That was the overwhelming wave of shock and despair that followed Shabbetai Zvi's unsuccessful bid to assume control of the tide of human history and, by the use of supernatural powers, to substitute his own messianic crown for that of the Sultan.

The belief that God will intervene in human affairs to redeem his chosen people through the actions of the Messiah was deeply rooted in Jewish consciousness; and since the time of Maimonides in the 12th century, it had come to be accepted as a fundamental principle of faith. To satisfy that longing for redemption, self-professed messiahs arose in every era, ranging from piously deluded simpletons to megalomaniac tricksters; and Jewish history is littered with a succession of tragic dramas of hope and disappointment.

A brief account of practical attempts to establish the Messianic Age by force of arms during the early years of Islam was included in chapter 8. Another peak of expectation was reached in the year 950 when Jews of both East and West became convinced that redemption was at hand. The rabbis of the Rhineland even wrote to colleagues in Jerusalem to inquire whether the Messiah had arrived, only to be rebuked for their ignorance and credulity. In that same year Ḥisdai ibn Shaprūt, the leader of Spanish Jewry and diplomatic advisor to Khalīf 'Abd al-Raḥmān III, sent a letter of inquiry to King Joseph of the powerful Jewish Khazar kingdom on the river Volga:

... I ask my master the King to let me know whether there is any tradition among your people concerning the end of time for which we have been waiting these many years, and during which we have been going from one captivity to another and from one exile to another; for one must be very strong indeed not to inquire about it. How can I remain silent about the destruction of the Temple of our glory, and about the remnant of our people escaped from the sword and passed through the perils of fire and water? We who were many are now few, and are fallen from our formerly high estate and now dwell in exile ...

Unfortunately King Joseph's reply to that poignant inquiry can have afforded Ḥisdai very little comfort:

> ... our eyes are turned to the Lord our God and to the wise men of Israel in the academies of Jerusalem and Babylon, for we live very far from Zion. But we have heard that because of the sins of the people the calculations have gone astray, and we know nothing ... We have nothing but the prophesies of Daniel. May the God of Israel hasten the redemption and gather our exiled and scattered people in our lifetime and in yours ...

Genuine or not, and scholars disagree, that exchange of letters well illustrates the urgent expectation of redemption always present in the minds of Jews, as well as the anguish caused by its inexplicable delay.

It was however the period of the aftermath of the expulsion from Spain that proved the most significant in the history of messianic speculation. To the bewildered Spanish exiles, as well as to those who remained behind as reluctant New Christians, the date of the redemption was no abstract speculation but a matter of pressing urgency. Surely what they were then enduring really were the travails prophesied to herald the coming of the Messiah: there could be no other explanation. Also knowledge of Kabbalah, developed in Spain, had spread to the ordinary people and gripped their imagination as never before. Kabbalah provided a complete explanation of what had happened in the world, what was happening and how it would all end. In the words of Gershon Sholem, mystical theory joined with messianic expectation after the expulsion, one reacting with the other to produce a climate of intense hope that was to have far-reaching consequences.

All previous attempts to calculate the coming of the Messiah having failed, the Jews of the 17th century again turned to their sacred books and this time convinced themselves that 1648 was the promised year of the redemption. 1648 did not usher in the Messiah but a series of massacres of Jews in Poland and the Ukraine, so devastating that contemporary chroniclers described them as the birth pangs of the Messianic Age. The scene was set for the imminent arrival of the Messiah; but when a messiah did come, it was not from Poland as might have been expected, but from the bustling port of Smyrna (Izmir) in Turkey where Jews lived contentedly under the benign rule of the Ottoman sultans.

Shabbetai Zvi was a learned young rabbi, afflicted by a recurrent mental illness which might these days be diagnosed as manic-depression but was then regarded either as possession by an evil spirit or simple madness. At roughly the same time as the first Polish survivors reached Turkey as refugees, Shabbetai's imagination shifted into a new dimension. He heard a divine voice proclaim:

You are the saviour of Israel ... the true Redeemer.

Shabbetai wandered for years through the main Jewish centres of the Middle East, at first welcomed as a pious young scholar, but then punished and driven out when local rabbis became exasperated by his bizarre behaviour during bouts of illness. At last he reached Gaza where, during one of his periods of remission, he visited the celebrated prophet Nathan to seek a cure for his troubled soul. Though the two men had never met before, Nathan had seen visions in which Shabbetai figured as the Redeemer: he therefore fell to the floor before Shabbetai and hailed him as the Messiah.

It was shortly after that, in 1665, that Shabbetai announced his mission to the world as the Anointed of the Lord God of Jacob, the royal Messiah from the House of David. After that proclamation in the Gaza synagogue, we are told that his face shone with heavenly radiance; and his majestic presence, frenzied singing and compelling authority so dominated his audience that all stood in awe of their king. Shabbetai had entered into one of his periods of manic exaltation.

He was fully supported in his new role by Nathan, who busied himself in reshaping messianic tradition to fit the unsuitable figure of Shabbetai Zvi. Nathan's messiah was not the expected all-conquering hero, come to lead his people to victory in battle against their enemies, but rather a man of suffering with a mission to wage a mysterious spiritual war against the powers of darkness. Again, contrary to traditional Jewish belief, the Messiah was not to be recognised by miraculous signs but simply by the faith he inspired in his followers. Nathan taught that personal salvation could not be achieved by penitence, prayer and good works alone; and that belief in the messiahship of his candidate was the essential requirement.

Nathan's call for immediate repentance to lessen the woes predicted to inaugurate the messianic era evoked an overwhelming response in the hearts and minds of Jews all over the world. They succumbed to an orgy of penitence and rejoicing, the like of which contemporary observers claimed had never been seen before. Thousands fasted for days at a time and spent their waking hours and most of their nights in prayer. In the north, men rolled naked in the snow: they beat their bodies with thorns, nettles and leather scourges. Others wore layers of nettles under their clothes against their skins: nettles were in such demand by Jews that in some places they were specially imported over long distances. Shops and businesses closed down and workers neglected their tasks – for was not the End of Days at hand? People tried to sell their immovable possessions in preparation for the End, when they expected to leave for Jerusalem to join the Messiah.

Only a small minority held out against the tide and urged that individuals would be judged by the deeds they perform in this world, rather than by faith in Shabbetai Zvi. But such opposition was submerged by the almost universal acceptance of the new creed; and even opponents found it hard to ignore the positive features of repentance on so grand a scale. Never before had the whole nation of the Jews – from the Holy Land to Egypt, the Yemen, Persia and Kurdistan: from Istanbul to Salonika, Venice and Rome: from Vienna to Prague, Hamburg and Amsterdam: from Poland and Lithuania to Alsace, Avignon and Morocco; and even in England and the Americas – been engulfed by such a mood of repentance and rejoicing. Never before had the rich and the poor, the learned and the ignorant, the pious and the indifferent, so eagerly accepted the claim of a pretender to the messianic throne. The reaction to the appearance of the half-crazed Shabbetai Zvi was unique in Jewish history. Jesus of Nazareth, it will be remembered, attracted comparatively few Jewish followers during his lifetime; and the religion later founded in his name derived its main support from pagan converts.

Flushed with success, Shabbetai set sail for Istanbul with the openly declared intention of seizing the Sultan's crown and placing it on his own head. But the Turkish authorities were waiting for him: Shabbetai was arrested on arrival, brought before the Grand Vizier and thrown into prison. It was a strange sort of imprisonment for after payment of heavy bribes, Shabbetai was granted a degree of personal comfort, allowed to receive visitors at will and even to take ritual baths in the sea, accompanied by crowds of admirers.

Shabbetai behaved quietly enough in Istanbul but on his transfer to the fortress prison of Gallipoli, his conduct became manic once more. He publicly pronounced the Ineffable Name – the most sacred of God's many names, the name of four letters considered so holy that only the High Priest could articulate it once a year at the climax of the Temple service for the Day of Atonement, and which has not been pronounced since the destruction of the Temple. Ignoring the prohibition against performing sacrifices outside the Temple of Jerusalem, he sacrificed a lamb on the eve of Passover and consumed it with its forbidden abdominal fat after reciting the blasphemous benediction:

Blessed are you, O Lord our God, who permits that which is forbidden.

It should be understood that such acts would have been considered outrageous in the extreme if performed by any other than the Messiah in the Messianic Age. Shabbetai perverted many other rituals and customs; and as the high point of his innovations, he abolished the solemn Fast of Av, which commemorates the destruction of the Temple and is the saddest day in the Jewish calendar.

By permission of his venal Turkish jailers who waxed fat on the proceeds, and the liberality of his followers, Shabbetai lived the life of a king in prison. He wore royal clothes, furnished his rooms with gold and silver objects, dined off gold plate encrusted with gems and was attended by a bevy of beautiful virgins: a retinue of learned kabbalistic rabbis followed him everywhere – but how the rabbis coped with the virgins is not recorded! Shabbetai held court to thousands of visitors from all over the world; and so numerous were the pilgrims to Gallipoli, that the Turks complained of soaring food prices in the locality. Messianic enthusiasm increased during Shabbetai's captivity; and expectation rose to dangerously high levels as fantastic stories of the wonderful doings of the King Messiah, and of new prophets who sprang up all over the Jewish world, multiplied without limit.

The fragile edifice of hope was finally shattered beyond repair by the intervention of a simple Polish rabbi called Nehemia who visited Shabbetai in August 1666. Nehemia's literal mind failed to understand Shabbetai's claim to be the Messiah. It should of course have been plain to all that Shabbetai, by his very nature, could not possibly fulfil the ancient prophesies concerning the Messiah – the warrior king from the House of David who would lead his people to victory over their enemies. But he had always relied on kabbalistic argument, on personal charisma and on his aura of manic illumination to cloud the issue and convince doubters.

The two rabbis debated furiously together for three days and nights, during which they ate little and slept even less. In the end, the exasperated Nehemia rounded on Shabbetai and accused him of lying and leading his followers astray. Nehemia rushed straight to the Turkish guards and declared his wish to convert to Islam. Once that had been accomplished, he denounced Shabbetai to the Turks as a dangerous imposter, bent on sedition.

All privileges at Gallipoli were abruptly cancelled and Shabbetai was taken under armed guard to Adrianople, one hundred and fifty miles away, where the Sultan was in residence. It seems that the Islamic authorities had advised against making Shabbetai a martyr by putting him to death, so he was brought to the Council Chamber and confronted by a group of high officials: the Sultan himself observed the proceedings from behind a heavily latticed screen. To cut a long story short, Shabbetai displayed no heroism and very little dignity. On being offered the choice of the turban or his head, he promptly apostatised to Islam to save his life. He was graciously received into the Muslim faith by the Sultan, who gave him an honorary post at court and granted him a substantial pension. In a resigned letter to his elder brother in Smyrna, Shabbetai commented sadly:

... and now let me alone, for God has made me a Turk.

and he ended with a quotation from Psalm 33:

For he spoke and it was done; commanded and it stood fast. (17.1)

Sultan Mehmed IV was greatly angered by Shabbetai's disclosure of the disloyalty of so many of his Jewish subjects, who ignoring all obligations to his person and empire, had expressed enthusiasm for their messianic king: such ingratitude seemed a poor return for the kindness with which Turkey had always treated the Jews. The Sultan's first reaction was to impose a terrible punishment on all the Jews of the Empire; but he was dissuaded from that course by his chief advisers. Instead, warrants were issued for the arrest of many leading rabbis and laymen with a view to their execution. However the Sultan's mother intervened on behalf of the Jews and procured an amnesty from her son. Turkish Jewry was thus saved from catastrophe; and even the arrested notables escaped with a mere reprimand. The Turks behaved with remarkable restraint throughout the incident: Jews were not molested or persecuted in any way nor was the apostasy of their supposed messiah used as a pretext for forced conversions to Islam. Had a similar event occurred within the boundaries of Christian Europe, the outcome would have been very different and the end result too terrible to contemplate.

Most Jews felt betrayed by Shabbetai and turned on him with

revulsion; but an influential minority called "believers" refused to accept that Shabbetai had been a fake, or even that he had been deluded. To them it was inconceivable that God could so cruelly have deceived the righteous and led his people into fraud. For some who had already tasted the flavour of redemption, even if only in their own minds, things could never be the same again. Refusing to submit to the sentence of history, they embarked on a secret inner life of their own whilst outwardly professing conventional Judaism.

The "believers" were sustained by a mystical theology developed by Nathan of Gaza and by those who came after him. This explained the mystery of the apostasy in terms that prepared the way for Shabbetai's Second Coming and the Redemption. Nathan taught that it was not possible for the Messiah to attain perfection until he had first descended into the realm of evil and emerged unscathed. The Messiah was not bound by the ordinary rules of the world but governed by profound mystical purpose. At the heart of Sabbatean belief was the disturbing doctrine, present just below the surface of most messianic movements, that a new age had dawned in which laws previously given by God to men were no longer valid. Extremists never found it difficult to extend that idea to include a positive obligation to break all the old laws in order to sanctify the new epoch. Believers in Shabbetai Zvi were not slow to follow suit, their crazier elements assuming with glee that they had been commanded to follow their Messiah into apostasy and the realms of sin. The paradoxical notion of redemption through sin became popular in radical Sabbatean circles, particularly among the apostates, and caused great scandal when details of ceremonies involving group adultery and incest leaked out. In general though, the vast majority of "believers" remained within the Jewish fold and differed from other Jews only in their secret beliefs and hopes. This hidden messianic movement, which included influential rabbis, survived until the 19th century; and a remnant of the descendants of those who converted to Islam, while remaining secret Sabbatean Jews, has retained its hidden identity in Turkey to the present day.

After the initial shock at the news of Shabbetai's defection had passed, the rabbis of the Ottoman Empire worked long and hard to steer their flocks away from the brink of the twin disasters of heresy and apostasy. They assumed unprecedented powers and used that authority to eliminate all internal democracy and intellectual freedom within their communities. In the end, they did manage to achieve their declared aim of blotting out the very name of Shabbetai Zvi from the collective memory – but that was at the cost of imposing a stultifying conservatism on most aspects of Jewish life, secular as well as religious. Their reaction, understandable in the immediate aftermath of the debacle, eventually became a straightjacket which impeded progress and modernisation at every turn. The long-lasting effect of all this on the Jews of the Empire was profound discouragement, which contributed yet another element to their steady intellectual and economic decline.

Jews were indeed made to suffer for their messianic aspirations in another part of the Muslim East – in Iran, whose Shi'ite rulers had already a long history of religious intolerance. As recorded by the English diarist John Evelyn in his "History of the late and final extirpation and exilement of the Jews out of the Empire of Persia" in 1669:

... In the reign of the famous Abas (Abbas I, 1587-1629), Sophy of Persia ... the nation being low and somewhat exhausted of inhabitants, it entered into the mind of this prince ... to seek some expedient for the revival and improvement of trade, and by all manner of privileges and immunities to encourage all contiguous nations to negotiate and trade amongst them; and ... in a short time the whole kingdom was filled with multitudes of the most industrious people and strangers that any way bordered on him.

It happened, that amongst those who came, innumerable flocks of Jews ran thither from all their dispersions in the East, attracted by the gain which they universally make wherever they set footing by their innate craft, sacred avarice and excessive extortions which they continually practice. And it was not many years but by this means they had so impoverished the rest, and especially the natural subjects of Persia, that the clamour of it reached the ears of the Emperor ... and indeed it was intolerable ...

How to repress this enormity and remedy this inconvenience ... he long consulted ... After much dispute it was at last found that the Jews had long since forfeited their lives by the very text of the Alcoran (Qur'ān) where it is expressed that if within 600 years of the promulgation of that religion they did not universally come in and profess the Mahometan faith, they should be destroyed ... His majesty commanded that all the rabbins and chiefs amongst the Jews should appear and make answer ...

The Sophy, easily perceiving the cunning and wary subterfuge ... told them that they were a people of dissolute principles ... and (he) therefore required of them to set a positive time when their Messiah was to appear ... but assuring them that he would both pardon and protect them for the time they should assign ...

The poor Jews contrived to give him this answer: that ... their Messiah should appear within 70 years, prudently believing that either they or the Emperor should be dead before that time ... (or that) all this should be forgotten or averted ...

The Emperor accepts the answer and immediately causes it to be recorded in the form of a solemn stipulation between them that in case there was no news of the Messiah within the 70 years assigned ... they should either turn Mahometan or their whole nation be destroyed throughout Persia and their substance confiscated: but ... if their Messiah did appear within that period, the Emperor himself would become a Jew and all his people with him ... The Jews were then for the present dismissed with a payment of two millions of gold for the favour of this long indulgence.

Since the time of this Emperor Abas to the present Sophy now reigning there are more than 70 years past ... By a wonderful accident ... a person extremely curious of antiquities, searching one day among the records of the palace ... found this writing ... intimating what had solemnly passed between him and the chiefs of the Jews in the name of their whole nation ...

Upon this the Sophy instantly summons a council, produced the instrument before them and requires their advice ... for there now began to be great whispers and some letters from merchants out of Turkey of the motions of a pretended Messiah, which was the famous Sabatai. This so wrought the Emperor and his council that with one voice they immediately conclude on the destruction of the Jews ...

... Proclamations are issued out and published to the people ... impowering them to fall immediately upon the Jews ... and to put to the sword man woman and child, but as such as should forthwith turn to Mahometan belief ...

Happy was he that could escape the fury of the enraged people ... (they) flew and made havoc of them ... falling upon the spoil and continuing the carnage to their utter extermination ...

5 Shabbetai Zvi
as sketched in 1667 by an eye-witness in Smyrna
from Thomas Coenen's Ydele Verwachtinge der Joden, Amsterdam 1669

6 The Sultan in procession
from a 16th century engraving by Antonio Tempesta

7 A European trader of 1593
from a contemporary engraving by De Bry

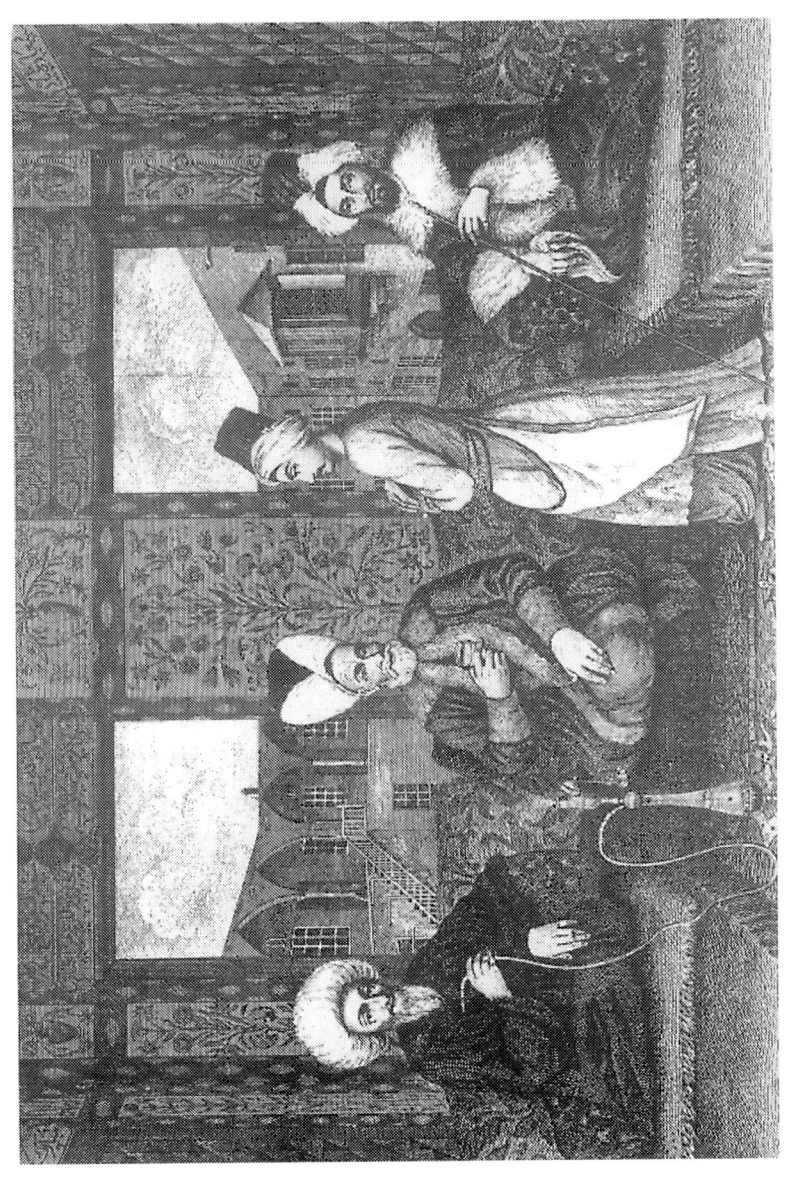

8 The Ottoman Governer, Quadi (Chief Justice) and Agha (Commander of the Janisaries) of Aleppo from A. Russell's *Natural History of Aleppo*, London 1794

CHAPTER 18

PROVINCIAL LIFE IN THE 18TH CENTURY

By the middle of the 18th century the Ottoman Empire was well past the pinnacle of its glory, when the magnificence of the Sultan's court had dazzled European ambassadors and his invincible armies had struck terror into the hearts of their royal masters. However, despite its decline, the Sultan still remained at the helm of a vast empire. His Jewish communities too, most of whose members had by then become accustomed to sharing the lot of the humblest of the Sultan's subjects, continued to provide a framework in which Jews governed themselves in relative freedom under their own laws, little more troubled by outside forces than were other minority groups.

There were, of course, many exceptions to the general pattern of poverty and obscurity into which the Jews of the Ottoman Empire were gradually descending. Individual Jews still used their medical skills to influence foreign ambassadors and high Ottoman officials – though rarely did they any longer treat the Sultans themselves. Daniel de Fonseca (d. 1740), a Portuguese Marrano, gained much esteem at the Ottoman court where he used his contacts to represent France in a dispute with Austria: he eventually retired to France where he joined high society and was described by Voltaire as "the only philosopher of his people". Yehudah Baruch, chief banker to Sultan Mahmūd I (1730-54), used his position at Court to get the Sultan to send agents to Maria Teresa in Vienna and talk her out of her intention to expel all Jews from Austria.

Jews long continued to act as bankers, moneychangers and tax farmers within the Empire because of their unique abilities; and it was many years before they were replaced as customs agents – in Egypt not until the 1770s. As only Jews knew the value of goods and what duties should be charged, most Muslim and European merchants just had to employ Jewish agents for this purpose.

Some Ottoman Jews had managed to evade the ban on employment imposed by European merchants by investing directly in countries such as Prussia, Denmark, Ragusa and Holland. They had thus gained the protection of those countries and even sometimes became honorary consuls, in turn securing similar protection for their families, business partners and friends. The prohibition against Jewish protégés lapsed towards the end of the 18th century when consuls began to sell their protection more widely and Jews used their acquired status as English, French, Swedish and Austrian nationals to prosper and amass fortunes.

Groups of European Jews – known as Francos – also settled in Aleppo, Damascus, the Holy Land and elsewhere. They dominated local commerce by use of Capitulations' privileges and extended their own protected status and prosperity to local Jewish agents and employees. In Damascus, for example, the Farhi family controlled the finances, banking and foreign trade of Syria for the better part of a century, partly because of the great ability of its members and partly because of their good relations with the Europeans: even as late as 1830, it is estimated that Jewish business houses were still handling almost 40% of the foreign trade of the city. In Egypt and North Africa, one member each of the leading Jewish families took up Austrian or French nationality and then used his status as a lever to benefit his whole clan. Thus was gradually created a new, Europe-oriented mercantile élite, increasingly cut off from the poverty-stricken masses of Ottoman Jewry who struggled on unaffected by the life-style of their more fortunate brethren.

This chapter focuses on Ḥalab (or Aleppo) in the north of Syria to illustrate the quality of life in general, and of Jewish life in particular, in the Arab provinces of the Ottoman Empire in the 18th century. Aleppo was chosen for several good reasons. First, because of the existence of Abraham Marcus's study of life in the town, based on the proceedings of its Sharī'a (Islamic) court: then because Aleppo was home to a resident colony of European merchants, including a large English contingent who kept records and wrote accounts of their life there; and finally because of the unique journals of Shalom ben Aharon ha-Cohen and his son-in-law Moshe Dwek ha-Cohen, who left Aleppo at the turn of the century to found a new Jewish community in Calcutta, India.

Ḥalab, with its population of about 120,000 in the 18th century, was one of the great urban centres of the Middle East: only Cairo with 250,000 people and Istanbul with 450,000 were larger. The city was ancient indeed, with a history going back beyond 2000 BCE Abraham was said to have milked his flocks there on his way to the Promised Land and Jews called the city Aram Zova, referring back to the time of King David. Local tradition claims that Ezra the Scribe paused in Ḥalab on his way from Babylon to Jerusalem and built a synagogue in Tedef, a few miles from the city. Its Jewish community was certainly in existence shortly after the destruction of the Temple in 70 CE

After the Turkish conquest of 1516, Ḥalab – or Aleppo as it is known in Europe – became the capital of the important Ottoman province of Northern Syria and the seat of its provincial government. Not only was Aleppo the administrative centre of an extensive area, but it was also a hub of regional and international trade and an industrial centre. Aleppo was considered one of the most pleasant and elegant cities of the Ottoman Empire. In it lived an accomplished, wealthy and powerful élite, possessed of learning and fine manners, proud of themselves and their city; and people from countries as distant as England and India came there to trade, study and settle.

Aleppo, strategically astride a main caravan route to the East – through Iraq to Persia, India and China – was well placed for internal trade within the Empire and external trade with Europe. Aleppo's commerce with Europe started as early as the 15th century and was much stimulated by the Capitulations agreements discussed in earlier chapters. Though its extensive internal trade was little affected, intercontinental commerce was badly hit by the opening of sea routes to India in the 1600s and again by the opening of the Suez Canal in 1869. However Aleppo long remained an important market town within the Empire as well as one in which European manufactured products, were exchanged for the raw materials of the East.

The inhabitants of Aleppo accepted without question that their city belonged to the Ottoman Empire and that the Sultan was its absolute ruler. The Sultan's government, which promised only physical security and justice in return for total obedience, existed for the Sultan's own private purposes and not to serve the general public. The people were not encouraged to identity with the Ottoman Turks or participate in the political life of the province: extravagant displays of patriotism were not expected of them, nor were they liable for conscription to the Turkish army. There was no opposition to the Ottomans for the inhabitants of the city had long been accustomed to rule by alien Muslim dynasties. National consciousness hardly existed; and it was not until the end of the 19th century that some of the Sultan's subjects first began to think of themselves as members of separate nations, entitled to independence.

Situated close to the boundary between Arabic-speaking and Turkish-speaking peoples, the population of Aleppo was diverse. It included Arabs, Turks, Kurds, Greeks, Serbs, Bulgars and many others who all spoke Arabic. Of the total population of some 120,000 in the middle of the 18th century, there were 4,000 Jews, 20,000 Christians of various denominations and 90,000 or so Sunni Muslims. Naturally the upper classes were much influenced by the Turkish culture of the ruling Ottoman élite; and knowledge of the language and fashions of Ottoman society was a useful passport to advancement.

This was a very unequal society containing a thin crust of the fabulously wealthy, a middle class estimated as about 30% of the population and the mass of the miserably poor. All accepted such inequalities as part of the natural order and lived side by side without open discontent. Indeed most would have agreed with the 18th century resident of the city who jotted the following thought in his diary:

Whoever claims that all people are equal must be hopelessly mad. (18.1)

It was a world keenly sensitive to status and to the differences between men, in which visible indications of wealth, lineage and occupation were all assessed with an assiduity that would do credit to one of Jane Austen's heroines. At the very top were the key government officials and their staff, all Ottoman Turks posted to Aleppo from Istanbul: below them came the military and religious leaders, members of the Ashraf (supposed descendants of the Prophet, of which there were several thousand in Aleppo) and the very wealthy. In the business world only the great export-import merchants could ever hope to achieve high status.

The pursuit of wealth was considered legitimate and natural, even amongst religious leaders:

Be known for wealth and not poverty.

and

Power on earth rests on wealth, in the hereafter on good deeds.

were two popular sayings of the time.

It did not occur to the government that helping the needy was any part of its responsibility. There were very few welfare institutions and the poor could depend only on the rich for succour: that situation had not changed very much in that respect by the 1930s when it was reported that:

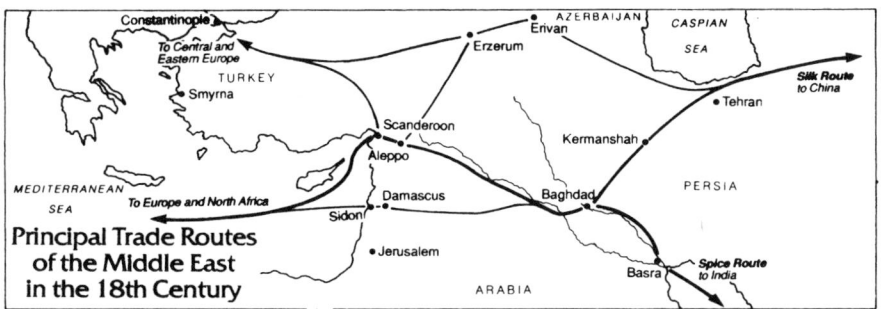

Principal Trade Routes of the Middle East in the 18th Century

There was no welfare state or big charitable institutions in Aleppo: it was left to the rich to take care of the poor ... The most wonderful food was served for Shabbat lunch after the men returned from the synagogue. We had our own pet beggars who came to the house to be fed every Saturday after the family had finished lunch. (18.2)

Religion was not a private matter, left to individual choice, but was woven into the very fabric of society. Its relevance was affirmed at every turn and the option of non-belief was inconceivable. Muslims, Christians and Jews were neighbours, business associates and professional colleagues: they spoke the same language, lived in similar homes, enjoyed similar food and had like pleasures and pursuits. All were able to practise most professions and trades and to belong to the same guilds: they often worked together under the same roof. Business partnerships cut right across confessional lines, as did patterns of residence. Although Jews and Christians lived in particular parts of the town, no neighbourhood was exclusively Jewish or exclusively Christian. Yet as members of distinct religious communities, organised around different beliefs, Christians and Jews were irreparably divided from the Muslims as well as from each other. As dhimmīs, protected subjects of subordinate status, they were subjected to special taxation, prohibited from proselytising or worshipping in public and separated from the Muslims by restrictions on clothing and other disabilities. However, as elsewhere in the Islamic world, these restrictions, except always for the jizya or poll tax, were imposed unevenly.

In 18th century Aleppo, dhimmīs were totally excluded from government and political power. The ban on building new churches and synagogues was enforced strictly. Riding on horseback was permitted; but limitations on clothes, shoes and headgear to differentiate dhimmīs from Muslims were always enforced to some extent. For example, men had to wear specially marked robes in the bathhouses and women could only attend at special times when Muslim women were not present. Such regulations were tightened from time to time, only to be relaxed later and especially after sums of money had changed hands.

It must be remembered that, though resenting the restrictions, Jews had no interest in merging with Muslims and losing their separate identity as a nation. Their leaders used Jewish law, taxes, enforcement agencies, education, endowments and social legislation to the full for the preservation of the community and the discouragement of out-marriage and conversion to Islam. The Jews of Aleppo maintained many international connections other than those deriving from trade, for their rabbis kept contact with colleagues throughout the Middle East and even in Europe: relations with Baghdad and the Holy Land were particularly close.

Aleppo had long attracted resident colonies of European merchants, mostly Frenchmen and Englishmen with a few Italians and Dutch, who lived and conducted their business in "khans" (closed courtyards containing commercial premises with living quarters above), located in the city centre and away from the residential quarters of the town. Their lives, properties and goods were extra-territorial, outside Turkish jurisdiction, and governed only by their own consuls. Although many lived in the city for years, they always remained expatriates and did not mingle with the local population. Few brought their wives with them or married local women; and even fewer bothered to learn Arabic or Turkish, preferring to conduct their affairs through Christian or Jewish intermediaries. There were between 100 and 400 European residents in Aleppo at any one time in the 17th century, and more later.

As described in 1675 by the chaplain to the English colony, Aleppo was one of the pleasantest cities in the Levant and compared favourably to most in Europe.

... from hence all the city shows most beautiful ... The buildings are all of stone and flat on top. They look white and very beautiful. Next you see the cupolas – which are in abundance, not only on their mosques but on many of their great buildings – rising over the rest of the buildings like so many pretty mountains over the plains ... Another adorning are the cypress trees, which are very high and green all over the town and which make a very pretty show ... And last of all the castle which seems to stand in the very midst of all. ... About the town are brave gardens and pleasant plantations ... being made more fruitful by a small brook which runs close by the town. (18.3)

By the middle of the 18th century Henry Maundrell, another English chaplain, described the social life of his compatriots as a continual round of visits to other Europeans as well as to the houses of Turks, Jews and Armenians. Their tables were stocked with a marvellous assortment of game and fish; and much of their spare time was spent in feasting, hunting and in games and picnics in the delightful countryside.

For descriptions of Jewish life in 18th century Aleppo we are fortunate in having a book written by Alexander Russell, who served as doctor to the English colony in the 1750s. At that time the Jews all lived close to their synagogue and were religiously observant and well behaved. According to Russell, this was so because it was:

... more difficult (for Jews) to conceal debauchery than it would be among a more numerous nation ... (18.4)

The community included poor people as well as prosperous bankers, merchants and shopkeepers; and Russell explains that when meat was available, the wealthy subsidised its price for the benefit of the poor. Such was the influence of the Jews on the town's commerce that trade was suspended on Jewish holydays when:

... even the Pashas and other grandees are sometimes obliged to postpone the dispatch of their own affairs (18.4)

and when even the departure of important trans-desert caravans had to be delayed. The festival of Succot (Tabernacles) made a great impression on the English doctor:

Turkish ladies at this season stroll in troops among the Jewish houses to see the tabernacles, and are seldom refused admission. Such as are acquainted with the family are entertained with coffee, sweetmeats and sherbets; and the others, after satisfying their curiosity, retire without ceremony ... They entertain hospitably at their houses, send presents of various kinds of sweetmeats to their friends, and all business is suspended. (18.4)

Within their own community, Jewish women were not segregated from men nearly as strictly as were Muslims. Their social centre was the hamām (bathhouse) where they met together for gossip on Friday afternoons after they had finished preparing for the Sabbath. It was only in the hamām that they could meet freely to show off their fine clothes and talk to strangers; and it was in the hamām that mothers often selected likely brides for their sons. All marriages were arranged by the parents but only rarely were unwilling couples forced together. Again, the custom had not much changed by the 1930s, when it was reported that:

A few of the young men emigrated to New York where they prospered. As soon as they became established there, they asked one of their relatives in Aleppo to choose a bride for them. The young man would then buy the trousseau, send this back to Aleppo and marry the girl by proxy. Amazingly, most of the marriages turned out really well. (18.5)

Polygamy, though not forbidden to Sephardim, was resorted to mainly when a wife refused to live with her husband or in cases of childlessness after a ten year wait, or when their was no male heir born to the marriage. In such circumstances the taking of a second wife, usually with the consent of the first, did occur; and that custom continued at least until the end of the 19th century. Russell mentions that it was considered scandalous to take a second wife in the absence of such cause – which implies that it happened sometimes. He quotes one amusing instance:

In one case a person of low condition had taken a second wife on account of his first wife's barrenness; and soon had the mortification of seeing both become pregnant. Both wives continued for several years to bear one child every fifteen months, which the pious Hebrews considered a punishment for not trusting to God's providence. (18.4)

Another custom mentioned by Russell was that of visiting the sick:

... men on their return from synagogue go in parties together from house to house to visit the sick; and it is sufficient for a person to be considered sick if he does not make his appearance at public worship. People, though really indisposed, often make an improper exertion to go to synagogue in order to avoid the fatigue of ceremonious visits. (18.4)

A more intimate picture of Jewish manners and attitudes of mind is provided by the journals of two travellers. In the year 1789, at the age of 26, Shalom ha-Cohen left his wife and home in Aleppo to seek his fortune in the East. After visiting Baghdad, Basra and Bombay he ended

9 A Khan in Istanbul

10 Moshe Dwek in his 55th year

up in Surat, then India's leading port and home to a thriving colony of sixty-five Arabic-speaking Jewish merchants. Shalom established himself quickly in Surat and was recognised by the East India company as the Chief Jewish Merchant and spokesman for the colony. Legend relates that he then sent back to Aleppo for his wife Sathie, only to be rebuffed by her parents who declared:

Even if you were to pave the way from Aleppo to Surat with gold and precious stones we would still not send you our daughter. (18.6)

The frustrated husband took a second wife the following year, choosing Naīma, the sister of his business partner in Baghdad. Two years later, Sathie's parents having relented, Shalom was re-united with his first wife in Baghdad and escorted her home to Surat. Naīma is said to have embraced Sathie at the entrance to the house and handed over its keys, saying:

You are my elder sister, so must keep the keys. We will live together in love and peace. (18.6)

Sathie died in childbirth and her infant was suckled and reared in love by Naīma, who had given birth herself some months earlier. In 1815 the two half-sisters were married from their father's house on the same day; and they and their husbands then set up home together in the kind of extended family so common at that time.

In 1796 the monopoly controlling the shipping of goods in and out of Calcutta was lifted and Shalom, accompanied by his shohet (ritual slaughterer) and a cook, set sail to investigate business prospects: the date of his arrival in 1796 is marked as the birthday of Calcutta's Jewish community. Shalom had an adventurous life in India, making and losing a fortune before serving as Court Jeweller first to the Nawab of Oudh and then to Maharajah Ranjit Singh. In Amritsar it was said that he was asked to value the 191-carat Koh-i-Noor diamond, later to be presented to Queen Victoria; and he earned the Maharajah's praise by declaring that as such a jewel could be acquired only as a gift or by the shedding of much blood, it was priceless. Shalom died in Calcutta in 1836 and was buried in the cemetery he had previously donated to the Jewish community.

Some thirty years previously, Shalom had written to his old friend and brother-in-law in Aleppo asking him to send one of his sons to Calcutta

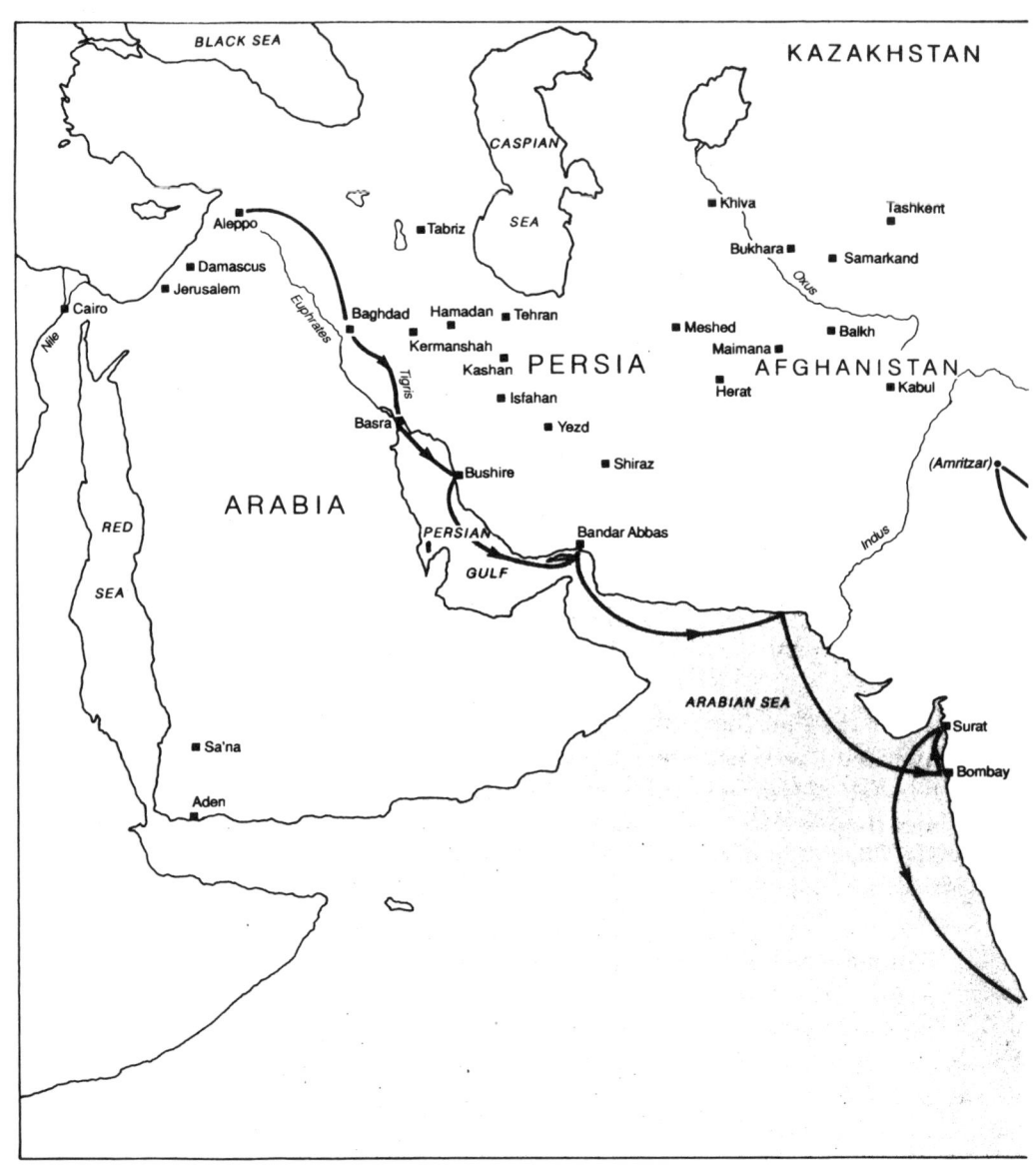

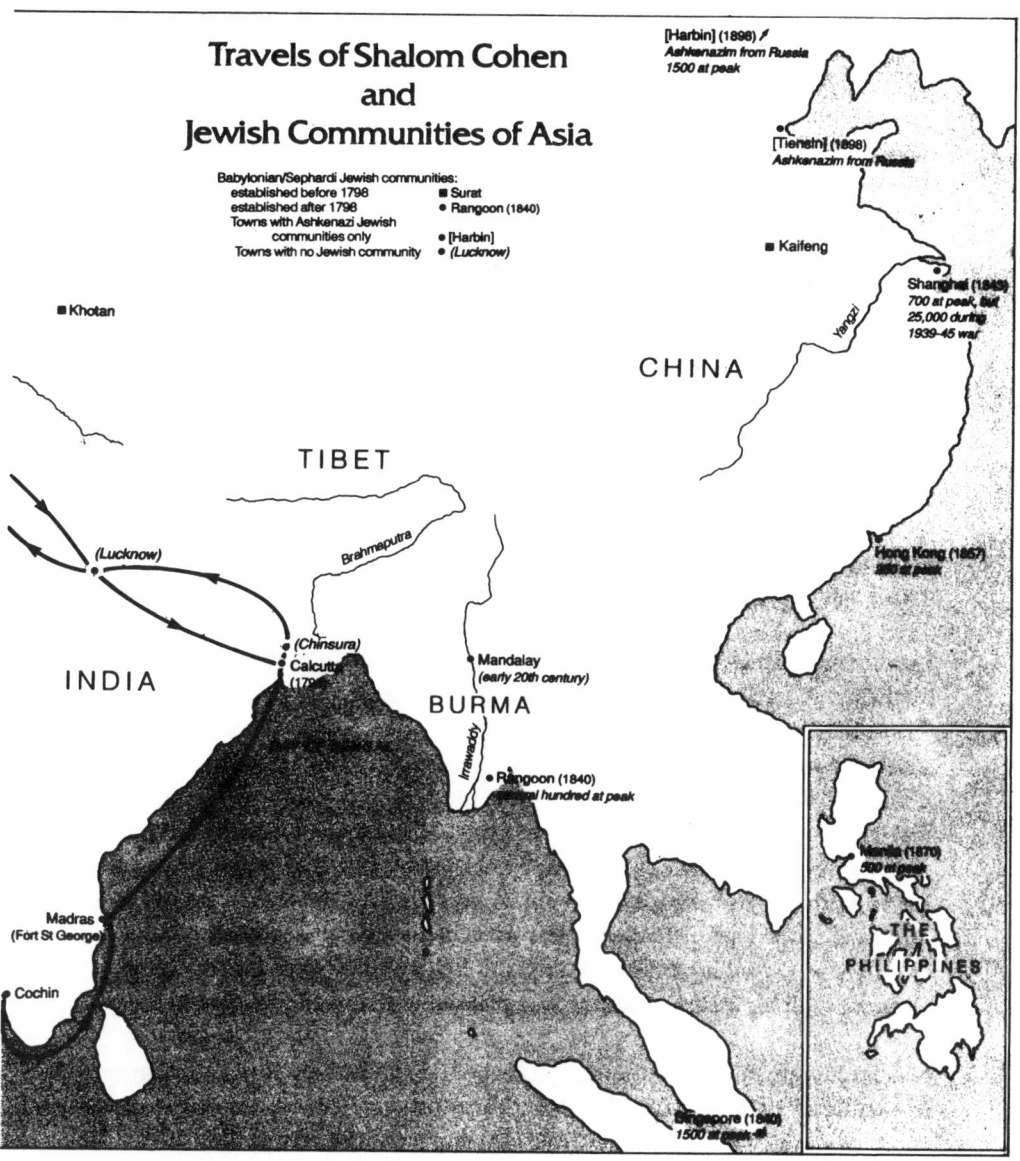

to marry Shalom's twelve-year-old daughter, Luna. His letter was received with joy and an enthusiastic reply returned:

... my dear son Moshe (Moses), the light of my eyes, the crown of my head, choicest of young men, is yours. And I trust in your affection that you will keep your eye on him. From this day on, he is your son ...(18.6)

Moshe dutifully set out for Calcutta, where he encountered his new family for the first time. Arriving at Shalom's house at midnight, he later recalled that:

... we met and I bowed before him and kissed his hand; and he also kissed and embraced me as a father his son. And so did all the other relatives living in the house ... and in the morning we rose early to the synagogue of my father-in-law, the crown of my head, which was in the house ... and I gave praise and thanksgiving for life and peace and for my having arrived. Blessed be He who does good and deals kindly ... amen. (18.6)

Luna was married to Moshe in Calcutta two months after her thirteenth birthday. Again, in the words of Moshe's old age,

... and I stayed in quiet and peace in the house of my father-in-law; and God, blessed be He, set me favourably in his sight and in the sight of his family ... I married my bride, my dove, my perfect one, Miss Luna – of women in the tent may she be blessed – daughter of my father-in-law, the crown of my head. And I lived with her and she found favour in my eyes and she also loved me as her own soul. And I give thanks to His great name for all the above that I had experienced ... And after the wedding, my father-in-law gave into my hand and possession all his affairs ... and he was pleased with my efforts. (18.6)

Moshe Dwek, a far quieter man, succeeded his flamboyant father-in-law as the head of Calcutta's Jewish community, which he served in many capacities and with great devotion throughout the remainder of his life.

Returning to commercial matters, Jews had at first derived little benefit from the presence of the European merchants and their consuls in Aleppo: in early days local Christians rather than Jews were the preferred intermediaries between the foreigners and Aleppo life. The Capitulations agreements allowed each consul to employ one or two dragomen (interpreters) from the local population: those fortunate protégés enjoyed full consular protection, involving exemption from

Turkish laws and taxes. Grossly abusing the privilege, the consuls began to dispense their protection more widely: first they extended it to the families and employees of their dragomen, then to the host of clerks, agents and salesmen employed by their merchants and finally to wealthy non-Muslims willing to pay generously for such protection and exemption from taxation. The Jews also pursued European patronage, though on a smaller scale, for as described earlier, a few of the most wealthy of them had invested directly in a European country and so managed to gain the protection of its consul in Aleppo.

Rich Italian-Jewish merchants, mostly from Livorno, also settled in Aleppo on the heels of the Europeans. They came to the country as protected foreign nationals and not as dhimmīs. Known as Francos, their thriving commercial enterprises employed many local Jews; and eventually they were also able to extend foreign protection to their own Jewish employees and their families. In Aleppo, Jewish opportunities improved still further when Raphael Picciotto, a member of one of the most prominent Franco families, became Austrian consul in 1784. (Habsburg-Lorraine kings, who ruled Austria, took over Tuscany from the Medicis).

Another though later source of foreign protection for Jews arose from British rule in India. Several Jewish families of Baghdad origin, who could prove that they had lived or traded extensively in Bombay or Calcutta, automatically achieved the status of British-protected subjects on reaching Aleppo.

Thus in Aleppo there came into being a community of Christians and one of Jews who were able to live and trade under the protection of foreign consuls, free from Turkish taxes and interference. The number of those privileged Christians and Jews rose steadily during the 18th century and further increased during the 19th century. In 1910, for example, the British Consul reported that 45 Jews of the city, comprising six different families, were registered as British subjects. The families concerned were Dwek (19), Gubbay (14), Shalom (5), Sassoon (4), Levy (2) and Btesh (1) – all names now well known in the Jewish communities of Manchester and London. (18.7)

Protected Christians and Jews considered themselves far superior in social standing to the dhimmīs and wore pretentious fur caps to mark that difference. Compared to dhimmīs they were indeed privileged, being both wealthy and free from oppressive restrictions. It is sad to report that, human nature being what it is, the protected Jews felt secure in their own privileges and did not always do their best to help their less fortunate brethren. They sometimes sheltered behind their exemption from Turkish law and refused to pay the internal taxes levied by the Jewish community. The number of wealthy Jewish taxpayers dwindled as a result of the extension of foreign protection; and the records contain threats by the Haham (Chief Rabbi) to excommunicate those whose refusal to pay their fair share of the taxes was imposing a further burden on the Jewish poor. The Ottoman authorities also came to resent these wealthy tax-dodgers, whose exemption affected state revenue and whose freedom from Turkish control was perceived as an affront to the dignity of the Empire. In 1806 an attempt was made to abolish all such privileges, including the fur cap, but this failed because of European pressure and was not repeated.

For those of Aleppo's Jews who had adopted British nationality, as opposed to another European nationality, the final irony came in 1914 when Turkey joined Germany in its war with Great Britain and its allies. All British subjects, including British-protected Jews, were rounded up by the Turks and interned in Iskenderun, Aleppo's port, until a neutral ship could be sent to rescue them. Even those Jews who could speak no English were unable to escape the consequence of their previous abdication from Ottoman life and were exiled together with their English compatriots.

CHAPTER 19

WESTERNISATION

The first step towards long-overdue reform of the Empire came in 1826 when Sultan Mahmūd II assembled his corps of Janissaries in the Maidan Square of Istanbul and massacred them to the last man, so removing a main obstacle to his Westernising reforms. The Janissaries, once composed of Christian converts and their descendants, had usurped much of the political power of the sultans during the long years of decline and had contributed to the chaos and misrule of the previous years, including repeated pillaging of Jewish communities. Paradoxically the destruction of the Janissaries was accompanied by the downfall of the last of the influential Jewish families of the capital who were closely allied to them. This was caused by the intrigues of Armenian Christian rivals for power rather than by anti-Jewish feeling as such; but it did seal the end of Jewish economic power in the capital.

The sultan's programme of fundamental reform which followed took the best part of a century to complete because of sustained opposition from the peoples of the Empire. In 1856 the sultan issued a firmān abolishing restrictions on non-Muslims and declaring all subjects of the sultan equal under the law: no more dhimmīs, no more poll tax, no more discriminatory regulations. One result was that the former dhimmīs, now equal citizens, were liable for conscription to military service; but as both Christians and Jews regarded that with horror, and as the Muslims did not want Christians and Jews in their army, a military substitution tax was imposed instead. Though this was in fact similar to the former poll tax, it had few of its humiliating overtones.

The system of internal autonomy for dhimmī communities (called millets) was reformed but not abolished altogether to avoid the impression of attacking the minority religions; and in response to European pressure, new millets were created for the Roman Catholic, the Bulgarian Orthodox and the Serbian Orthodox communities. At the same time secular institutions of law, justice and education were established alongside the existing religious ones, with the clear aim of eventually superseding them.

The sultan's reforms were strenuously resisted. Traditional Muslims viewed them with horror, Christians feared the diminution of their privileges and most Jews were too conservative to contemplate change of any kind. In 1835 the sultan reorganised the internal government of the Jewish community by appointing its first Haḥambashi (Chief Rabbi) as a government official in charge of all religious and administrative affairs of the Jews of the Empire. A series of regulations followed, fully defining the duties and powers of the Haḥambashi to regulate his community.

In Istanbul and elsewhere in the Empire the Jews resisted all modernising measures with implacable ferocity, whether in the state as a whole or in their own community. The reaction was led by the rabbis: most of them interpreted all change as a direct threat to Jewish survival and refused to have any part of it. In particular, the rabbis strenuously resisted all attempts to end their monopoly of control over justice and education; and they used their power of excommunication ruthlessly against anyone who dared send a child to a secular school – even to the few Jewish schools daringly opened by wealthy philanthropists. They equally opposed the sultan's attempt, through the Haḥambashi, to introduce councils of lay notables to assist in the running of the community. The military medical school, provided by the sultan with a kasher kitchen and facilities to enable Jewish students to fulfil their religious duties under rabbinic supervision, was shunned by order of the rabbis; and as a direct consequence Jews who had once led the way in Turkish medical practice had to step aside and allow eager Armenian and Greek physicians to take their places. Even the opening of Jewish hospitals, encouraged by the sultan and paid for by wealthy donors, was long delayed for similar reasons.

When the ultra-conservative Jewish mob of the capital rioted over the opening of a secular Jewish school, and then again over a modest proposal by the Haḥambashi to introduce a lay element into the government of the millet, the sultan himself intervened. In 1865 he presented the Jews with a new constitution, similar to the one worked out themselves by the Armenian millet. This limited the previously exclusive domination of the rabbis and provided a role for the laity in the government of the community; but that too proved a failure for the rule of the rabbis was unshakeable. Only in Egypt did Jews take advantage of the new liberalising measures, with the result that its Jewish population increased from under 4,000 in the middle of the 19th century to 25,000 by its end.

So for much of the 19th century most Jews missed out of the brave new world then unfolding and remained deeply rooted in the past: only the small mercantile élite described earlier allied themselves with the modernisers. Christians however eagerly lapped up the new educational opportunities and all else on offer by the reforming Turkish state: they wore modern clothes, educated themselves in the Western manner and increasingly entered Ottoman society and its administration on something like equal terms.

At first it was only the tightening of central Ottoman control over its provinces that had any real effect on the Jewish condition; for that made it harder for provincial governors to exploit their own Jewish communities for personal gain. The Turks always did their best to protect the Jews; and their failures were due more to weakness or indolence than to positive ill will. A marked improvement, for example, was noticed in the condition of the Jews of Libya after 1835 when the previously autonomous local regime was replaced by direct Ottoman rule.

However, help was on its way from an unexpected source, from Europe and in particular from the Jews of France. Founded in Paris in 1860, the Alliance Israélite Universelle created a network of European-type Jewish schools throughout North Africa and the Middle East. It was those schools that enabled Jews to acquire the rudiments of secular education for the first time, as well as some knowledge of French and English. Once again they were able to start competing with their Christian rivals; and for the first time in centuries they began to look to the West, not just with nostalgia but as the key to survival and worldly success.

Not only did the Alliance schools help to bring the long isolated Sephardim of the Middle East back within sight of the mainstream of European life, but its European-trained teachers and inspectors ensured that Jews could no longer be oppressed in secret by local Turkish governors. From the date of the Alliance's foundation, the full glare of international publicity was brought to bear on all cases of wrongdoing, with beneficial effect.

The history of the Alliance Israélite Universelle, how the leaders of French Jewry undertook the romantic mission of undertaking the "regeneration" of their less fortunate brethren in North Africa and the Middle East, is one of the most fascinating stories of recent Jewish history.

Though the Jews of France were the first in Europe to be fully emancipated, their feelings of insecurity had not much diminished by the middle of the nineteenth century. Modern racial anti-semitism, as opposed to the medieval religious variety, was born and nurtured in post-revolution France as well as in Germany: its rise caused French Jews to interpret every attack on their fellows abroad as an attack on themselves, a threat to their position in French society. Incidents such as the Damascus Affair in which Jews were accused of murdering a Capuchin friar for ritual purposes, and the Mortara affair in which a Jewish child was kidnapped and brought up as a Christian under the Pope's personal protection, were all reported by the French press with menacing overtones, thus increasing their existing unease.

To the semi-assimilated French Jews of the period those of the Near East were a poor benighted lot, backward, obscurantist and in dire need of "civilising" influences from the West. That help, in the form of an extensive network of French schools to replace the traditional Talmud Torah system, was eagerly grasped as a lifeline by those Jews of North Africa and the decaying Ottoman Empire able to do so. It was the only sure way of escaping from the trough of helpless poverty into which they had descended.

The founders of the Alliance expressed an ardent wish to:

... moralise those who have been corrupted and not condemn them, enlighten those who have been blinded and not abandon them, raise those who have been exhausted and not rest with pitying them ... (19.1)

In other words, the Alliance sought to re-make the Jews of North Africa and the Middle East in the idealised self-image of the Westernised French Jews of its day. In time the Alliance created an alternative network of power and influence to that of the traditional communal leaders; and it slowly but surely moved from the margins to the very centre of Jewish life in the Ottoman Empire.

It must be appreciated that only a small proportion of the Jews of the Ottoman Empire was exposed to the European influence of the Alliance schools, and even then many parents could not afford to keep their children in school for more than three or four years of advanced elementary education. A few children proceeded from the Alliance to higher French or other European schools; and it was they who eventually formed the new Jewish middle class.

Despite its splendid work, the Alliance was bitterly opposed in conservative religious quarters and accused of alienating its pupils from their traditional Jewish roots. In its enthusiasm for all things French and European, for the new world ahead, it was said to have failed to foster appreciation of the old, diminished respect for religion and opened a gulf between secularly educated children and their more pious parents.

It is true that the Alliance schools with their vocational training, their education of girls and women and their initial hostility to Zionism, were very different from the traditional religious schools of the poverty-stricken Jewish areas of North Africa and the Middle East: also that there was often antagonism between the staff of the Alliance and traditional rabbis in the areas in which it operated. But the Alliance always intended its schools to foster Judaism, which it regarded as a "moral religion" and as

... the source of joy and energy which has enabled Jews to live through centuries of persecution and oppression without equal in history. (19.2)

As well as secular subjects, the study of Judaism and Jewish history constituted an important part of the Alliance's curriculum, both at local level and at its teacher-training college in Paris; but many Western-trained Alliance teachers despised what they regarded as the superstitious religion of the traditionalists. Though secular Jewish history was taught by French-trained teachers in the schools, religious instruction and Hebrew were relegated to the care of "backward" local rabbis and thus were marginalised and rendered less attractive to ambitious pupils.

A very elderly Paris-trained ex-Alliance teacher recently expressed his views on the mass of Middle Eastern Jews, those taught only in a traditional Talmud Torah. Though poor and ignorant, with no secular education or knowledge of European languages, he saw them as people of genuine piety untinged with fanaticism, modest and with a high standard of morality. It must be said that few echoes of that respectful recognition of values other than those of semi-assimilated Westernised Jews emerge from surviving Alliance records. The accusation that the Alliance's work led directly to a loosening of religious ties and the rapid assimilation of many of its graduates remains the sole question mark on its splendid record of achievement.

It was thus through secular European-style education and increasing contact with merchants from Europe, for whom Jews often acted as agents, that Sephardim of the Ottoman Empire began to trade and travel to the West. A few of the leading families, but by no means all, were helped by acquiring European nationality. The more energetic started moving to countries such as British India and cosmopolitan Egypt, where European influence was strong. Others migrated directly to

Western Europe and to North, Central and South America, where they were eventually joined by the remainder of their brethren fleeing from the rising tide of Arab and Islamic nationalism.

Part 4

Dissolution

CHAPTER 20

COLONIAL PERIOD AND INDEPENDENCE

Despite increasingly desperate attempts at reform, including the "Young Turk" revolution of 1908 which overthrew the autocratic Sultan Abdul Hamīd II, the Ottoman Empire was unable to contain the rising discontent of its Christian subjects backed by the great powers of Europe. Most of its European territory was lost when the peoples of Serbia, Greece and Montenegro gained their independence in the bitterly fought Balkan wars of 1912-13.

Though many Jews had supported the reform movement of the "Young Turks", one aspect of their policy of equal citizenship proved a mixed blessing: the abolition of restrictions on the religious minorities was accompanied by the abolition of their special privileges. For the first time ever, all citizens including Jews became liable for conscription to the Ottoman army. Rather than accept this, many thousands of young men emigrated, mostly to the United States of America: the final emptying of the reservoir of Sephardi Jewry in the Balkans and Anatolia had started.

The First World War of 1914-18, in which the Ottomans were on the losing side, completed the process of dismemberment: the Empire was divided up between the victorious allies, Istanbul was occupied by British, French and Italian forces, and a Greek army overran most of Anatolia. Kemal Atatürk, a new and radical Turkish leader, then managed to drive the Greeks from Anatolia and persuade the allied forces to withdraw from Istanbul. In 1923 Atatürk proclaimed the new Turkish Republic, restricted in area to the old heartland of Anatolia and a tiny European spur; and in a complete break with the past, he declared Turkey a secular state organised on European lines.

The mass emigration of Jews from the territories of the old Ottoman Empire, which had continued during the Balkan wars, accelerated as a result of the disturbances caused by the First World War and subsequent events. Few of the Sephardim who then remained in the Balkans managed to survive the Second World War of 1939-45.

The fate of the largely Jewish city of Salonika, which fell to Greece in 1912, is a good illustration of those changes. Though King George of the Hellenes had promised equal rights for all minorities, Salonika was soon transformed from a thriving cosmopolitan trading centre into a provincial Greek town. Some 70,000 Jews, displaced from their homes in the city centre by the great fire of 1918, were prevented from returning. The declaration of Sunday as a compulsory day of rest sealed Salonika's new status as a Greek Christian city for it abolished the centuries-old tradition in which all work ceased on the Jewish Sabbath. As anti-semitic incidents proliferated, Jews began leaving for Palestine, France, Italy, England and the United States. Salonika's Jewish population dwindled even further after a nasty pogrom in 1933. The Germans conquered the town in 1942 and deported its remaining Jews to the extermination camps of northern Europe where, with very few exceptions, they perished.

All traces of former Jewish autonomy in Turkey ended in 1923 with the establishment of Ataturk's secular republic. Jews became ordinary citizens of the state, subject to its laws without exception. They could no longer control their own marriages and divorces, nor impose taxes to maintain their synagogues and charitable institutions. Jewish schools were secularised, with the teaching of religion in them strictly forbidden; and Turkish replaced French as the language of instruction.

Turkey steadfastly refused German demands to surrender its Jews for deportation during the dark days of the Second World War of 1939-45. Sadly though, its traditional policy of sheltering Jewish refugees was shattered in 1941 when the ship Struma carrying 769 Jewish fugitives from the Balkans anchored in the Golden Horn. Yielding to pressure from the British Colonial Office, which wished to prevent Jewish immigration to Palestine at all costs, none of the Jews was allowed to land. Two months later, Turkish ships towed the Struma out into the Black Sea, where it blew up with the loss of all lives on board.

The imposition of a harsh capital levy on Armenian, Jewish and Greek businesses in 1942, bore very heavily on Jews who were predominantly urban traders. Faced with a charge of 184% on their capital, most Jewish businesses were totally ruined and the community shrank even further. The situation eased in 1949 when the remaining Jewish community of at least fifty thousand was again allowed a measure of autonomy in its internal affairs. By then, Jews were freely attending government schools and universities and were well represented in the professions and even in parliament. However, growing unease at the rise of Muslim revivalism, kept in check only by the power of the army, caused well over half the remaining community to emigrate, mainly to Israel. Some ten to fifteen thousand Jews now live in the Turkish Republic.

One result of the First World War of 1914-18 was the division of most of the Arab provinces of the former Ottoman Empire between the victorious powers, each of which promised to lead its mandated territories to eventual independence. The Jews of the Middle East, who adapted readily to European rule, prospered in the colonial period but did less well as independence approached and they suffered from a popular backlash encouraged by the emerging nationalists. All prospects of peaceful accommodation between Arabs and Jews vanished in 1948 when the sight of the Jews of Palestine gaining their own independence in the teeth of Arab opposition was just too much for Muslim susceptibilities. In country after country, Jews either fled voluntarily or were encouraged to leave, thus ending for ever the ancient Jewish communities of the Middle East, many of which had pre-dated the first coming of the Arabs in the 8th century.

Great Britain took over Palestine after the First World War and divided it into the two separate territories of Palestine and Transjordan. Transjordan, in which Jews were not allowed to settle, eventually gained its independence as the Kingdom of Jordan; but Palestine, promised in the Balfour Declaration of 1917 as a national home for Jews, became a battleground between Jews and Arabs. Britain finally abandoned Palestine in 1948, after which the armies of its neighbouring Arab countries invaded in an unsuccessful attempt to stifle the newly declared state of Israel at birth.

The Kingdom of Iraq, also under British control, flourished during the first part of the inter-war period. Jews, who constituted one-quarter of Baghdad's population, dominated the city's trade. Better educated than their neighbours and speaking some English because of the Alliance schools, they were favoured by King Faisal and his British advisors. The king proclaimed:

Freedom of religion, education and employment for the Jews of Baghdad, who had played such an important part in its welfare and progress.

Jews were appointed to high positions in government; and several served in Parliament and the Senate. It was a good period for Iraq as a whole and for its Jewish community in particular. King Feisal died shortly after Iraq gained its independence in 1932. Significantly, Hitler came to power in Germany that same year, Mein Kampf was translated into Arabic and a German embassy opened in Baghdad. The new government of Iraq lost little time in proceeding against its minorities: Assyrian Christians were massacred and Jews dismissed from official positions. After a military coup in 1936, things went from bad to worse for the Jews, with a multiplication of restrictions and disabilities. A pogrom that followed the suppression of the revolt against the pro-British government in 1941 prompted a large number of Jews to leave the country, most of them fleeing to India and Persia. Once started, the emigration of Iraq's Jews continued steadily with the wealthier ones leaving for Europe and America and the remainder for Israel. Over 107,000 Jews, stripped of all their possessions, were airlifted to Israel in 1952, after which a mere 6,000 Jews remained in the country; and even they had departed by the mid 1980s.

After defeating an Arab bid for independence, French colonial rule between 1920 and 1945 brought much benefit to the Syrian provinces of the old Ottoman Empire, which were divided into Muslim Syria and Christian Lebanon. With the French came law and order as well as liberty, fraternity and equality, allegedly absent from British colonies. The fertile countryside recovered after centuries of neglect; and once again great flocks of sheep and fields of cotton and wheat provided exports, which enriched the Arab farmers and landowners. Trade with the West in which Jews, assisted by French-language education from Alliance schools, took a full part, was the key to prosperity and a comfortable life for a middle class of many hundreds of Jewish families, far removed from their poverty-stricken brethren still living in the old Jewish quarters of Aleppo and Damascus. In the 1930s, graduates of the Alliance schools who had gone on to the French Lycée for further education became the community's first doctors, lawyers and other professionals. The Syrian Jewish community rapidly dissolved after popular disturbances following the decision of the United Nations in 1947 to partition Palestine into Jewish and Arab states; and that of Lebanon also disappeared shortly afterwards.

11 Photograph of the Staff of Alliance School in Tunis
taken in 1886

12 Photograph of King Faisal of Iraq
    with the leaders of the Jewish community of Baghdad
    taken in the 1920's (courtesy Naim Dangoor)

Egypt, declared a British protectorate at the outbreak of the First World War in 1914, was host to a community of some sixty thousand Jews, attracted by the economic opportunities of a booming economy coupled with the framework of law and order provided by the country's British masters. The community included prominent bankers, financiers and businessmen whose names became household words in Egypt and who mingled freely in the highest circles of Egyptian society. The Jews of Egypt maintained their own hospitals, schools and other charitable institutions and were often able to assist and shelter refugees from persecution abroad. The size of the community remained reasonably constant until 1948, after which it rapidly shrivelled away as a result of Egypt's long war with Israel.

Algeria, wrested from the Turks by the French as early as 1830, became an integral part of France; and following the Crémieux Decree of 1870, many of its Jews were granted French citizenship. They too were threatened by Hitler's rise to power in Germany and by sympathetic anti-semitic echoes from elements in the French settler population. After France's defeat by Germany in 1940, its government abrogated the Crémieux decree and disenfranchised Algerian Jewry, causing much misery in the process. The Jews as a whole stood aside from the bitter struggle with France in which independent Algeria was forged. They owed much to France but all the same were reluctant to betray the land and its Muslim inhabitants in whose midst they had lived for so many centuries. However, Algerian nationalists launched several vicious attacks on Jews in 1962; and that was the signal for mass departure shortly before the country finally achieved its independence. In very similar manner, the Jewish communities of Tunisia and Libya also came to an end. Morocco alone, under the benevolent rule of its sultan, still hosts a significant Jewish presence.

And so by 1970, the only remaining and secure Jewish communities in the Muslim world were those of Morocco and Turkey; and even they had been reduced to shadows of their former strengths. The once proud Jewish communities of Islam have ceased to exist and their achievements are remembered only in the pages of history books, now rarely opened by other Jews. Though overlooked by a Christian world obsessed with the plight of Palestinian refugees, it must never be forgotten that the obliteration of the ancient Jewish communities of the Middle East was part of the heavy price exacted by the Arabs for the establishment of the modern state of Israel in their region and for their own attempt at religious and cultural regeneration.

CHAPTER 21

ISLAMIC FUNDAMENTALISM

The descendants of the Arab warriors who poured out of Arabia in the 7th century to overcome the mighty empires of Persia and Byzantium and conquer a vast swathe of territory in the name of Islam can have had few doubts about the purpose of their grand enterprise or of its future. Their belief in God was absolute: so too was their faith that the steady expansion of the boundaries of Islam and the rapid conversion to their faith of so many millions of people from both within and without their territories was the sure sign of God's approval of them and their mission. Islam was God's final and perfect revelation to mankind, superseding the corrupted versions contained in Judaism and Christianity. The course of history, the working of God's purpose in the world, was clear: Islam would spread until the whole world would be ruled by Muslims in the final age of mankind – the time Jews call the Messianic Age, and Christians the Kingdom of God.

All went well for the first five hundred years. Not only did Arab and Muslim arms triumph almost everywhere, but their victories were rewarded with widespread prosperity and the establishment of an advanced new civilisation without parallel at the time. It was only later that things started to go wrong. Christian Europe began to exert pressure on the frontiers of Islam; and within the Muslim world, alien rulers from Central Asia intensified old conflicts, ruined the economy and oppressed the native peoples of the Empire. Muslim self-confidence faltered as the result of these unaccustomed checks to the serene advance of Islam – with resulting turbulence and hardship.

What must have seemed the natural course of history was fully restored with the rise of the Ottoman Turks in the 15th century and the advance of their seeming invincible armies to the gates of Vienna, capital of the Hapsburg Empire and the heart of Christian Europe. The respite was brief though; for the long decline of the Ottoman Empire from the 18th century onwards, accompanied by the inexorable rise in the power of the Christian West, sapped Muslim confidence in the worth of their own society and its values. The collapse of the Islamic world in the modern period, with its total domination by Europe and America, produced an acute internal crisis, the final resolution of which remains uncertain.

Most modern Muslim thinkers accept the fact of their society's deep malaise and look back with nostalgia to their ancient glory. They all agree that fundamental internal reform is needed to stop the rot but differ as to how this may be accomplished.

It is unlikely that those Muslim leaders who seek to modernise their countries and bring them closer to Western models believe fully in the vision of the eventual triumph of Islam. Kemal Atatürk in Turkey and the last Shah of Iran both accepted Western social and political values in preference to those of traditional Islam. They imitated most aspects of Western society and sought to confine Islam to a personal religion, separate from government and public affairs. The Turkish army, heir to the Atatürk revolution, still struggles to preserve his secular state; but in Iran, the last Shah's westernising reforms were totally swept away in a ferocious fundamentalist backlash. The Egyptian and Algerian forms of nationalism have so far managed to keep Islamic fundamentalism at bay, but at high cost; in Egypt, Muslim fundamentalists have been executed regularly since the time of President Nasser, and in Algeria the death toll has been truly horrific.

Ronald Nettler's book "Past Trials and Present tribulations" contains a penetrating analysis of the Muslim Fundamentalist view of the Jews. Traditionalist Muslim thinkers attribute all present failures to God's punishment for neglecting Islam – and where have we heard that argument before? If people will only return to their faith and live in accordance with the holy Shari'a then, as surely as day follows night, world history will again be set on its proper course culminating in universal acceptance of divine rule under Islam. The Christian West, responsible in their eyes for Islam's present humiliation, has only acted as God's agent in this chastisement: the real fault lies with Muslims themselves, and with no one else.

The fundamentalists go even further by totally rejecting the compromises adopted by modern Islam as it has developed, and insisting on a literal return to the attitudes and laws of the earliest Islamic community. Even more important in its effect on others is their belief in the concept of jihad (holy war), which they interpret as a permanent state of active warfare between Islam and its enemies; and they really do mean it, as the West and Israel have learnt to their cost. In addition, the traditional glorification of those who sacrifice their lives as martyrs in the cause of Islam has made jihad a highly potent weapon in the struggle. For fundamentalists, jihad extends also to their own secular national rulers and to all fellow Muslims who betray Islam by refusing to live under its ancient laws.

Jews have become a prime target in this harsh and uncompromising fundamentalist ideology. Gone are the days of casual contempt and easy tolerance. A far harder approach has been substituted, in which all the negative attitudes to Jews in traditional Islamic sources are emphasised at the expense of the more pragmatic and accepting practical approach of Muslims throughout the ages.

The reasons for this dramatic change are not hard to find. Jews were always closely allied to the Muslim rulers and never endeared themselves to the masses; fundamentalism arose from within the masses of the people, especially those suffering from extreme poverty and repression. In the old Islamic world, Jews presented no threat and were hardly worth hating. It was only when they occasionally forgot their assigned status in Muslim society and rose to prominent positions of wealth and power that they provoked hostile reaction. However the feeling that Jews must never be allowed to get out of line has always run deep within the Islamic religious establishment: a good example of the flaring of latent resentment is contained in a report by Ibn Baṭṭūṭa, a Moroccan traveller of the 14th century:

While we were sitting with the Sultan a sheikh entered ... The Sultan greeted him; and the qadi (Islamic judge) and the faqīh (Muslim theologian) rose in his honour. The sheikh sat in front of the Sultan and above the Qur'ān readers.

When I asked the faqīh who the sheikh was, he laughed but made no reply. So I repeated the question and was told "He is a Jewish doctor whom we all need: that is why we honoured him as you saw".

What had happened made me furious and I said to the Jew "Oh you accursed and son of an accursed! How dare you sit above the Qur'ān readers when you are a Jew? I continued to vilify him, raising my voice. The Sultan was astonished and asked the meaning of my words. The faqīh explained them to him; and the Jew became angry and left in a foul mood.

When we had dispersed, the faqīh said to me "Bravo and may Allah bless you ... You certainly taught him who he is". (21.1)

The Europeans, who so humiliated the Islamic world in the 19th and 20th centuries, introduced their own novel idea of the equality of all men and totally rejected the concept of dhimmīs as subordinate subjects, however well protected they may have been. Muslim rulers, from the reforming Ottoman sultans of the 19th century onwards, co-operated with the Europeans and adopted many of their attitudes. Thus Jews gradually lost their status as dhimmīs and emerged from the obscurity into which they had descended during the long decline of the Ottoman Empire into the full light of day as people equal to others in their legitimate aspirations. They were eager to join the new world opened under European influence and many of them prospered, some few exceedingly, under European tutelage.

Traditional Muslims, horrified to see the frustration of God's grand design as their world plunged into crisis, were outraged to see the Jews, in league with Europeans, emerge from their proper place in society. Jews thus became a symbol of Muslim humiliation; and the establishment of Israel, in which Jews ruled over Muslims on their own sacred territory, was the last straw. In this context, some Jewish fundamentalist attitudes and actions inevitably inflamed, and continue to inflame, Muslim resentment.

Casual contempt for Jews was transformed by fundamentalists into a virulent hatred that was uniquely modern. That in turn spawned an anti-semitic literature in which Jews were demonised to an extent only previously seen in Christendom. The Muslims learned well from Christian anti-semites, and from Nazis in particular: they equalled if not surpassed them in their writings. However, despite everything, one must always remember Salo Baron's comment that there was never an Auschwitz under Islam – or anything like it.

It was only too easy to justify this new attitude by reference to Islāmic history as portrayed in the Qur'ān and the Hadīth (Traditions) – but suppressing all the more tolerant passages. The Jews are one of the Peoples of the Book, the recipients of an earlier revelation from God; but they killed God's prophets and falsified his words. The Jews of Medina rejected the hand of friendship extended to them by Muḥammad and conspired with his enemies against the early community of Islam, insidiously undermining its message by sowing doubt amongst its supporters: their actions compelled the Prophet to suppress them. From this it is not so large a step to the sentiments expressed in the following quotation from the writings of Sayyid Qutb, one of the fathers of Islamic fundamentalism:

The Jews have confronted Islam with enmity from the moment the Islamic state was established in Medina ... the Muslim community continues to suffer the same Jewish machinations and double-dealing which discomfited the early

Muslims ... This is a war which has not been extinguished ... for close on fourteen centuries its blaze has raged in all the corners of the earth and continues to this moment ... (21.2)

Much influenced by one of the late King Faisal of Saudi Arabia's favourite texts, the 19th century forgery The Protocols of the Elders of Zion, Qutb went on to blame the Jews for the internal degeneration of the Muslim world:

Just as, in the past, it was the Jews who had disrupted the early Islamic community ... it was the Jews who had more recently undermined Islam by installing a generation of fifth-columnists in its midst, posing as true Muslims but in reality betraying the Muslim cause ... The Jews have installed ... a massive army of agents in the form of professors, philosophers, doctors, researchers ... some even from the ranks of the Muslim religious authorities ... intending to break the creed of the Muslims by weakening the Sharī'a in many ways ... with this and that they fulfil the ancient role of the Jews... (21.2)

In this fearful scenario it will not be long before Yassir Arafat himself is referred to as a Jewish agent. Sayyid Qutb was sentenced to death and executed by President Nasser's government in Egypt in 1966; but that did not stop the spread of his ideas. It is a sobering thought to consider the motivation of the scores of young men in the Middle East today who queue up for the privilege of turning themselves into human bombs, with the sole aim of killing as many Jews as possible – any Jews, whether soldier or civilian, man, woman or child.

The emergence of fundamentalism is the prime symptom of the present malaise in the Islamic world; and it is perhaps understandable that a small minority of Muslims seek to return to a mythical golden age when confronted with the huge problem of corruption in their own society with its immense disparity between rich and poor – but hardly realistic for a mass following comprising so large a part of the human family. Looking at the list of significant dates at the back of this volume, it is hard to detect an actual turning point in the relative fortunes of East and West. In the 1550s architects were hard at work designing two of the world's finest buildings; and how Sinan's Sülemaniyé mosque complex in Istanbul compares with Michelangelo's work at St Peter's in Rome can long be debated. But from the mid 17th century onwards, the Christian West rapidly overtook the Islamic East in the world of ideas as well as in natural sciences, technology and the quest for economic prosperity.

Can Islamic fundamentalists really hope to turn their backs on the world represented by Jefferson and modern democracy, by Freud and Einstein, and find a viable alternative in the doubtful myth of spiritual certainty in the distant past? Islam really will have to find a way to renew itself in a more moderate and accommodating manner, recognising and building on the advances made by humanity since the days of the Prophet. The hope is that fundamentalism will be left behind one day, just as a dangerous fever eventually subsides and quits the human body. Whether this will happen, and when, is difficult to predict and fortunately well beyond the scope of this book.

So far as Islam and the Jews are concerned, their old relationship disappeared for ever with the extinction of the ancient Jewish communities of the Muslim world. In future, Muslims will have to accept that the idea of the Dhimma and the mind-set it represents – when a Jew must humbly take his place behind a Muslim and when petty obstruction is accepted as a part of the natural order – is dead beyond recall: what might have been a tolerably fair attitude to Jews in the 10th century is monstrously inappropriate in the 20th and best forgotten. For their part, Jews would do well to study their own history with rather more care than they have done so far, and give due credit to Muslims for the many good things they shared in their past lives together.

Hatred of the 'other' is a common factor in the attitudes of most religious fundamentalists, be they Muslims or Jews, and is not the prerogative of Muslims alone. We should not forget that there are extremists on both sides of the Jewish/Muslim divide whose actions display total disregard for the human rights of others.

It is a pity that the necessity of recording the ordered sequence of historical events should have resulted in this book ending with the ugliness of fundamentalist anti-Jewish outpourings rather than with a description of one of the more fruitful episodes in the centuries-long relationship between Muslims and Jews. An honest attempt has been made in these pages to portray all aspects of that relationship, the bad times as well as the good times; and it is for the reader to decide whether, on the whole, Jews fared well or badly under the rule of Islam.

MAIN SOURCES AND GUIDE TO FURTHER READING

This book is intended as a primer, a first introduction to the subject. Information on its sources, including a guide for further reading, is given below.

Introduction:

Civilisation on Trial by Arnold Toynbee contains stimulating chapters on the shift in historical perspective between the East and the West.

Chapters 1 & 2:

Salo Baron's monumental *A Social and Religious History of the Jews*, volume 3, includes chapters on the World before Islam, on Muḥammad and the Khalifate, and on A Protected Minority. John Glubb's *The Life and Times of Muḥammad* is an excellent, non-scholarly account of Arabia and its Prophet, highly sensitive to the nuances of the Bedouin life-style. Karen Armstrong's *Muḥammad* is a Western attempt to understand the origins of Islam.

Chapters 4 & 5:

Bernard Lewis's *The Jews of Islam* is both an authoritative and a very readable account of Islam's relationship with its Jews. This is required reading for anyone approaching the subject for the first time.

Chapter 6:

In *Zahor*, Yosef Yerushalmi expounds his fascinating theory on traditional Jewish indifference to the recording of secular history.

Chapters 7 & 13:

For the history of the Arabs and of the Middle East in general, refer to Philip Hitti's classic *History of the Arabs* and to the much more recent *The Middle East* by Bernard Lewis. Both books are outstanding in their different ways.

Chapters 8 & 9:

The History of the Jewish People, ed. Ben Sasson, includes an interesting chapter on the history of the Babylonian exile prior to the coming of Islam.
Based on his research into original documents, Walter Fischel's *Jews in the Economic and Political Life of Islam* deals in fascinating detail with Jews in Abbasid Baghdad, Fatimid Egypt and the Mongol empire.
S. Fawzi has contributed a useful essay on the Jewish Academy in Abbasid Baghdad, to *Studies in Muslim-Jewish Relations*, volume 1, edited by Ronald Nettler. Mark Cohen's *Jewish Self-Government in Medieval Egypt* is also of much interest.

Chapter 10:

S D Goitein's monumental *A Mediterranean Society* must remain the standard work of information on Jewish life of the time, based on the revelations of the Cairo Geniza. Volume 1 was used extensively in this chapter.

Chapter 11:

Eliahu Ashtor's *The Jews of Muslim Spain*, despite the rather irritating style of its English translation from the Hebrew, is the most comprehensive study of the Jews of al-Andalus.

Chapters 14-16 & 19:

Stanford Shaw's *The Jews of the Ottoman Empire and the Turkish Republic*, though very pro-Turkish in approach, deals in useful detail with most aspects of Jewish life in the Ottoman Empire and the Turkish Republic.
Constantinople – City of the World's Desire 1453 – 1924 by Philip Mansel contains a fascinating picture of Ottoman and Turkish life.

French Jews, Turkish Jews by Aron Rodrigue is a valuable study of the work of the Alliance Israélite.

Chapter 17:

The work of Gershon Scholem, and in particular his *Sabbetai Sevi* and *Major Trends in Jewish Mysticism*, is essential reading for an understanding of the impact of Kabbalah on the Jewish world.

Chapter 18:

The Middle East on the Eve of Modernity by Abraham Marcus is the principal in-depth study of 18th century Aleppo relied on in the text.

Dr. Alexander Russell's *The Natural History of Aleppo* is a rare book, available only in specialist collections such as the British Library.

The correspondence of the British consuls in Aleppo is preserved at the Public Records Office, Kew.

The Jews of Calcutta by Flower Elias and Judith Elias Cooper contains a charming account of Jewish life in Aleppo and India based on contemporary documents, including the journals of Shalom Cohen and Moshe Dwek.

Chapter 21:

Ronald Nettler's *Past Trials and Present Tribulations* contains a spine-chilling critique of Sayyid Qutb's essay *Our Struggle with the Jews*.

In General:

The valuable collection of translations of original documents contained in Norman Stillman's *The Jews of Arab Lands* has been used extensively throughout the book. This documentary history is very well worth reading in its entirety. Also of interest is Mark Cohen's *Under Crescent and Cross: The Jews in the Middle Ages*, the most recent scholarly work on the subject

LIST OF QUOTATIONS

The sources of most of the quotations used are included here, together with reference to more easily obtained books in which the entire texts may be found. Translations have been adapted freely for clarity of meaning rather than for complete accuracy.

Chapter 3

1 Early 8th century source quoted in Akhbār Majmū'a. From *The Jews of Arab Lands* by Norman Stillman p.156

Chapter 5

1 Al-Turtushi, quoting 7th century 'Abd al-Rahman ibn Ghanam. From *The Jews of Arab Lands* by Norman Stillman p.157

2 Late 8th century. Abū Yūsuf (Quadī of Khalīf Harun al-Rashīd) Kitab al-Kharaj. From *The Jews of Islam* by Bernard Lewis p.31

3 Yahya al-Antakī. From *The Jews of Islam* by Bernard Lewis p. 42

4 Mahmūd ibn 'Umar al-Zamakhsharī (1075-1144). From *The Jews of Islam* by Bernard Lewis p.14

5 Late 8th century. Abū Yūsuf (Quadī of Harun al Rashīd), Kitab al-Kharaj. From *The Jews of Arab Lands* by Norman Stillman p.159.

6 Al-Qalqashandi. A Fattal, Le Statut, p.242

Chapter 8

1 The Revelations of Simon ben Yohai. See *A History of Messianic Speculation in Israel* by A H Silver, p.43

2 Al-Muqaddasi, late 9th century. From *Jews in the Economic and Political Life of Mediaeval Islam* by Walter Fischel, p.7

Chapter 9

1 N M Adler, edit. *The Itinery of Benjamin of Tudela*, p.38. Also in *The Jews*

of *Arab Lands* by Norman Stillman, p.252
2 From S.Fawzi, *The Jewish Academy in Abbasid Baghdad* (Studies in Muslim-Jewish Relations, vol.1), p.198
3 ditto, p.193
4 Sa'id al-Andalusi, Tabaqat al-Umam. From *The Jews of Arab Lands* by Norman Stillman, p.210
5 Translated by David Goldstein in *The Jewish Poets of Muslim Spain*, p.80
6 From *A Social and Religious History of the Jews* by Salo Baron, vol.3, p.153
7 Ibn Muyassar, p.2. Quoted from Persian Literature under Tartar Dominion, E G Browne. Also in *Jews in the Economic and Political Life of Mediaeval Islam* by Walter Fischel, p.89
8 Source quoted in *Jews in the Economic and Political Life of Mediaeval Islam* by Walter Fischel, p.21
9 The Arab historian Suyuti. Quoted in *A Social and Religious History of the Jews* by Salo Baron, vol.3, p.153
10 Cairo Geniza fragment (Oxford collection), translated by L. Ginsberg
11 Source quoted in *Jews in the Economic and Political Life of Mediaeval Islam by Walter Fischel*, p. 23
12 ditto, p.24
13 ditto, p.28

Chapter 10

1 Ibn Jubair, a contemporary Spanish Muslim traveller. Quoted in *A Mediterranean Society* by S D Goitein, vol.1, p.70
2 Geniza letter quoted in *A Mediterranean Society* by S D Goitein, p.92

Chapter 11

1 Early 8th century source quoted in Akhbar Majmu'a. From *The Jews of Arab Lands* by Norman Stillman p.156
2 Sa'id al-Andalusi, Tabaqat al-Umam. From *The Jews of Arab Lands* by Norman Stillman, p.210
3 Contemporary poet. See Luzzatto p.66.

From *The Jews of Muslim Spain*, Eliyahu Ashtor, vol.1, p.229

Chapter 12

1 From the Megilla of Samuel b. Hosha'ana, ed. Jacob Mann p.433. Quoted in *The Jews of Arab Lands* by Norman Stillman, p.202
2 Geniza letter translated by S D Goitein and included in *Letters of Medieval Jewish Traders*. Quoted in *The Jews of Arab Lands* by Norman Stillman, p.250
3 Quoted in *A Social and Religious History of the Jews* by Salo Baron, vol.3, p.125
4 ditto, p.157
5 Abu Isḥaq of Elvira, translated by Bernard Lewis in his *Islam in History*, p 159. Quoted in *The Jews of Arab Lands* by Norman Stillman, p.214

Chapter 13

1 Chronicon Syriacum, Bar Hebraeus. Source quoted in *Jews in the Economic and Political Life of Mediaeval Islam* by Walter Fischel, p.91
2 Wassaf. Source quoted in *Jews in the Economic and Political Life of Mediaeval Islam* by Walter Fischel, p.108
3 Bar Hebraeus. Source quoted in *Jews in the Economic and Political Life of Mediaeval Islam* by Walter Fischel, p.109
4 ditto, p.117

Chapter 14

1 Zinberg, p.5. Quoted in *The Jews of the Ottoman Empire and the Turkish Republic*, Stanford Shaw, p.32
2 M Lattes, Likkutim de-Vei Eliahu. Quoted in *The Jews of the Ottoman Empire and the Turkish Republic*, Stanford Shaw, p.30
3 Seder Eliahu Zuta, Eliahu Capsali. Quoted in *The Jews of the Ottoman Empire and the Turkish Republic*, Stanford Shaw, p.30
4 ditto, p.33

5 Franco. Quoted in *The Jews of the Ottoman Empire and the Turkish Republic*, Stanford Shaw, p.33

Chapter 15

1 Fr. Jean-Baptiste de Saint-Aignan. Quoted in *The Jews of Islam*, Bernard Lewis, p.140
2 Ailot dam be-Turkiya, Uriel Heyd. Quoted in *The Jews of Islam*, Bernard Lewis, p.43

Chapter 17

1 Coenen, p.86. Quoted in *Sabbatai Sevi*, Gershon Scholem, p.686

Chapter 18

1 Quoted in *The Middle East on the Eve of Modernity*, Abraham Marcus, p.37
2 Victoria Shammah. Quoted in *The Sephardim*, Lucien Gubbay and Abraham Levy, p. 84
3 From *Aleppo in Devonshire Square*
4 *The Natural History of Aleppo*, Alexander Russell. Parts also quoted in *The Jews of Arab Lands* by Norman Stillman, p.318
5 Victoria Shammah. Quoted in *The Sephardim*, Lucien Gubbay and Abraham Levy, p.84
6 From the journals of the two men, and associated traditions, as translated in *The Jews of Calcutta*, Flower Elias and Judith Elias Cooper (privately published by the Jewish Association of Calcutta)
7 Public Records Office, Kew.

Chapter 19

1 Manifesto 1860 by the six founders of the Alliance. Quoted in *French Jews, Turkish Jews*, Aron Rodrigue, p.22
2 From *Instructions*, Alliance Israélite Universelle. Quoted in *French Jews, Turkish Jews*, Aron Rodrigue, p.80

Chapter 21

1 Quoted in *Past Trials and Present Tribulations*, Ronald Nettler, p.9
2 From *Our Struggle with the Jews*, Sayyid Qutb. Quoted in *Past Trials and Present Tribulations*, Ronald Nettler

LIST OF ILLUSTRATIONS

1 Tīmūr's tomb in Samarkand
2 Mehmet the Conqueror
3 The 'tugra of Suleiman the Magnificent
4 Moses Hamon
5 Shabbetai Zvi
6 The Sultan in procession
7 A European trader of 1593
8 The Ottoman Governer, Quadi and Agha of Aleppo
9 A typical Khan
10 Moshe Dwek
11 Staff of Alliance school in Tunis, 1886
12 King Faisal of Iraq with the leaders of the Jewish community

Front cover: The Alhambra, Granada.
Back cover: The Damascus Keter and Carpet Page detail from a 13th century Spanish Bible (Courtesy of the Jewish National and University Library, Jerusalem)

LIST OF MAPS

1 Arabia and the two great empires in the 5th century
2 Trade routes through Arabia
3 Boundary of the Islamic world in 900
4 Sway of the Geonim in the world of Islam
5 Routes of Jewish traders from Baghdad in the 9th century
6 The Seljūk empire at its peak
7 Invaders from the east: the Mongol empire
8 The Ottoman empire at its peak
9 The expulsions of 1492-1502
10 The flight of the Marranos
11 Principal trade routes of the Middle East in the 18th century
12 Travels of Shalom Cohen

SIGNIFICANT DATES

30	Crucifixion of Jesus of Nazareth		
70		Destruction of Temple in Jerusalem	
219		Rav returns to Babylon from the Holy Land and founds Academy of Sūra	
325	Council of Nicea. Jesus declared God		
476	Collapse of Western Roman Empire		
500		Completion of Babylonian Talmud	
618		Persians conquer Jerusalem	
632			Death of Muḥammad
661			Ummayad Khalifate of Damascus founded
694		Judaism banned in Visigothic Spain	
711			Arab conquest of Spain
732	Charles Martel defeats Arabs at Poitiers		
750			Abbāsid Khalifate of Baghdad founded
751			First paper mill in Samarkand
800	Charlemagne crowned Holy Roman Emperor		
850 (circa)		Amram Gaon composes first prayer book and sends it to Barcelona	
909			First Fatimid Khalīf in N. Africa

929			Ummayad Khalifate of Córdoba established
942		Death of Sa'adia Gaon of Sūra	
969			Fatimids conquer Egypt
970		Death of Ḥisdai ibn Shaprūt, Nasī of the Jews of al-Andalus	
991		Death of Ya'cūb ibn Killis, Vizier of Fatimid Egypt	
1030-56		Samuel served as Vizier of Berber Kingdom of Granada	
1040		Birth of Rashi	
1055			Tugrul as Grand Sultan in Baghdad
1066	Normans conquer Britain	Murder of Joseph ha-Nasī, Vizier of Granada	
1071			Turks defeat Byzantines at Manzikert
1095	Pope Urban II launches Ist Crusade		
1099	Jerusalem captured by Crusaders		
1146		Almohads conquer Muslim Spain. Judaism banned	
1187			Saladin takes Jerusalem from Crusaders
1204		Death of Maimonides	
1206			Temujin assumes title of Chinghiz Khan
1215	Magna Carta. King John shares power		

1242	Mongol armies reach gates of Vienna		
1250			Mamlūks take over Egypt
1258			Hūlagū sacks Baghdad. End of Abbasid Khalifate
1279			Mongols complete conquest of China
1290		Jews expelled from England	
1291		Murder of Sa'd ad-Daula, Vizier of Mongol Iran	
1295-1304			Mongol Il-Khan converts to Islam
1347	Outbreak of Black Death in Europe		
1380			Tīmūr starts his wars of conquest
1391		First pogroms in Christian Spain	
1396			Bayazīd I, Sultan of Rūm
1450	Invention of printing. Use of paper widespread in Europe		
1452	End of Byzantine Empire	Turks invite Jews to settle in Istanbul	Constantinople falls to the Turks
1492	Columbus sails for America	Expulsion of Jews from Christian Spain	
1498	Vasco da Gama's ships reach India		
1517	Martin Luther launches the Reformation		
1527			Babur conquers Hindustan for Islam

1529	First Turkish seige of Vienna. Europe under threat		Turkish armies reach gates of Vienna
1535			First Capitulations Agreement
1550			Sinan starts work on Sülemaniyé mosque in Istanbul
1558	Michaelangelo designs dome of St. Peter's in Rome		
1561		Duke of Naxos founds Jewish colony in Tiberias	
1565		Publication of Shulḥan Arûch	
1566			Death of Suleiman the Magnificent
1633	Galileo tried and condemned in Rome		
1649	Execution of King Charles I of England		
1664	Outbreak of plague, followed by Great Fire of London		
1665		Shabbetai Zvi proclaimed Messiah	
1683	Turkish threat to Europe finally repelled		Turkish armies decisively defeated outside Vienna
1686	Newton's Principia Mathematica		
1776	American War of Independence		
1798			Napoleon invades Egypt
1789	French Revolution		
1791		Jews of France emancipated	

1805			Muḥammad 'Alı, Khedive of Egypt
1807	Slavery abolished in England		
1818	Consolidation of British rule in India		
1826			Mahmūd II massacres his Janissaries
1839	First Opium War between England and China		
1848	Marx and Engels publish the Communist Manifesto		
1856		Foundation of Alliance Israélite Universelle	Dhimma abolished in the Ottoman Empire
1869	Opening of the Suez Canal		
1870		Crémieux Decree emancipates Jews of Algeria	
1871		Completion of Jewish emancipation in England	
1883			French protectorate of Tunisia
1896		Cairo Geniza discovered	
1899	Freud publishes his Interpretation of Dreams		
1905	Einstein publishes his Theory of Relativity		
1908			Young Turks depose Ottoman Sultan
1912-13		Salonika falls to Greece	Balkan Wars
1914			British protectorate of Egypt
1914-18	First World War		End of Ottoman Empire
1917		Balfour Declaration promises national home for Jews in Palestine	

1922			Egypt independent
1923			Atatürk proclaims Turkish republic
1932			Iraq independent
1939-45	Second World War	The Holocaust	
1943			Syria independent
1945	First atomic bomb on Hiroshima		
1946			Jordan independent
1948		Declaration of State of Israel	
1952			Libya independent
1962			Algeria independent

INDEX

Abba Arikha 54
Abbas, Abbasids 44, 52, 58, 65, 67, 75, 76
Abbas I, Shah of Iran 127
Abd al Rahman I 76
Abd al Rahman III 77
Abraham 18, 26
Aden 10, 84
Adrianople 99, 125
Afghanistan 19
Agriculture 12, 24, 46, 47, 48, 49, 70
Aharon ibn Amram 60-64
Ahwaz 61, 63
Aleppo 2, 130-137
Algebra 45
Algeria 153, 155
Ali ibn Isa 61-63
Ali, Khalif 20, 24, 29
Alliance Israélite 145-147, 151
Al-Llah 10
Almohads 65, 80, 84
Alp Aslan 92
America 114, 148, 152, 154
Amram Gaon 76
Amritsar 137
Anatolia 92, 96, 105, 115
Ancona 111
Anti-semitism 69, 117, 118, 145, 150, 157
Antwerp 101
Apostasy 36, 48
Arabia 9-13, 46
Arabic language 1, 24, 43
Arabs, the 4, 21, 40, 43, 46, 74
Aramaic 24
Arghūn, Il-Khan 93-94
Arian Christianity 9, 73
Armenians 50, 117, 143, 144
Ashi, Rav 54
Ashkenazi, Solomon 111
Ashkenazim, Ashkenazi tradition 4-6, 55, 69, 72, 99, 109, 110
Ashraf 132

Ashtor, Eliahu 76
Asia – see: Central Asia
Assyrian Christians 152
Astronomy 45
Atatürk, Kemal 149, 155
Austria (see also: Hapsburgs) 129, 141
Azerbaijan 100

Babli, Natan ha 41
Babylon, Babylonian Jewry 4, 39, 76
Baghdad 4, 40, 44, 46, 52, 58, 90, 94, 100, 134, 136, 137
Balfour Declaration 151
Balkans 7, 96, 98, 105, 115, 118, 150
Banks, banking, bankers 45, 50, 58-64, 69, 107, 111, 129, 135
Baron, Salo 156
Baruḥ, Yehudah 129
Basra 136
Battūta, ibn 156
Bavaria, 99
Bayazıd I, Sultan 96
Bayazıd II, Sultan 100, 101
Bedouins 9, 20,43, 65, 90
Belgrade 100
Believers, the 126
Benjamin of Tudela 52
Berbers 74, 75, 79, 90
Beth Shearim 12
Bills of Exchange 45, 67
Blood libel 111, 118
Bombay 136
Britian – see: United Kingdom
Btesh family 141
Budapest 100, 101
Bukhara 88, 92
Bursa 99
Bustanay, Exilarch 24, 52
Byzantine Empire, Byzantines 7, 9, 12, 20, 21, 29, 43, 96,

Cairo 130

Cairo (Old Cairo) – see: Fustat
Cairo Geniza 41, 64, 66, 84
Calcutta 130, 137-141
Cambridge 41
Canton 45
Capitulations 115, 117, 130-131, 140
Catholic Christianity 73
Capsali, Rabbi 100, 110, 111
Caro, Joseph 108
Cemeteries 36
Central Asia 3, 85, 88
China 3, 40, 45, 58, 92, 95, 131
Chinghiz Khan 92
Christian Europe – see: Europe
Christian Spain 80, 81, 87
Christians, Christianity, Christian Church 21, 24-27, 29, 107
Churches 36, 107
Class, class consciousness, status 70, 132
Cohen, Shalom 130, 136-140
Columbus, Christopher 3
Commerce – see: Merchants.
Concubines 46, 112
Conscription 131, 143, 149
Constantinople 7, 68, 98, 99
Conversion to Islam, to Judaism 2, 12, 36, 49, 69, 73, 83-87, 125
Córdoba 46, 57, 74, 76, 77, 84
Copts 24
Crémeiux Decree 153
Crimea 114
Crusades 37, 85
Customs dues, agents 33, 67, 77, 106, 129

Damascus 43, 44, 94, 99
Damascus Affair 146
Dardanelles 96
David, King 29, 52
Day of Judgement 18, 49
Denmark 129
Devshirme system 96-97, 112, 117
Dhimma, dhimmıs 31-38, 75, 94, 107, 118, 133, 141, 143, 156, 158
Diplomacy, diplomats 69, 78, 105
Doctors – see: Medicine
Dover 20
Dragomen - see: Interpreters
Dress, dress regulations 35, 58, 69, 107, 118, 133
Dubrovnik – see: Ragusa
Dwek family 141
Dwek, Moshe 130

Egypt 1, 46, 50, 66, 83, 89, 92, 95, 100, 130, 144, 147, 153, 155
England – see: United Kingdom
Ethiopia 10, 12
Eunuchs 46, 112
Europe, Christian Europe, Western Europe 3, 6, 70, 131, 148, 152, 154
Evelyn, John 127
Exchequer 59
Exilarch 29, 41, 51-54

Faisal, King 151
Farhi family 130
Farming - see: Agriculture
Fatimids 30, 34, 46, 64, 65, 67
Finance, financiers – see: Banking
First World War 151
Fischel, Walter 60
Fonseca, Daniel de 129
France 68, 115, 117, 118, 129, 134, 145-147
Francos 130, 141
Franks, Kingdom of, Land of 9, 76
Fundamentalism, Islamic 4, 28, 154-159
Furat, ibn al- 49

Fustat (Old Cairo) 25, 41, 42, 46, 65, 66

Gabriel, Angel 15,
Gallipoli 123, 124
Gaza 122
Gazali, al- 69
Geniza – see: Cairo Geniza
Geography 45
Geometry 45
Geonim, the 4, 41, 52-58
Georgia 90
Germany 42, 68, 99, 146, 150, 152
Ghazan, Il-Khan Mahmud 95
Ghuzz – see: Oghuzz
Gibraltar 74
Goitein, S.D. 49, 66
Granada 21, 36, 74, 80, 86-87
Great Britain – see: United Kingdom
Greece, Greeks 117, 149-150
Gubbay family 141

Hadiths 14, 157
Hahambashi 144
Haj 10
Hakam II, al- 57, 77, 79
Hakim, Khalif al- 35, 83
Halab – see: Aleppo
Hamadan 34, 49
Hamid II, Sultan Abdul 149
Hamon, Joseph and Moses 111
Hapsburgs, Hapsburg Empire 114, 115, 119, 129
Hebrew language 27-28, 78
Hejaz 32
Himyar 9-13, 19
Hindus 26
Hisham II, Khalif 79
Histories, the 14
History, Jewish 39-41
Holocaust 6
Holland 115, 117, 129, 134
Holy Land – see: Palestine
Holy Sepulchre 83
Hungary 99
Hulagu Khan 92

Husayn 24, 52

Ibn Battuta 156
Idris ibn Abdullah 46
Imam 30
Incense 10
India 3, 45, 131, 141, 147, 152
Industry 24, 46, 106, 115
Ineffable Name, the 123
Interpreters 105, 134, 140
Inheritance 37
Iran (see also: Persia) 30, 38, 84, 94, 100, 127, 131, 152, 155
Iraq 24, 27, 29, 94, 151, 152
Isa, Abu 49
Islam 1, 20, 26-29, 154
Israel, State of 1, 4, 152, 153, 157
Istanbul 109, 110, 113, 115, 123, 130, 143, 149
Italy, Italians 20, 66, 68, 75, 134

Jaén 80
Jahiz, al- 48
Janissaries 97, 112-113, 117, 143
Jaxartes, River 88
Jehoiachim, King 51
Jerusalem 9, 17, 18, 27, 30, 31, 47
Jerusalem, Academy of 30, 68
Jesus 17, 18, 26, 123
Jews, Jewish people 21-26, 43, 47-50, 116-119
Jihad 155
Jizya – see: Poll Tax
Jordan, Kingdom of 151
Joseph ha Nagid, ibn Samuel 80, 86
Joseph, King of the Khazars 120
Josephus 39
Jubair, ibn 66
Judaism 1, 26-29, 68, 73

Ka'aba 10, 14
Kabbalah 108, 121-128

Kairouan 24, 41, 47, 65
Karaites 41, 56, 109
Karakhamids 90
Khadijah 14
Kharaj 33
Killis, Yacub ibn 64
Kipchaks 90
Kufa 24

Ladino 116
Lebanon 152
Letters of Credit 59
Levant Company, English 106
Levy family 141
Lewis, Bernard 92
Libya 90, 145, 153
Lithuania 6, 104
Livorno 117, 141
London 104
Louis the Pious, King 76
Lucena 80
Luria, Isaac 108

Mahmud II, Sultan 143
Maimonides 34, 55, 69, 84
Malikite School of Islamic Law 32, 34, 77, 79
Malta 46
Mamluks 65, 70, 88, 113
Manzirert, battle of 92, 96
Map-making 45
Mar Zutra, Exilarch 9-13
Marcus, Abraham 130
Marranos (secret Jews) 81, 101, 111, 129
Marriage 37
Mecca 10, 14-19
Medicine, doctors 45, 50, 60, 69, 72, 77, 106, 117, 144, 156
Medina 15-19, 75, 157
Mehmet II the Conqueror, Sultan 41, 97-99, 107, 110, 114
Mehmed IV, Sultan 125
Mendes, dōna Gracia 111
Merchants 10, 21, 24,

49, 53, 58, 66, 105, 107, 111, 135, 147
Messiah 4, 9, 12, 16, 30, 40, 48, 49, 83, 93, 120-128
Middle East, the 1, 3, 7, 90, 145, 46
Millet system 143
Misrahi, Rabbi Eliahu 110, 111
Mitelene, duke of 111
Mongols, the 54, 87, 88-95, 96, 114
Montenegro 149
Morocco 66, 85, 90, 153
Moses 17, 18
Moshe ben Hanoch 79
Mortara Affair, the 146
Mu'tasim, Khalif 88
Mu'tatid, Khalif 59
Muhammad 14-19, 20, 157
Muqtadir, Khalif 59, 60-63
Murad II, Sultan 96
Murad III, Sultan 111
Musa ibn Nusair 74
Musta'arab Jews 109

Najran 12, 19
Nasi, Joseph duke of Naxos 111
Nasser, President 155, 158
Natan ha-Babli 53
Nathan of Gaza 122, 126
Natronai bar Habibae 76
Nehemia, Rabbi 124, 126
Netira ibn Yosef 60
Nettler, Ronald 155
New York 136
North Africa 3, 7, 24, 46, 49, 65, 73, 75, 100, 130, 145, 146

Oguzz 90
Onon, river 92
Opthalmology 45
Oral Law, the 27, 41, 56
Orthodox Christianity 7, 9, 24
Ottoman Empire, the Ottomans 1, 6, 37, 38, 47, 89, 95, 96-

116, 154
Oudh, Nawab of 138
Oxus, river 88

Palestine 12, 25, 46, 55, 66, 100, 151
Palestinian Academy 55
Paper 40
Peking 92
Persian Empire, Persians, (see also: Iran) 7, 9, 12-13, 20, 21, 43, 46, 51
Philosophy 27, 45, 69
Phoenicians 73
Piccioto family 141
Poetry, Arabic and Hebrew 12, 27, 45, 78, 80
Poland 6, 104, 117, 121
Poll tax 19, 21, 32, 98, 107
Polygamy 72, 136
Portugal 82, 101
Protocols of the Elders of Zion 158
Prussia 119, 129
Pschat 28
Public office 36, 59, 69, 86, 78
Pumbeditha Academy 54-57, 68, 76

Qomm 24
Qur'an 12, 14-15, 26, 27, 32, 157
Qutb, Sayyid 157-158

Radhanites 58
Ragusa 101, 129
Rahman, Abd al 46
Rashid al Din 95
Resh Galuta – see: Exilarch
Responsa 56
Rhodes 100, 101
Roman Empire, Eastern - see: Byzantine Empire
Romaniotes 99, 109
Rome, Western Roman Empire 7
Russell, Dr Alexander 135-136
Rûm, Kingdom of 96
Russia 90, 92, 114

Sa'ad ad Daula 87, 93-94
Sa'adia Gaon 57, 60
Sabbath, the 9, 18
Saladin 34, 67
Salonika 99, 108, 109, 111, 150
Samarkand 40, 88
Samuel ibn Nagrila, Nagid 80, 86
Sardinia 20, 46
Sarfati, Rabbi 99
Sassoon family 141
Saul, King 19
Second World War 150
Seljuk, Seljuks 90, 96
Sephardim, Sephardi tradition 4, 5, 109, 117, 147
Serbia 149
Serene 49
Sfez, Batto 34
Shalom family 141
Shaprut, Hisdai ibn 57, 64, 120
Shari'a 30, 155
Sherira Gaon 41, 56
Shi'a Islam 29-30, 44, 83
Sholem, Gershon 121
Sicily 20, 46, 65, 90, 99
Silk 10, 58, 77
Singh, Maharajah Ranjit 137
Sisebut, King 73
Slaves 10, 37, 44, 58, 70, 71, 74, 76, 77, 88
Slavs 79
Smyrna 121
Spain 1, 6, 20, 21, 73-82
Spices 10, 58
Status in society – see: Class
Struma 150
Suez Canal 131
Suleiman the Magnificent, Sultan 100, 101, 115
Sunni Islam 26, 44, 83, 92, 95
Sura, Academy of 54-57, 68, 76, 79
Surat 137
Synagogue, synagogues 27, 53, 36, 101
Syria 21, 24, 46, 50,

66, 75, 100, 130, 131

Talmud 4, 27, 47, 54-56, 68, 76
Tamberlane – see: Timur Lang
Tariq ibn Ziyad 74
Tatars – see: Mongols
Taxes, taxation 24, 52, 75, 105, 106, 108, 129, 142
Temujin – see: Chinghiz Khan
Textiles 72, 77, 106, 114, 115
Tiberias 47, 108, 111
Timur Lang 54, 95, 96
Tiran, Straits of 12
Torah 12, 16
Trade 10, 12, 25, 58, 69, 105, 106, 114, 115, 117
Traditions, books of - see: Hadiths
Transjordan – see: Jordan
Translations 45
Travel 25, 47, 66, 67
Transoxiana 88
Trinity, the 17, 28
Tugrul 90
Tunisia 34, 46, 65, 90, 153
Turkic-speaking peoples, Turks 37, 46, 88-95, 92
Turkish Republic 149, 153

Ukraine 121
Umar I, Khalif 31, 36
Ummayads, dynasty and khalifate
United Kingdom 3, 104, 115, 117, 142
Urban II, Pope 85

Victoria, Queen 137
Vienna 92, 99, 114, 129, 154
Visigoths 9, 73, 74
Voltaire 129

Women 44, 71-72, 112, 134, 135, 147
Written Law, the 27, 41

Yemen (see also: Himyar) 34, 84

Yerushalmi, Yosef 39
Yitzhak Gaon 24, 55
Yohai, Simon bar 48
Yosef ibn Pinhas 60-64
Young Turks 149
Yudghan 49

Zahir, al-, Khalif 32
Zionism 147
Zoroastrians 21, 24, 26, 88
Zutra – see Mar Zutra
Zvi, Shabbetai 120-128